Dr. Holmes in 1892

Other titles in this Chelsea House series:

LIFE AND LETTERS OF
OLIVER WENDELL HOLMES
JOHN T. MORSE, JR.

VOLUME II

INTRODUCTION BY

EARL N. HARBERT

American Men and Women of Letters Series

GENERAL EDITOR

PROFESSOR DANIEL AARON

HARVARD UNIVERSITY

CHELSEA HOUSE
NEW YORK, LONDON

1980

Cover design by Stanley Dunaj

Library of Congress Cataloging in Publication Data

Morse, John Torrey, 1840-1937.
    Life and letters of Oliver Wendell Holmes.

    (American men and women of letters)
    Reprint of the ed. published by Houghton, Mifflin,
Boston.
    1. Holmes, Oliver Wendell, 1809-1894.   2. Authors,
American--19th century--Biography.   3. Physicians--
United States--Biography.   I. Title.   II. Series.
PS1981.M6 1980   818'.309[B]   80-21475
ISBN 0-87754-171-X

Chelsea House Publishers
Harold Steinberg, Chairman & Publisher
Andrew E. Norman, President
Susan Lusk, Vice President
A Division of Chelsea House Educational Communications, Inc.
133 Christopher Street, New York 10014

CONTENTS
VOLUME II

LIST OF ILLUSTRATIONS

VOLUME II

MEMOIRS AND CORRESPONDENCE

CHAPTER XIII

OCCUPATIONS : METHODS OF WORK

DR. HOLMES was a man of many tastes, which pressed close upon each other through his life in a procession broken by no intervals of tedium. He had the mechanical ingenuity which is, or used to be, the proverbial gift of the Yankee. He was always "tinkering" at one contrivance or another. When the first enthusiasm about the microscope had passed, the train of thought awakened thereby led him to make a clever invention, — the small stereoscope for hand use. I recollect the first one of these clever adaptations, made — all save the lenses, of course — by his own hands, and to which only small improvements in the way of finish were afterward added. If he had taken out a patent for this he would have made a large sum of money, would perhaps have become, for those times in Boston, a rich man. Why he did not do so I cannot say, — whether it was from a bit of that sentiment which has so often led physicians to refrain from burdening their inventions with the added cost of a royalty, or whether he did not give much consideration to the mercantile value of what he had done. I can say, however, that I often heard him speak of the sums which he had thus "lost," and never heard him express any regret that his invention had not been laid beneath this fine for his benefit.

Here too is an intimation of Dr. Holmes's skill in another handicraft. I venture to publish the note, since Mr. Sumner is dead without progeny; if it is a little caustic, it is also amusing in its presentation of a quite familiar trait of the egotistical statesman: —

TO GEORGE ABBOT JAMES.

296 BEACON STREET. *April* 22, 1886.

DEAR MR. JAMES, — If I do not put down a few words on paper now, I shall be apt to forget to do it in the various distracting preparations for the voyage.

I remember the dinner you refer to, well. I recall more especially Mr. Sumner's learned discourse on book-binding.

How formidable a little cheap knowledge looks to those who are wholly ignorant of its familiar terms! I recollect that the word "forwarding" made almost a sensation, as Sumner spoke of it. What is "forwarding"? It includes all that part of a bookbinder's work which is necessary for the preservation of a volume.

All the rest is "finishing," — coloring the leather, gilding, and ornamentation of every kind.

I think we were all interested in Sumner's dinner-table lecture, — I am sure he enjoyed giving it as much as any old Professor discoursing to a class of students.

When you hear a distinguished personage using long words or technical phrases that frighten you and make you think how learned he is and how desperately ignorant you and all your acquaintances are, as soon as the speech is over, and the company separates, go to your dictionary or cyclopædia and look out his polysyllables, and ten to one you will get him off his high horse in five minutes.

If he quotes a Latin sentence, see if Bohn's *Handbook* has n't got it. If a line from any English poet or prose-writer, look in your Bartlett's *Familiar Quotations*. This will probably fetch him.

I bound a book myself once. I don't believe Sumner ever did. — But I liked his talk about it, and hunted up the sources of his knowledge.

At one time the Doctor was seized with an ardent desire to learn to play upon the violin. I think there was not the slightest reason to suppose that he ever could learn, and certainly he never did; but he used to shut himself up in his little "study," beside the front door in the Charles Street house, and fiddle away with surprising industry, and a satisfaction out of all proportion to his achievement. After two or three winters he reached a point at which he could make several simple tunes quite recognizable, and then finally desisted from what would have been a waste of time had it not been a recreation.

Photography he took up in the old days of "wet process," when it was by no means the easy and fashionable amusement which modern inventions have made of it. He arrived at a great degree of skill, and found amusement in it for many years.

He had a lifelong enthusiasm for great trees. In his youth, travelling about the country on his lecturing tours, he always had a measuring tape in his pocket, and used to stretch it around the girth of any especially big fellow with as much interest as fashionable young ladies show in taking the circumference of each other's waists. His memory was loaded with statistics, and even when he was in England, he still could pull out a bit of string to see whether or not the giants of Old England surpassed those of New England. It was amusing, he once said, to "see how meek one of the great swaggering elms would look, when it saw the fatal measure begin to unreel itself." An especial one of these cis-Atlantic monsters he remembered well, "as we measured the string which was to tell the size of its English rival. As we came near the end of the string, I felt as I did when I was looking at the last dash of Ormonde and The Bard at Epsom. Twenty feet, and a long piece of string left!—Twenty-one.—Twenty-two.—Twenty-three.—An extra heart-beat or two.—Twenty-four!—Twenty-five, and six inches over!!"

In 1885, when he was living at Beverly Farms, he used to walk over to see "the finest oak he could remember." "I never pass it," he said, "without a bow and a genuflexion." It stood upon some land belonging to me, and I often found him looking at it with an expression of eager admiration. He said to me once: "Ah, J., you think that you own that tree; but you don't, *it owns you!*"

In time he came to be recognized as such an authority as to big trees that he was even consulted by Professor Asa Gray, the famous botanist of Harvard University, and he made this reply: —

TO MRS. ASA GRAY.

January 24, 1871.

MY DEAR MRS. GRAY, — I am a little overwhelmed with my new reputation as a gardener; yet as I have succeeded in raising as many cauliflowers and cabbages that did not head, as many rat-tail carrots and ram's-horn radishes, in our Cambridge sand-patch, which we called a garden, as any other horticulturist could show grown from the same surface of ground, I *have* some claim to the title.

To answer Mr. Robinson's question: I never saw more than two or three good photographs of American elms. The best is a large one of the "Johnston Elm," about three miles from Providence, one of the finest trees, as it was when I used to visit it, in New England. This was sent me, framed, by my nephew Dr. Parsons, of Providence, who may be in possession of the negative. It might of course be reduced, though it would not quite come up to the first direct photograph. I have stereographs of the Boston Elm, before its present condition of decadence, and one of the Washington Elm, the last a fair specimen of the tree, but neither of them equal to the great Johnston Elm. On the whole, I think it would be hard to get anything more satisfactory and easily obtained than a copy of my photograph of this great tree, which will be at his or your husband's service at any time, if a copy is desired. The original is a picture of perhaps eight or ten inches square.

The Autocrat of the Breakfast-Table says: "I have brought down this slice of hemlock to show you. Tree blew down in my woods (that were) in 1852. Twelve feet and a half round, fair girth; nine feet, where I got my section, higher up. This is a wedge, going to the centre, of general shape of a slice of apple-pie in a large and not opulent family. Length, about eighteen inches. I have studied the growth of this tree by its rings, and it is curious. Three hundred and forty-two rings. Started, therefore, about

1510. The thickness of the rings tells the rate at which it grew. . . . Look here. Here are some human lives laid down against the periods of its growth, to which they corresponded. This is Shakespeare's. The tree was seven inches in diameter when he was born ; ten inches when he died. A little less than ten inches when Milton was born ; seventeen when he died. Then comes a long interval, and this thread marks out Johnson's life, during which the tree increased from twenty-two to twenty-nine inches in diameter. Here is the span of Napoleon's career, — the tree does n't seem to have minded it."

This was a bit of autobiography. He had such a tree-section, and devoted much minute toil to sticking into the rings on its big tabular surface a countless forest of little pins, each one tagged with the date of some event which was occurring when that ring of the tree was forming.

" I like books, — I was born and bred among them, and have the easy feeling, when I get into their presence, that a stable-boy has among horses. I don't think I undervalue them, either as companions or instructors." Thus said the Doctor, speaking through the mask of the Autocrat. In fact, he was a bibliophile, but was not a bibliomaniac. He was an expert in judging the physical qualities of a book ; he loved the clear old type of some of the earlier printers, and the strong wood-cuts made by a past generation. But mere rarity, or a purely artificial first-edition valuation, meant very little to him. If any admirer of his wants a good picture, by description, of his library, it can be found at the beginning of the Professor's second paper.

Cicero and Bacon have uttered two notable passages about books, and Holmes has a sentence which may go with them: "Some books are edifices, to stand as they are built; some are hewn stones, ready to form a part of future edifices; some are quarries, from which stones are to be split for shaping and after use." And here is a bit of drollery from his address at the opening of the Medical Library at Boston: "A library like ours must exercise the largest hospitality. A great many books may be found in every large collection which remind us of those apostolic-looking old men who figure on the platform at our political and other assemblages. Some of them have spoken words of wisdom in their day, but they have ceased to be oracles; some of them never had any particularly important message for humanity, but they add dignity to the meeting by their presence; they look wise, whether they are so or not, and no one grudges them their places of honor."

May it be said, without irreverence, in speaking of Dr. Holmes's tastes, that he had a considerable infusion of the "sporting man" in his composition? One of his most cherished memories of his early days in Europe was, that he saw *Plenipotentiary* win the Derby; and he always kept a lively interest in the incidents of the turf. He knew the points and the style of the favorites and the winners as they succeeded each other, and he carried in his memory with extraordinary accuracy the records of the time made in all the important "events." His erudition concerning the race-horse sometimes astonished men who had always fancied that they themselves knew a good deal about these things, but never imagined that his mind could be busied with them.   He was like his own Major Rowens: "He knew a neat, snug hoof, a delicate pastern, a broad haunch, a deep chest, a close ribbed-up barrel, as well as any other man in the town.   He was not to be taken in by your thick-jointed, heavy-headed cattle, without any go to them, that suit a country parson, nor yet by the 'gaänted-up,' long-legged animals, with all their constitutions bred out of them, such as rich greenhorns buy and cover up with their plated trappings."   And in another place, sketching this Yankee with such marvellous skill that it seems cruel to cut out a piece from so fine a whole, he tells us that the Major "had no objection, either, to holding the reins in a wagon behind another kind of horse, — a slouching, listless beast, with a strong slant to his shoulder, and a notable depth to his quarter, and an emphatic angle at the hock, who commonly walked or lounged along in a lazy trot of five or six miles an hour; but, if a lively colt happened to come rattling up alongside, or a brandy-faced old horse-jockey took the road to show off a fast nag and threw his dust into the Major's face, would pick his legs up all at once, and straighten his body out, and swing off into a three-minute gait, in a way that 'Old Blue' himself need not have been ashamed of."   The picture is enough to make an old country jockey "wriggle," as Dr. Holmes said that the *Biglow Papers* made him do.   He even held horse-racing to be so important an interest of humanity that, in the preface to a late edition of *The Professor*, enumerating the amendments made necessary by sundry striking changes and advances which had taken place in the world since its first publication, he included among them that "the speed of the trotting-horse has been so much developed that the record of the year when the fastest time to that date was given must be very considerably altered."

Neither was he altogether oblivious even of the prize ring; he had the *Boxiana* prints, and he knew well the great deeds, doughty though brutal, of Heenan and Sayers and Yankee Sullivan and other champions. This interest, however, was chiefly from the side of physical development; and when he visited some of these heroes, and studied their muscles with admiration, it was only in the hours of peace; I never heard of his going to see a pugilistic "set-to." The truth is that the Doctor was a great lover of fine, symmetrical, powerful growth, whether in tree, horse, or man, and he hugely liked the fellow who *could* fight, and who would do so upon due occasion. There are a few combats in his books, described with much gusto; Bernard Langdon's fine muscles are affectionately depicted, and made effectively useful; and the sketch of the Southerner knocking down the butcher is like some of the English bouts of Town and Gown. He liked mere *size*, too, and used to find infinite amusement in holding friendly chats with the "giants" at the shows.

He was for many years, in mid-life, a zealous boating-man, and before "improvement" had gouged up the bottom of Charles River to make building - lots along its banks, in the good old days when there was an extensive and beautiful estuary of real water there, he was one of the first to pull upon those lively and often sizeable waves, in a boat of the "long, sharp-pointed, black cradle" pattern. In this he was to be seen making long excursions when the season permitted; and he had the contempt of a true expert for

"those miserable tubs, tugging in which is to rowing
the true boat what riding a cow is to bestriding an
Arab." There is a delightful sketch of this pursuit
in the seventh paper of *The Autocrat.*

These things were occupations; but of sheer hard
work Dr. Holmes did as much as any man, even in
the industrious communities of the Eastern States.
People did not give him credit for this, or at least
very insufficiently. Half of those who thought of him
forgot his work at the Medical School altogether,
and the other half fancied that he could repeat from
year to year his lectures on the unchanging science
of anatomy, much as the clergyman can pull out
of the traditional barrel any old sermon that comes
to hand, and preach it again for, it may be, the
twentieth time. One could hardly help feeling that
those easy, colloquial reports of the chats at the
Breakfast - Table might have been jotted down or
talked off to a stenographer in the same conversational way in fact, in which they purported to have
been uttered in fiction. Never were greater errors.
The lectures were revamped every year with genuine
hard labor. Keeping abreast with new ideas, even
in anatomical studies, meant something; preparation
each day called for some time and thought; and the
tax of delivery, of holding the attention of the tired
and disorderly medical students of those days, was a
considerable drain on the nervous force. President
Eliot, who knew whereof he spoke, paid him very
handsome compliments upon the amount and serious-
ness of his labor as a professor and instructor.

As for the matter of literary composition, it was a
very painstaking process with Dr. Holmes. His wit

and humor and thoughts flowed exuberantly enough; but he was a most careful, accurate writer. Not only when he dwelt upon, but when he even alluded to, any topic whatever, whether in the way of science or history, or argument or idea, or of literary or theological discussion, — whatever it might be, — he made sure by minute investigation that his knowledge was thorough, and that his use and treatment were correct. His hand was always on the Cyclopædias, the Dictionaries of biography, the innumerable works of reference of every conceivable kind, which stood in serried ranks beside his table. When he was writing the essay on Jonathan Edwards, he showed me how he was doing the work: he had some large quarto blank books, with the pages divided into liberal sections by lines from top to bottom; the requisite space was set aside for each division of the topic in the biographical, the theological, and the critical departments; the names of writers who had written of Edwards, disputed with him, criticised him, or in any way contributed to the Edwards study, were set at the heads of the several columns; and synopses of their views were then set down, in such orderly contra-position as was possible. When he had finished this huge tabulation, the Doctor expected to be master of everything of value concerning his subject. "I can't afford," he said, "to lose *anything.*" Yet he had selected Edwards as the topic for an article, because he had for years been greatly interested in that terrible theologian; and before he entered upon this minute and elaborate preparation for writing, he was already so thoroughly informed that he could have delivered, extempore, a lecture which would have seemed the fruit of patient study.

In this connection, a couple of letters written by

Dr. Holmes to his friend Dr. Weir Mitchell will be of interest: —

BOSTON, *March* 27, 1871.

MY DEAR DR. MITCHELL, — I will give you my own experience very briefly, and then that of another which came to me with the most singular "aproposity," as one of my young barbarians has it.

I cannot work many hours consecutively without deranging my whole circulating and calorific system. My feet are apt to get cold, my head hot, my muscles restless, and I feel as if I *must* get up and exercise in the open air. This is in the morning, and I very rarely allow myself to be detained indoors later than twelve o'clock. After fifteen or twenty minutes' walking I begin to come right, and after two or three times as much as that I can go back to my desk for an hour or two. In the evening it is different. I always try to stop all hard work before eleven o'clock and take a book of light reading to clear my mind of its previous contents. So it is that I can hardly say I ever have a proper "brain-tire," because other systems give the alarm first. I should say rather that too long brain work gives me a sense of disgust, like over-feeding, than one of actual fatigue. It sometimes happens that my brain gets going and I cannot stop it — a very common experience — and then I lie awake, but *this* again is different from physical fatigue of the thinking organ. I want to sleep and cannot, — I count — I do sums — I repeat passages from memory, but the underthought keeps grumbling on like the bass in a Beethoven symphony. In a word my brain, as a rule, will not let itself get fatigued. It becomes *disgusted*, rather, and throws up work. In composition, especially poetical composition, I stand on the bank of a river and hold myself very still, watching the thoughts that float by on the stream of association. If they come abundantly and of the right kind, there is a great excitement, sometimes an exalted state, almost like etherization, incompatible with a sense of fatigue while it lasts, and followed by a relief which shows there has been a tension of which I could not be conscious at the time. So much for myself. — While your letter was in my hand Dr. Edward [H.] Clarke, our first medical practitioner, Professor of Materia Medica in our school, came in, and knowing him to be a thinker, I questioned him.

He was the first scholar of his class in the Academic department at Harvard, — the only first scholar I remember who ever studied medicine. He studied too hard in the first part of his course, and was restricted by his advisers to two or three hours' work a day. The effect, he tells me, was this : He learned to work his brain *very hard* during the short time he gave to study, — a habit which he has kept up to this day, so that he says he can get up a new lecture of an hour in less than an hour's time, which for such a lecturer to say means a good deal. As a consequence of this forced labor he experiences a distinct sense of cerebral fatigue. There is a kind of pressure he experiences, such that he habitually clasps his hands over his head as if to "hold his head down." *After such severe mental labor he wishes to lie down and rest.* But after moderate, prolonged mental work he likes exercise as I do. He is very averse to the crowded hour or two's work on account of the effects which he describes.

To return to myself, I cannot express the loathing with which my mind turns away from a subject it has got enough of. I like nine tenths of any matter I study, but I do not like to *lick the plate*. If I did, I suppose I should be more of a man of science and find my brain tired oftener than I do. Mental nausea takes the place of mental fatigue with me. I believe in the depleting, nerve-straining qualities of our climate, etc. Brown-Séquard told us his animals do not *bleed* so much in America as they did in Europe! Is not that a startling statement?

Pardon my hasty letter, written only an hour or two after the receipt of yours, and believe me

Always truly yours.

TO THE SAME.

BOSTON, *March* 30, 1871.

DEAR DR. MITCHELL, — I shrink with a blush of ingenuous modesty from having my name connected publicly with the idiosyncrasies I told you of in my free and easy letter. The *facts* of course you can use, if you can disguise them so as not to have them fastened upon me. But I felt as if I were condemning my own intellect, according to the judgment of many persons. I have often regretted not having forcibly trained myself to the exhaustive treatment of some limited subject, and if I thought I should live to be a hundred years old I would devote ten years of the time, as it is, to such specialized study. You remember the story of the grammarian who had given his life to the study of certain nouns, and who regretted on his death-bed that he had not restricted himself to the consideration of the genitive case. When I

read your paper on the poison of the rattlesnake I felt
that such a labor as that, patient, thorough, leaving
nothing to be gone over again, was just the sort of
work I ought to have been compelled to begin, and
led by other influences to carry to its completion.
But my nature is to snatch at all the fruits of knowledge and take a good bite out of the sunny side —
after that let in the pigs.

A thoroughly detestable statement; but let it stand,
for there is too much truth in it.   You can see I do
not want to have it shown up as my particular form
of mental weakness — shall I say, or only special development.   It seems like putting a master key to the
strong box that holds my intellectual treasures, such
as they are, into the hands of any malignant — and I
think we have such, who like to use anything they
can get hold of relating to any of their betters.

Enfin.   I think you might use my experience, as
to the surfeit of a subject coming before the sense of
fatigue, without making it clear who the person was
that made this revelation.

Nobody but myself could tell it in full with all the
reservations, qualifications, conditions of every kind,
compensations, philosophical justifications, crack-put-
tying subterfuges, and counterclaims to discursive
intelligence, which render life tolerable with such a
vicious and kicking brain as I have described my will
as bestriding.

I am glad my discourse interested you, and though
I am afraid you will not think much of me after these
two letters, you must remember that I have at least
the merit of appreciating your sincere and thoroughly
satisfactory labors.

Very accurate and painstaking was he concerning the literary finish of his works. He wrote a simple, what may be called a gentlemanlike style, and of great purity, but crowded with allusions, so that it was truly remarked by one of his critics, and has been often repeated by others, that the greater the scholarship of the reader, the greater also the pleasure which he would derive from Dr. Holmes's writings. The same thing was true of Thackeray; both wrote for educated and well-read audiences. I remember once hearing a gentleman of some reputation in literature say — actually in addressing the Board of Overseers of a distinguished seat of learning — that he did not approve of teaching young men to write "good English," to use words accurately and to construct sentences grammatically; on the contrary, he said that he wanted an infusion of the wild rough inaccuracies of the great new West! He was the victim of a foolish notion, that one of the available ways to show "American independence of England" was by devising a degraded dialect of the English language for use in the United States. Nor was he alone in this feeling that a coarse and imperfect form of speech was good enough for us; there was, for a while, a mild pseudo-literary fad in this direction. Dr. Holmes looked upon it with disgust and indignation, making his opinions known with his usual outspoken courage, and exemplifying them by his own action, with the result that he was for a while subjected to some abuse, which he endured with tranquillity, or rather with indifference. An English writer, in the *Quarterly Review*, has a passage on this matter, which I desire to quote:

"Opinions so directly contrary in many respects to the main direction of American movement brought

Holmes at one time into disrepute with the more advanced of his countrymen. He was accused of attaching excessive importance to conventionalities of dress, manners, and speech; he was charged with using his influence to starve and paralyze literary originality. To us it seems that his attitude was abundantly justified. The debt which the best American literature and all who in the Old World and the New appreciate its mixture of freshness and refinement owe to Holmes is very great. How great the debt was has not yet been fully recognized by his countrymen. When young America demanded that the political revolution which separated the Old and New Worlds should have its literary counterpart in a similar revolt, Holmes threw all his influence into the opposite scale. He urged, with keen satire as well as with the force of example, that even a Republic must recognize the laws of conventional decorum, and that those who enter the Temple of the Muses outrage propriety if they ostentatiously flaunt their working-dress. To him, as much as to any other man, we owe it, that the Versailles of American literature has not been invaded to a greater extent than it has by the vocabulary and manners of the ' Halles.' "

Dr. Holmes occasionally discussed with Richard Grant White, who had made a close study of the English language, the use of one or another word or phrase; and these two letters may be interesting.

TO RICHARD GRANT WHITE.

March 28, 1868.

MY DEAR MR. WHITE, — I was greatly pleased with your kind letter, and enjoyed the two articles from the *Galaxy* exceedingly. I hunted up the

"jewelry," and found it in *The Professor at the
Breakfast-Table*, page 27, in quotation marks it is
true ; but, I am inclined to think, not so much as being a questionable word as because it is one of the
stately names applied to paltry things by our pinch-
beck plebeians.   I do not know, however, that I have
used the word ; at any rate I think I shall be on the
lookout for it hereafter.   I was delighted with your
vindication of " some " three or four, etc.   It is a
beautiful, brief, erudite *excursus*, and as I followed
you from the Frog Pond to the Danube my heart
swelled with the thought that so good a judge as yourself counted me not unworthy to handle the words
that Alfred and Shakespeare and Bacon had spoken.
I am so pleased with your hits at several detestable
expressions that I must pick them out.   " Retiring "
for going to bed, — I have had my shy at that in *The
Autocrat*, page 241.   " Proven " for proved.   Will
you believe me when I tell you that Lowell uses
" proven " (in his very last article, if I remember
right, in the *North American*) ?   I could not believe
my eyes, and accused him of *lèze* majesty to the face,
as Paul withstood Peter.   It shows how the best of
us are liable to be caught.   I once used the expression " In our midst."   Edward Everett took me to
task for it, and showed me an old review in which Dr.
Gilman, of Charleston, S. C., had attacked him for
the same phrase.   The " consummation " criticism is
pyramidal.   I think I have seen the word so used
myself.   I tell a story in one of my books of a marriage between two servants, I saw or heard — (not con-
summated but " transpire," to use the " newspapor-
ial " or " reportorial " dialect), in which the question
was thus put by the Rev. Baron Stow, Baptist minis-

ter of this city: Wilt thou have this *Lady*? and, Wilt thou have this *Gentleman*? Was not this an euphuism of solar, nay of systemic, dimensions?

TO THE SAME.

September 27, 1868.

MY DEAR MR. WHITE, — I have been reading your article in the *Galaxy*, which you kindly sent me, with pleasure and interest, as I read all your philological articles. You will indulge me in a comment or two. If I am not mistaken, the two first lines of nursery poetry you give on page 518 are both slightly in error. "Hush, my *babe*, lie still," etc., it is, as I remember it. "*Now* I lay me down to sleep" is, I think, the correct version. I do not see why you should object to "experience" as a verb. It is necessary to avoid a paraphrase, unless we return to the old use of *experiment* as signifying to learn by trial, etc.; and we want that as signifying to try in order to learn. What would our country deacons be if they had not "experienced religion"? I can beat your stories about *limb* for leg. A schoolmate of mine, a girl of some fourteen or fifteen years old at the time, — niece of an American celebrity of the first water, — had occasion to mention to me, a year or two younger than herself, a misfortune which had happened to her mother (it was a fracture of the *femur*, in surgical language) — "Since mother broke" — (she hesitated) — "her *foot*." I assure you this is a genuine recollection. — "*Gentleman*" and "*lady*." Did you ever see one of my failures called *The Professor at the Breakfast-Table*? If you did, and looked at the 182d page, you saw an account of the use of these words for "man" and "woman" in the marriage service. I should have said "*stop* at So-and-So's" was a Yankee vulgarism. Our country folk always say they are *stopping* at cousin Jehoiakim's, etc. *Smock* is a vulgar word, onomato-poetically vulgar; *shift* will do better; both sound *naked; chemise* does not call up the bare body. We clothe the nude word by Frenching it.

I hate *shew* for shewed, in spite of your analogies. I only hear it from the half-breeds, or now and then from a careless person who has caught it in bad company.

Has Mr. Bergh the h final? I am not sure. I find your article very pleasant, with its light, good-natured satire, as well as instructive.

Somebody must have made some very foolish criticisms, which called forth this letter: —

March 7, 1891.

MY DEAR LADY, — I am very much obliged to you for taking the trouble to tell me the story of your first acquaintance with my poems. The particular one, "The Music Grinders," was unlucky in having two or three words which alarmed your teacher, who was, I suppose, of the prunes and prisms variety of pedagoguesses! If her injured shade still wanders on earth, it may see by my later editions that "filthy" is changed to "odious," which I hope she recognizes as rendering the line presentable! As for "oath" and "curse," I am sorry to say they stand as of old; but I suspect readers are tougher now than they used to be. Your letter gives me pleasure, and I am grateful to you for it.

When the Doctor had brought any of his work to the point of finish which suited him, he was very chary of alteration by any one else. I fancy that he was seldom subjected to it; for a matter of the kind, stated in the following paragraph from one of his letters, was referred to by him with a frequency indicative of its being an unusual occurrence.

"*I* very rarely adopt the suggestion of another person; but I have done such a thing and sometimes been sorry, and sometimes glad, that I have done it. Edward Everett corrected, as he thought, a line for me, and I accepted his alteration; forty years afterwards I restored the original reading. So you see I am not like to call you to account for not accepting my suggestions."

When a lady suggested a slight verbal improvement in a line of "The Last Leaf," he rendered an elaborate and public acknowledgment, which would have been big enough as thanks for a whole stanza.

This accurate habit of mind of the Doctor filled him with an anxious and ever-present fear of plagiarism. The dread of unwittingly committing a literary theft seemed at times actually to haunt him; he said that he did not expect that such an accident would *never* befall, but he pleased himself with the belief that his extreme precaution had made it at least of rare occurrence.

As for repeating himself, that was a different matter, — objectionable, but entirely honest. He did it sometimes. What he said on the subject was very happily put: —

"You don't suppose that my remarks made at this table are like so many postage-stamps, do you, — each to be only once uttered? If you do, you are mistaken.

He must be a poor creature who does not often repeat
himself. Imagine the author of the excellent piece of
advice, 'Know thyself,' never alluding to that sentiment again during the course of a protracted existence!
Why, the truths a man carries about with him are
his tools; and do you think a carpenter is bound to
use the same plane but once to smooth a knotty board
with, or to hang up his hammer after it has driven its
first nail? I shall never repeat a conversation, but
an idea often. I shall use the same types when I like,
but not commonly the same stereotypes. A thought
is often original, though you have uttered it a hundred
times. It has come to you over a new route, by a new
and express train of associations."

He was himself the victim of a very curious, of
course entirely accidental, theft of this kind. When
The Innocents Abroad appeared, it bore on its un-
blushing front a dedication which had already done
the like service for the Doctor's *Songs in Many Keys*.
Mark Twain referred to the incident humorously at the
Atlantic Breakfast; told how indignant he was when
a friend charged him with the act; how penitently,
when he found the charge to be true, he had written to Dr. Holmes; and how kindly the Doctor had
replied, saying that he believed that all writers at
times worked over the ideas of others unconsciously,
and conceiving the development to be their own.

So careful was the Doctor with his "copy" that he
received the liberal praise of his printers, a thing
which I fancy has befallen few authors, at least before
the advent of the typewriting sisterhood. Mr. Houghton bore tribute to his neatly written white pages,
bearing few interlineations, and those very carefully
made; and said that so few corrections had to be made

in going through the press that the Doctor " caused us
but little trouble."   On one occasion, in sending a
poem to a newspaper, he wrote, in the accompanying
note : " Poems are rarely printed correctly in newspapers. This is the reason so many poets die young.
Please correct carefully."

Yet all the Doctor's care could not always save him
from the inevitable errors of the printing-house. In
one of his papers occurred the sentence : " If all the
medicine were thrown into the sea, it would be the
better for mankind and the worse for the fishes." But
instead of "*fishes*," the printed page made him say
"*physicians*." The sentence as he intended it to be
excited criticism enough, but the proof-reader's amend-
ment changed criticism into a storm of indignation.

The Doctor practised a pretty strict economy in what
may properly be called his literary business. The
wit and humor and wisdom in his brain were his stock
in trade, just as are the merchant's goods in his ware-
house. He designed to deal with them, guard and
save them, and exchange them to as good advantage
as possible for the paper money of the Republic, —
which I take to be the proper adaptation for us of
the good old phrase, " the coin of the realm." The
Autocrat says : " What do you think an admiring
friend said the other day to one that was talking good
things, — good enough to print ? ' Why,' said he,
' you are wasting merchantable literature, a cash
article, at the rate, as nearly as I can tell, of fifty
dollars an hour.' "   Dr. Holmes appeared to be lavish
in this fashion himself.   I remember one evening two
or three of us, then young collegians, were sitting at
his dinner-table, in the Charles Street house, when
The Autocrat had just taught him what sums he could

win by his brains; he talked on most charmingly for an hour or two after the cloth was removed; then suddenly stopped short, sprang up, exclaimed: "Why! I believe I 've wasted a hundred dollars worth on you boys to-night," and vanished merrily and in a twinkling. In fact, however, he was by no means wasteful; and whenever, wherever, however he turned out a good article, to use the language of trade, he took care in due season to get the value of it. "It is a capital plan," said the Autocrat, "to carry a tablet with you, and, when you find yourself felicitous, take notes of your own conversation." Now the Doctor never did this, of course; but the best things which he said, the best bits in his letters, were very sure to be encountered afterwards in print. He gathered up the fragments, that nothing should be lost.

Occasionally the exuberance of Dr. Holmes's merriment bubbled up in the shape of puns. The best opinion will probably declare that the collection of these trifles, which occupies a few pages in an early paper of *The Autocrat*, is a disfigurement. But such gay sparkles, when they occur in ordinary correspondence, should find criticism silent. These letters, though some of the puns are local, and so a little occult, may amuse the pun-lover: —

TO DR. WILLIAM HUNT.[1]

21 CHARLES STREET, *May* 25, 1863.

MY DEAR DR. HUNT, — Wendell has been doing very well, but of course without any notable change.

---

[1] At the battle of Fredericksburg, May, 1863, Lieutenant-Colonel Holmes, whose regiment formed a part of the corps of Major-General Sedgwick, was severely wounded in the heel. He was carried homeward, and on the way he remained for a while in Philadelphia, where he was under the care of Dr. Hunt.

There has been very little pain, no mark of inflamma-
tion, nothing but what belongs to the healing process.
Dr. Bigelow probed the wound yesterday and found
one portion of bone movable, and another part fixed
but denuded. He is in excellent spirits, not at all
nervous, as when he was last wounded, is very reasonably tractable, avoids stimulants, smokes *not* enor-
mously, feeds pretty well, and has kept tolerably quiet
until to-day, when Dr. Bigelow let him ride out, and
is, on the whole, a quite endurable patient.

Again I must thank you for your kindness in taking
charge of him, and pouring oil and wine into his
wounds — in a metaphorical sense. If I contributed
in any way to your enjoying your visit to Boston, it is
nothing to the aid and comfort you have rendered
him again and again, at a time when skilful and careful treatment were perhaps a matter of life and death,
or of permanent injury, at the least, on one hand,
and harmless scars on the other.

Dr. Bigelow has done nothing but keep the wound
open as you did. He makes him use a little plug of
carrot for that purpose, which is handy enough, and
seems to agree very well with the wound.

There is something wrong about your quotation,
non animal, etc., etc. I understood that you purchased a *horse*, whereas the line refers to the *female*

. . . " qui trans *mare* currunt."

I should like to see you in the saddle upon your
Vermont steed; it would so remind me of the *Green
Mountings.* — Also, I pinched W.'s heel a little the
other day and asked him into what vegetable I had
turned his carrot. No answer.

Why, into a Pa's nip ! was my response.

The weather here is very cold and the spring puns are very backward. Early Joe Millers, though forced so as to be up by the 1st of April, are like to yield but a poor crop. The *art o' jokes* don't flourish. I wish you to see that we are some *punkins* here in Hub town, though you have the *demirep-utation* of making worse puns and more of them in your city than are made in any other habitable portion of the globe. The tendency is hereditary, no doubt — all vices are. Did not Alexander the Great inherit his tendency to get drunk from his father, the notorious *Fill-up of Macedon?* — Good-by, my kind friend and my son's friend, whom I have delicately commemorated in my " *Hunt* after the Captain."

P. S. I have at last found a man who has asked me about W.'s heel *without referring to Achilles!* " An Address without a Phœnix! "

TO F. A. ANGELL.

March 31, 1864.

DEAR SIR, — I often wonder how a man gifted with a beautiful but too suggestive name, like yours, manages to get through the world and keep his temper. What infinite changes must have been rung upon the celestial title you bear! How every quotation in which it occurs must have grown so odiously familiar to your ears that you can see it rising to the lips of the man who is going to utter it, while it is yet a mere unformed idiotic purpose in his feeble consciousness! How many times *per annum*, taking one season with another, do you hear: —

" Angels and ministers of grace defend us " ?

How large a proportion of your friends, as nearly

as you can compute the amount, are in the habit of saying, when you call to see them : —

Like *ditto* visits, few and far between ?

Do your flatterers speak of all the rest of mankind as being made a little lower than the *ditto?* Are you not told several times a week, on an average, that no woman could resist your suit, as she could not refuse to be changed into a *ditto?* Have you ever corresponded with *Deville*, the famous phrenologist in the Strand, London? I presume he is descended from the same stock with yourself, but that some ancestor of his must have fallen and had his name changed. Sir Roderick *Imp*ey Murchison is probably a branch of the same family. I should fear that after a certain length of time it would become unendurable to live in a perpetual atmosphere of pleasantries suggested by one's name. Did you ever pass a whole evening with friends where it was not played upon? Have you turned misanthropic, and do you shun society in consequence of the perpetual attempts made on your good name? There is one family in this city you ought to know; of course I mean the *Wings*. I have always understood they were connected to you in some way. Your complimentary letter almost "raised a mortal to the skies." I hope mine has not, by its trivialities, "brought an *etc.* down."

TO MISS LOUISE IMOGEN GUINEY.

April 18, 1889.

I thank you for your pleasant note, dear Miss Louise, and I wish you all happiness in your projected visit to Europe. You must not think of *chang-*

ing your Guiney until you get back among your own people here in New England.

Hoping that you will soon be in circulation among us once more,

I am faithfully yours

O. W. HOLMES.

Mr. Charles Francis Adams tells me that one forenoon, when he and Mr. Schurz were calling on Dr. Holmes, a copy of Worcester's *Unabridged Dictionary* lay on his desk. The Doctor told them that a canvasser for *The Century Dictionary* had just called, teasing him for a subscription. "No," said the Doctor, "I'm too old—eighty years—I shan't live to see the Century finished." To which the encouraging book-agent: "Nay, Doctor, you won't have to live so very much longer to use our book; we've already got to G." "And you may go to —*l*, if you like!" exclaimed the little Doctor; and the canvasser went — somewhere.

Dr. Holmes's medical line of thought, in topic, illustration, expression, was so prominent in his writings that some persons regarded it as a blemish. Others, more wisely, considered that it broadened his horizon, furnished him with many happy suggestions, and especially gave him a useful habit of accuracy and thoroughness. The (London) *Lancet*, speaking of him as a distinguished example of the physician in literature, says of him, very well, as it seems to me: "In him the physician—now as anatomist or physiologist, now as psychologist, now as diagnostician — was ever present and ever speaking. He wrote no book without drawing largely upon his scientific experience; he displayed in all his literary workmanship, in thought as much as in expression, an accurate tolerance — a

capability of taking the large view, with a resolve to
be correct about small things—that we make bold to
say, as he would often proudly say, had been largely
developed by his particular training; and many of his
wittiest little parables and paraphrases, many of the
most characteristic sayings of those three charming
rulers of the breakfast-table, were the direct outcome
of his medical learning." Moving in a different direction is the remark of his kinsman, Colonel Henry
Lee, a gentleman whose opinion is well worth having
on any matter relating to Dr. Holmes. He said, addressing the Massachusetts Historical Society after the
Doctor's death: "Fortunate for Dr. Holmes were his
practice and his lectures for thirty-five years. It gave
him promptness, accountability, resolution, touch with
the world. It was this commerce with the world that
widened his observations and his sympathy."

Though all the world thinks of Dr. Holmes as a
wit, he was in fact a writer with very grave and serious purposes. From a long line of pious ancestry he
inherited a conscience which was ever vigilant and
almost tyranically dominant. Nothing would have
humiliated him more than to be regarded as a writer
whose chief object, or at least principal achievement,
had been the entertainment of his readers. He was a
man profoundly in earnest, deeply conscientious. He
wrote under an ever-present sense of responsibility.
No temptation of fame, influence, or popularity would
ever have induced him to state anything which he did
not believe, or to withhold or exaggerate or mis-color
what he did believe. The accuracy and propriety
which have been imputed to him in the form and substance of his writings extended to the moral element
in them. He was extremely careful to say with preci-

sion that which he truly thought. The result was
that in all the thirteen volumes of his collected Works
there is probably not a line which he would wish to
expunge. He was an entirely cleanly writer. Thirty
years ago, this would have been assumed rather than
mentioned, but the sudden dash towards the pig-sty,
which has been made by so many writers lately,
makes it desirable to declare that Dr. Holmes was not
of this herd. He had too much respect for himself, for
his fellow men and women, and for literature, which
he loved, to write grossly. English and American
writers might declare their prurient books to be discussions of " social problems," and Frenchmen might
allege that all nastiness is reality, and all reality
is nastiness. The Doctor was not to be thus deceived. He rarely referred to this style of book, but
when he did it was with curt condemnation. The
Lancet, a newspaper whose praise is worth having, in
the article just now quoted, further says : —

" *Si sic omnes !* For the public nowadays is suffering from a surfeit of medicine in its literature.
Heredity and the transmission of physiological or
psychological taints; sexual problems; problems in
mental pathology, form the essence of the work of a
large school of writers. Sometimes the work is well
done and sometimes extremely ill done. Now and
again the great romancer will by a few illuminating
words supply a real contribution to the scientific side
of psychology; more often we are asked to solace ourselves after the day's work with long-drawn questions
pruriently put and left unanswered by a string of pom-
pous deductions. And so we say : Ah, if all were
like the Autocrat of the Breakfast-Table ! Would
that all our advanced novelists would recognize, first,

that it is necessary to know before instructing and to see before leading, if the ditch is to be avoided; and, second, that there is wisdom in restraint and an art in remaining silent, — that furibund descriptions of animalism, if accurate, are inappropriate in general literature, and that to display to common gaze a dissection of the morbid imaginings of the sick mind may be an act of positive indecency. Oliver Wendell Holmes was a man who knew. Whither he would lead, his readers might always be content to follow without fear of the ditch. His science was sound, his wisdom indubitable, and his powers of observation and introspection were of the acutest. And how did he use them? Not by shirking the responsibilities laid upon him by his possession of exceptional knowledge, as great men have done before now through fear of giving offence; on the contrary, his whole work is pervaded by his particular learning. And not by persistently presenting to the mental eye the dissected body or the sick soul, the charnel-house, the bordel, or the asylum; on the contrary, his multifarious writings are absolutely free from the taint of nastiness. Oliver Wendell Holmes used his beautiful endowments in the highest way for the good of all, neither burying his talents nor prostituting them. He was removed by a lovable, modest, sympathetic nature from all possibility of writing the harmful; he was removed by a true and highly cultivated artistic sense from the common error of spoiling a picture by overloading it with unnecessary details ; lastly, and chiefly, he was removed by his assured place as a man of scientific education, undoubted learning, and equally undoubted literary genius from all temptation to medical or linguistic display. From this position, with the conscientiousness of the skilled workman and the unpremeditated charm of the poet, he poured out broad lessons of human sympathy and preached a genial, yet shrewd, gospel of kindliness."

"It is a good rule," wrote the Doctor, "for the actor who manages the popular street drama of Punch not to let the audience or spectators see his legs." But he could not follow his own rule; in point of fact probably no writer ever exposed his legs more audaciously, untiringly, than did the good Doctor. The (London) *Spectator* said, after his death: "Dr. Holmes is almost the only man in modern literature in whom the work and its author cannot be separated, and the personality, like the work, stirs an emotion of warm and lasting friendship." "None reveals his personal temperament more clearly," said George William Curtis; and an hundred writers have said the same thing in their respective ways. It was not possible, of course, that the observant Doctor himself should be ignorant of the truth. Hark to his words:—

> What have I rescued from the shelf ?
> A Boswell, writing out himself !
> For though he changes dress and name,
> The man beneath is still the same,
> Laughing or sad, by fits and starts,
> One actor in a dozen parts,
> And whatsoe'er the mask may be,
> The voice assures us, *This is he.*

And in *The Poet at the Breakfast-Table* he says: "*Liberavi animam meam.* That is the meaning of my book and of my literary life, if I may give such a name to that parti-colored shred of human existence."

In point of fact Dr. Holmes's personality poured through his books like a stream in flood time through meadows, soaking and saturating them. He was in every page of the Breakfast-Table Series; he was never far or long away in the novels; he lurked in the stanzas of a large proportion of the lyrics. In a word it is fair to say that he was omnipresent; that those irrepressible legs were always keeping up their lively play before the spectator's eye. He did not work like the ant, by manipulation, acquisition, and dealing with outside materials; but he spun his books out of himself, as a spider spins his web from his vitals. The man who can do this thing well can do the most popular writing in literature. He must be an egotist; but he must be precisely the right kind of egotist, for if he is not so, the sensitive taste of readers — who are very fastidious upon this point — will reject him.

Now Dr. Holmes certainly was an egotist; not, however, in an offensive sense of the word. Alongside of all his kindliness, his philanthropy, there ran ever the deep strong current of his own purpose. Whatever was the work which he happened at any time to have in hand, he gave himself to it with very great zeal; his interest in the occupation of each passing hour was intense; he was absorbed in his own aims, labor, plans, thoughts, ideals; and he allowed nothing to interfere to any serious extent with their development. He was very rigid in protecting himself against undue interruptions. To an endless stream of bores, who encroached upon his time, he was singularly courteous; and yet all the while he was cautious and watchful; he could afford to give these people about so many hours; when that allowance had been devoured, the portcullis fell, sharply, relentlessly, and there was no more trespassing, no

more time-filching that day. Of course this was absolutely necessary, for the visiting stream would have
risen to the proportions of a drowning torrent, had it
not been cautiously kept under control, — a task in
which his wife was of infinite, untiring service to him.
There is a story — just how it may be mingled of
truth and jest I do not undertake to say — that he
kept on hand a little pile of autograph extracts from
his writings, and that when the visitor had reached the
extreme limit of a call, yet seemed unaware of the
fact, the Doctor would kindly hand him one of these
extracts, courteously asking him to take it as a keep-
sake. "They can't stop after that, however tough,"
he said. "I call the extracts my *lubricant;* it greases
the way to send them off."

Of these invaders some had a good right to come;
others came to see a great man, and others came to
let the great man see them. As a cat may look at a
king, so an ass may look at a lion, — and there came
a great number of the more ignoble animal. Some
hunters also desired to entrap this lion for their
own uses and purposes, and in order to propitiate the
beast, they for the most part offered him the sweet
titbits of flattery. The amount of this sort of food
that was stuffed down his throat in the last forty
years of his life would have been fatal to any digestion
which has ever been created. He understood his
danger well, and wrote of it: "So far as one's
vanity is concerned it is well enough. But self-love is
a cup without any bottom, and you might pour the
Great Lakes all through it, and never fill it up. It
breeds an appetite for more of the same kind. It
tends to make the celebrity a mere lump of egotism.
It generates a craving for high-seasoned personalities,

which is in danger of becoming slavery, like that following the abuse of alcohol, or opium, or tobacco. Think of a man's having every day, by every post, letters that tell him he is this and that and the other, with epithets and endearments, one tenth part of which would have made him blush red-hot before he began to be what you call a celebrity!" In time the diet had its influence upon the Doctor. In his old age many people said that he was vain, and they spoke not altogether without truth. Old age of course is egotistical, perforce; the old man, stripped of his comrades, unable to share in current activities, is thrust back by the violence of unkindly circumstances upon the memory of those past incidents *quorum magna pars fuit.* It may be admitted that egotism and vanity found in Dr. Holmes's nature a soil sufficiently congenial to nourish them to tolerably fair growth in his declining years; but if there be a grain of truth in this, at least it is also true that the traits appeared in their amiable and attractive form, and that he was so simple, frank, honest, in his enjoyment of the good opinion of others, that every one was cordially glad to give the kind old man the harmless gratification of praise. I quote Colonel Lee again, the best of authorities: "He has been called vain, by himself and others; but it was vanity of an amiable and childlike kind, — confessed, and so apologized for; not denied or disguised or justified. It was not made offensive by superciliousness, nor contemptible by unmanliness, nor malignant by envy. Had he visited Rotten Row, and gazed at the well-born, well-dressed, well-mounted equestrians, he would have exulted over their bright array, and not have growled out, as Carlyle did, 'There is not one of them can do what I can do.'"

Yet, after all, who can be better quoted than the
Doctor himself? His books and his letters contain
many scores of passages wherein he says in his light,
humorous, outspoken way, with the twinkle in the eye,
and the twitch at the mouth, that the flavor of flattery offends not his palate. He assured his friend
Mr. Appleton: "I was always patient with those who
thought well of me, and accepted all their tributes
with something more than resignation." He thanked
Mr. May for sending him the *Standard:* "Its praise
is extravagant, so far as my poem is concerned, but
I have always been struck with the fact that a man
bears superlatives about his own productions with
wonderful fortitude." The Autocrat says: "I purr
very loud over a good, honest letter that says pretty
things to me." And again: "*Non omnis moriar* is
a pleasant thought to one who has loved his poor
little planet, and will, I trust, retain kindly recollections of it through whatever wilderness of worlds he
may be called to wander in his future pilgrimages."
There is such a fragrance of humanity and fellowship
about this passage, that any one would wish to minister pleasant words to him who wrote it. In truth
the Doctor's vanity was of the sympathetic variety;
it did not seek, and was not to be put off with, mere
intellectual appreciation. He did not crave admiration
so much as a genial community of feeling. He did not
so much desire that you should laugh at his witticism
as that you should join him in laughing at it; or, if
there was satire, the twinkle in your eye must be the
return flash for that which parted from his own; and
if his sentiment called forth your tear, he valued it as
a companion drop with his. Who could fail to feel
kindly to a vanity of this sort? It was in perfect

accord with the Doctor's nature. In fact he had a kind of right to it. He had always shown kindliness and sympathy towards all the rest of mankind. Was he called upon to rule out himself alone from the benefit of his admirable traits; and must he do this only in order to respect a foolish modern prejudice against egotism? The requirement would have been indeed unreasonable!

Beneath the superficial gratification which he gathered from flattering words, he kept his cool observation and accurate measurement of facts. What he said in *The Poet at the Breakfast-Table* put the truth very well: "He looked pleased. All philosophers look pleased when people say to them virtually, 'Ye are gods.' The Master says he is vain constitutionally, and thanks God that he is. I don't think he has enough vanity to make a fool of himself with it, but the simple truth is he cannot help knowing that he has a wide and lively intelligence, and it pleases him to know it, and to be reminded of it, especially in an oblique and tangential sort of way, so as not to look like downright flattery."

This letter is not altogether inapropos, at this point: —

TO SAMUEL WILKS, M. D., GROSVENOR STREET, LONDON.

July 10, 1875.

MY DEAR SIR, — I have kept your letter as we leave a Bon Chrétien or a Rare-ripe — I hope you have that pear and peach — to mellow a little on my table, before saying these few words to let you know how much pleasure it has given me. I do not say that I have never had words as flattering to my self-love as yours; but I cannot have often had such words from any whose good opinion I should value so highly. For in the mean time, while my transatlantic fruit was ripening, I have read the four pamphlets you have kindly sent me, and found the reason why you were at home in my pages, — because the very qualities which you managed to find in them were already in your own intelligence, because your gamut of sensibilities was as wide in its extent as you were pleased to think my own. You speak so frankly, I must tell one or two of my own secrets. I do not know what to make of it sometimes when I receive a letter, it may be from Oregon or Omaha, from England or Australia, telling me that I have unlocked the secret chamber of some heart which others, infinitely more famous, infinitely more entitled to claim the freedom, have failed to find opening for them. This has happened to me so often, from so many different persons, men and women, young and old, that I cannot help believing there is some human tone in my written voice which sometimes finds a chord not often set vibrating. My mode of life is rather solitary than social, though I have contributed my share of hilarity to scores of festivals, and am almost entitled to be called the laureate of our local receptions of great personages, from Prince Albert Edward downward. I have long ceased to practice, but keep my professorship in the Medical School of Harvard University, which occupies and amuses me for seven months of the year. I go to a dinner-party once in a while, and once a month to the Saturday Club, where I meet Emerson, Longfellow, Lowell, and in other years used to meet Agassiz, Sumner, Motley, Hawthorne, and many others of more or less name and note. But I live quietly with my wife, by choice. My children (three) are all married, and

I find my contemporaries getting old. But I find my sympathies not less active because I live a good deal out of the busy world, and because I find myself so much at home among what are called elderly people, not of course recognizing myself as one of them. I suppose that is the reason I have made so many friends. But I am also willing to take credit for certain intellectual qualities, which you estimate at their full value at least; and this gives your letter a special significance, for I have read the four pamphlets you have sent me, and found so much in them that was in harmony with my own way of thinking, and so much, that was your own, of good sense and of ingenious observation, that your praise means a great deal to me. I feel very grateful to you for having the courage, I might almost call it, to say in good honest English what you felt about my books and myself. It is the best reward of authorship to be greeted in terms of friendship, nay something like affection, by those whose own words have cheered, comforted, consoled, strengthened, stimulated, if not instructed. I thank you from my heart for your most grateful letter.

Dr. Holmes was upon the whole very fortunate in escaping any severe criticism, — for, of course, opposition to his views, religious or other, could not be called criticism. He himself said some unkind things of the critics ; e. g., " What a blessed thing it is that Nature, when she invented, manufactured, and patented her authors, contrived to make critics out of the chips that were left." But, strange to say, these gentlemen did not retaliate ; perhaps they felt that they would meet too little sympathy in any severe handling of an author who was more than popular, who was really beloved, and who had the happy knack of uttering satire without giving offence. So in prudence, or kindness, or both, they generally gave him only fair words. *The Nation* once made a savage onslaught upon him, and succeeded in penetrating his philosophy and hurting his feelings. It was a triumph which was won, I think, only on this single occasion. But whether wounded or not, whether misrepresented or not, he had the good sense to avoid controversy. " If a fellow attacked my opinions in print, would I reply ? " asks the Autocrat. " Not I. Do you think I don't understand what my friend, the Professor, long ago called *the hydrostatic paradox of controversy ?* " — which enigmatic phrase he explained thus : " If you had a bent tube, one arm of which was the size of a pipe-stem and the other big enough to hold the ocean, water would stand at the same height in one as in the other. Thus discussion equalizes fools and wise men in the same way, and the fools know it."

Probably the " literary filter," referred to in the following letter, was not a perfect disinfectant ; but it is certain that the principle laid down generally controlled the Doctor's action.

April 28, 1859.

My dear Sir, — I owe you many thanks for your kind and thoughtful note. I understand the article appeared, that it was well written, that it applied the usual terms to me, and so forth. I not only do not intend answering this or any other attack, but I do not mean to read one of them. If what I say cannot hold water, I am not going to stop the hole with " soft sawder." As I write from my convictions, after ample opportunity of seeing the utter hollowness of all the pretensions to the exclusive possession of truth and goodness by the people who claim to be our spiritual dictators, I shall not trouble myself whether they like it or not. If something did not pinch, there would be no squeak.

I received this morning two letters from distant places expressing the greatest delight and sympathy, and I feel sure that there are good people enough to rally round every honest speaker, and see that he is not lynched for exercising the great inalienable right of every soul born into the world. I have a private committee of friends, to whom I have assigned the duty of reading all attacks on me and my doctrines. I sometimes ask them whether these attacks are clever or dull, what they take hold of, if they use epithets, and so on, and caution them to keep the papers out of my way. This patent literary filter of mine is a great convenience, it saves my temper, and allows my best friends to attack me as much as they like without my having to be aware of it ; so that while my assailant thinks I am busy with his article I have forgotten my own even, and am busy on next month. Be sure that your expression of interest was very welcome, all the more so for knowing what hard things some others would be saying. I could not help answering [?], notwithstanding your plenary indulgence and unconditional absolution.

CHAPTER XIV

THE Doctor glided gently and imperceptibly into
the period of old age. He came to it in excellent
condition both of mind and body, for he had led a
well-regulated life. He could tell of himself the tale
of Adam in "As You Like It." Wine, tobacco, and
late hours had never impaired his vigor, and as he
had grown older he had grown always more abstemi-
ous. He had been hard-working, but never really
overworked, and he had never taken either work or
play nervously and tensely. Above all, he had been
but little preyed upon by anxieties; in the middle
path between poverty and riches, he had probably
moved along that road which really gives the most
generous measure of content and comfort. He had
strolled pleasantly and at his own pace along the side
paths, by the enchanting hedgerows, quite apart from
the hurly-burly of the highway where the throng
hurried and jostled along, the millionnaires and the
beggars crowding, hustling, and cursing each other.
Thus leaving this procession, which could find no leisure for enjoyment, to push and tumble along as best
it might, he meantime advanced pleasantly, falling in
now and again with good company, moving through
the changing shade or sunshine, enjoying all the possible beauty and peacefulness of the journey through

life. In this way, by degrees, he became old, and
hardly knew it — would have forgotten it for a long
while, perhaps, had he been a less close observer of
facts, or if others had not called his attention to the
climbing figures of the anniversaries.

On December 3, 1879, there took place in Boston
a redoubtable feast, not so much a merry-making as
a stupendous compliment. It was given by the publishers of *The Atlantic Monthly* in honor of the contributor who, more than any other one man, had caused
its prosperity, who had been to it the life-blood racing
through its veins. The celebration took place, as the
lawyers say, "*nunc pro tunc*," on December 3d, as afore-
said, but "as of" August 29th next preceding; for
on that summer's day, unseasonably placed for social
gatherings, Dr. Holmes had reached the scriptural
limit of life. It was a very brilliant affair, and truly
famous, that Atlantic Breakfast; every one of any
account in literature either came to it, or regretted in
becoming phrase that he could not come. There were
poems and speeches, and really, though such things
are apt to be a trifle stilted and artificial, this was a
handsome success. Mr. Howells had been asked to
sit at the end of the banqueting-table opposite Dr.
Holmes, and the Doctor afterward wrote to him the
following note: —

TO WILLIAM DEAN HOWELLS.

December 14, 1879.

MY DEAR MR. HOWELLS, — I have never said a
word to you about our Breakfast, which you con-
ducted so admirably. It hardly seemed necessary,
where everybody agreed as to your share of it, that
any one should tell you what you must know so well.

You showed, I thought, great tact, and *savoir dire* and *faire* in your management of the south pole of the festival. Of course I was pleased — how could I help being pleased — with the penetrating and nicely accented praise you awarded me. We know the difference between a smudge of eulogy and a stroke of characterization. Even in putting the holiday dress of adjectives on the person who is asked to come and hear himself canonized, there is all the difference in the world between those who know how to make it fit without pinching or bagging, and the kind, well-meaning friends who think, if they only take cloth enough and dictionary-spangles enough, though "the garment of praise hides all your points and betrays all your malformations," they have done all that a demigod could ask for. In return, I must congratulate you on the brilliant and commanding position you have fairly won for yourself. You have brought us an outside element which Boston needed, and have assimilated all that Boston could do for you (if you can be said to have needed anything) so completely that it seems as if you had cheated some native Esau out of his birthright.

I hope you will live to see your septuagenarian breakfast and many a breakfast on the other side of it, not only famous, but happy in all that surrounds you.

Perhaps some such extreme measure as this celebration was necessary in order to impress upon the Doctor and the world the chronological fact upon which it was based, viz., that he was now at that age at which a well-constructed person should die, and of course had been an old man for at least ten years past.

But what is more absurd than truth can often be!

If Scripture and chronology thus conspired against the sprightly Doctor, they conspired in vain. Neither in body, mind, nor morale, did this vivacious, genial gentleman, a comrade for the young as for the old, seem a "trespasser upon the domain belonging to another generation." Being, however, an experienced physician and an intelligent man, he knew perfectly well the inevitable course of brain cells and tissues, and such-like crude components of the human experiment, and he knew that deterioration must have begun, and that the only question was as to the greater or less rapidity with which it would advance. Upon this point he did not mean to be deceived; he did not intend that the outside world should measure a decadence concerning which he was not himself accurately informed; he meant to be on his guard, and to have as few unpleasant remarks made behind his back as might be. So he began to keep upon himself the close and intelligent watch of the trained observer. It was noticed by those who knew him well that the faculty for keen and accurate observation, which all his life long had been one of the most striking of his mental traits, was now turned in its full force upon himself. If this was largely for the sake of self-knowledge and self-protection, yet it was not wholly so; for he felt a curious interest in studying old age from that only actual specimen from which any man can be sure that he is studying correctly; it was like vivisecting one's self; and he became absorbed in the process and the results. It was both a scientific investigation and a study of man.

That this could be altogether pleasant can hardly be imagined; but this memoir has been very ill-written if the reader has not divined that with the kindliness

and humanity of the Doctor's temperament, there
were linked the kindred virtues of unconquerable
cheerfulness and buoyancy, with the courage which is
the natural comrade of these traits. It was not with
grimness of spirit that he faced the advance of Time,
as one resolved to do battle; his geniality did not
grow out of a strenuous effort of the will; he only
aided the liveliness and optimism of his amiable nature by a cool resolution; and his philosophy was not
defiant, but serene.

In this way for fifteen years more he continued not
only uniformly cheerful, but much of the time light-
hearted and even merry. He had not very long before
described himself, with his clear self-knowledge, in a
letter to Motley: —

"How strangely — with what curious suggestions
and reminiscences, your Shelley neighborhood experiences come over me! I have always kept in my memory those 'Lines written in dejection near Naples,' or
some of them, from which I think you quote. I have
said a thousand times (I trust my memory now): —

> I could lie down like a tired child
> And weep away this life of care
> Which I have borne, and still must bear,

and the rest. But it was as a mood, and not as an
habitual or very real feeling, for my temperament is
too lively to be kept down long by the common burdens of this life of care. My spirits have, I think,
grown more equable, and I am sure my temper has
grown easier with years. But there I go again

> Ὁ δε βαρβιτος χορδοις
> 'Egomet' μουνον ηχει.

I hope my Greek letters are right, — you may put in

accents and aspirates to suit yourself, as Lord Timothy Dexter told his readers to do with their stops."

He declared that he had a "right to rest after a life which had been tolerably laborious;" yet it was obviously his intention to curtail his work no faster than the gradual shrinkage of his faculties should make desirable. It was natural that the first lopping off should be the lectures at the Medical School. Accordingly, on October 9, 1882, we find him intimating to Dr. Weir Mitchell his purpose in this direction: "I have not told you that I am very soon to resign my professorship. I have been thinking of it for some time, and very lately received a proposal from my publishers so tempting that I could not resist it. I hold on for a couple of months to give the Faculty and the Corporation of the University time to look round for some one to complete the course I have begun. Thirty-five years here — this is my thirty-sixth course — two years Professor at Dartmouth — that is long enough, isn't it? They say they don't want me to give up, but I had rather spend whatever days are left me in literary pursuits. So I expect to start the scimetar[1] through a good many volumes of prose and verse — yours, I hope, among the earliest." And to Dr. Fordyce Barker: "I am glad to look forward to rest from my official duties as professor. I say look forward, for they want me to lecture a little longer, at any rate, and I shall hold on until about Thanksgiving time. I should have liked, on some accounts, to lecture two or three years longer. We have a grand new College building about five minutes' walk from my house. My colleagues do not seem to

[1] The paper-cutter, which we have already heard of, *ante*, p. 352.

be tired of me, and my duties have been made most agreeable to me in every respect. But I found I could make a very advantageous arrangement with my publishers, and I accepted the opening which presented itself rather suddenly, just as our winter course was about to begin. I shall have a freedom I shall be glad of, and shall write when I feel disposed, — which, I think, will be pretty often when I have no routine duties to keep up a steady drain on my vital resources."

On November 28, 1882, he delivered his Farewell Address to the Medical School. "I have delivered my last anatomical lecture," he said, "and heard my class recite for the last time." He gave something like an apology for having held his office so long, as though there might be some danger or suspicion that Science had advanced faster than an old man could keep pace with her: "But while many of the sciences have so changed that the teachers of the past would hardly know them, it has not been so with the branch I teach; or, rather, with that division of it which is chiefly taught in this amphitheatre. *General* anatomy, or histology, on the other hand, is almost all new; it has grown up, mainly, since I began my medical studies. . . . If I myself needed an apology for holding my office so long, I should find it in the fact that human anatomy is much the same study that it was in the days of Vesalius and Fallopius, and that a greater part of my teaching was of such a nature that it could never become antiquated."

He closed thus: "Let me add a few words which shall not be other than cheerful, as I bid farewell to this edifice which I have known so long. I am grateful to the roof which has sheltered me, to the floors

which have sustained me, though I have thought it
safest always to abstain from anything like eloquence,
lest a burst of too emphatic applause might land my
class and myself in the cellar of the collapsing struc-
ture, and bury us in the fate of Korah, Dathan, and
Abiram. I have helped to wear these stairs into hol-
lows, — stairs which I trod when they were smooth
and level, fresh from the plane. There are just thirty-
two of them, as there were five and thirty years ago,
but they are steeper and harder to climb, it seems to
me, than they were then. I remember that in the early
youth of this building, the late Dr. John K. Mitchell,
father of our famous Dr. Weir Mitchell, said to me,
as we came out of the demonstrator's room, that some
day or other a whole class would go heels over head
down this graded precipice, like the herd told of in
Scripture story. This has never happened as yet; I
trust it never will. I have never been proud of the
apartment beneath the seats, in which my preparations for lecture were made. But I chose it because
I could have it to myself, and I resign it, with a wish
that it were more worthy of regret, into the hands of
my successor, with my parting benediction. Within
its twilight precincts I have often prayed for light,
like Ajax, for the daylight found scanty entrance, and
the gaslight never illuminated its dark recesses. May
it prove to him who comes after me like the cave of
the Sibyl, out of the gloomy depths of which came
the oracles which shone with the rays of truth and
wisdom!"

The students presented him with a silver loving-
cup, an appropriate gift; for if later classes might
have teachers equally efficient, no one else was likely
to inspire such personal affection as had been felt for

Dr. Holmes. He had not been forewarned of this, and being taken unawares was near to being overcome by a sentiment which it was inevitable that he should feel. He would not try at the moment to utter his thanks in words, but wrote afterward: —

"This gift, of priceless value to me and to those who come after me, will meet another and similar one of ancient date, which has come down to me as an heirloom in the fifth generation from its original owner. The silver teapot, which serves the temperate needs of my noontide refection, has engraved upon it, for armorial bearings, three nodules, supposed to represent the mineral suggesting the name of the recipient, the three words, *Ex Dono Pupillorum*, and the date 1738. This piece of silver was given by his Harvard College pupils to the famous tutor, Henry Flynt, whose term of service, fifty-five years, is the longest on the college record. Tutor Flynt was a bachelor, and this memorial gift passed after his death to his niece, Dorothy Quincy, who did me the high honor of becoming my great-grandmother. Through her daughter and her daughter's daughter it came down to me, and has always been held by me as the most loved and venerated relic which time has bequeathed me. It will never lose its hold on my affections, for it is a part of my earliest associations and dearest remembrances.

"But this loving-cup, which comes to me not by descent, but as a testimony that my own life as a teacher has not been undervalued, but thought deserving of such an enduring memorial, must hereafter claim an equal place in my affections with that most prized and cherished of all my household possessions. I hope that when another hundred and fifty years have passed away, some descendant of mine will say, as he lifts this cup and reads the name it bears: 'He, too, loved his labor and those for whom he labored; and the students of the dead nineteenth century remembered their old teacher as kindly, as gracefully, as generously, as the youth of the earlier eighteenth century remembered old Father Flynt, the patriarch of all our Harvard tutors.'"

The University made him Professor Emeritus.

I fancy that the official records do not contain a remark made by the Doctor on this occasion, apropos of the fact that when he began his labors there were six instructors, and now there were seventy: "But it is not every animal which has the most legs that crawls the fastest."

The following spring, April 12, 1883, the members of the medical profession of New York gave a grand dinner at Delmonico's in honor of Dr. Holmes. Mr. Evarts, George William Curtis, Whitelaw Reid, and others, spoke, and the Doctor of course read a poem. It was another very handsome and flattering compliment, — a golden milestone in the journey.

One by one friends and contemporaries, and the associates who had sat around the table of the dearly loved Saturday Club began to drop away, had in fact begun long ere Dr. Holmes reached his seventieth birthday. Agassiz had died in the last month of 1873. In 1877 Motley died; in 1882 Longfellow, and Emerson followed. The Doctor began to feel, he said, that the old Club was, for him, a gathering of ghosts.

He had always been greatly attracted by the gentleness and urbanity of Longfellow, and he made some remarks about him at the meeting of the Massachusetts Historical Society, and wrote some verses for *The*

Atlantic Monthly. "But" he said, "it is all too little, for his life was so exceptionally sweet and musical that any voice of praise sounds almost like a discord after it; and yet, as he cannot sing his own requiem, we must utter ourselves as nature prompts us to." [1]

Of these departed friends, Dr. Holmes was called upon to write the lives of two, John Lothrop Motley and Ralph Waldo Emerson.

Mr. Motley died in May, 1877, and Dr. Holmes wrote the customary brief memoir for the Massachusetts Historical Society. Naturally enough, this was expanded into a small volume, for publication. It was fairly supposable that the Doctor was especially well equipped for the task. The two men were nearly of an age, — Motley was born in April, 1814; and though the five years of difference was an untraversable space in their youthful days, afterward, when maturity had arranged the perspectives of life, they became close friends, and in no other letters does Dr. Holmes betray such warm personal feeling as in those to Motley. It may be said that he had fallen prone beneath the fascination of the handsome gentleman and brilliant historian. Therefore when now he was asked to narrate the career of his illustrious friend, the Doctor came to it with a full heart and an ardent pen. Yet he did not produce an entirely satisfactory book. Throughout, it is vivid, eloquent, and illumined with many charmingly written pages. It is a glowing, generous eulogy, an idealized picture of a man whose nature, moral, mental, and physical, held out a lure which Dr. Holmes's temperament was unable to resist. What, in fact, he did may be justly expressed in words used by himself upon another occasion: "Bidding

[1] Note to Paul H. Hayne.

the dead past unbury its dead, in new and gracious aspects; recalling what was best in their features, and clothing them in the embroidered garments of memory."

He wrote to Mr. Motley's daughter, Lady Harcourt, when the book was about to be published : —

"I hardly dare to think that I have told the story of your father's life in a way to satisfy you, even as an outline. I confess, I feel as if no one could do it to please in every way, and to the full extent, one who knew him so intimately and loved him so dearly. But I have at least tried to do him justice, and I feel sure you will give me credit for having done my best to honor his memory."

Thus much, at least, there was no doubt that he had achieved. The volume was distinctly what is called "a tribute." It was a labor of love, an outpouring and lavishment of praise; but it was not history, not even biography. Undoubtedly there was excuse for this; for, from the elements involved, the task of composition could hardly have been more difficult. Twice Motley had been in public life, and twice had left it under circumstances which were the more unfortunate because they were extremely discreditable to other persons whom, otherwise, the nation justly held in high honor. It was no easy matter to enter the labyrinth of charges, criminations, and aspersions which ensnarled these incidents, and the Doctor keenly appreciated that to do his task well was almost impossible. He wrote anxiously to his old friend, John O. Sargent : —

February 3, 1878.

MY DEAR JOHN, — I am more obliged to you than I can tell for your outspoken, intimate, and truly confidential letter. No higher compliment can be paid to one than to trust his discretion with the inside view of many details of life and character of those in whom he is interested, — details which he ought to know, but many of which he ought also to keep to himself. There is nothing that surprises me in what you say of our old friend; I have talked and corresponded with many of those who knew his character and history best, and I was, during his last visit more especially, in the most intimate daily relations with him at a time when his heart opened itself most freely. I had, besides, been almost his only regular correspondent in this country for some twenty years or more. So I knew his strong and weak points pretty well. If I had my will, I would never write anybody's biography or memoir, for we all want to draw perfect ideals, and all the coin that comes from Nature's mint is more or less clipped, filed, "sweated," or bruised and bent and worn, even if it was pure metal when stamped — which is more than we claim, I suppose, for anything human.

But I write this note to thank you again and again for your great kindness in taking so much pains to give me a true picture of our impulsive, passionate, ambitious, proud, sensitive, but always *interesting* friend. It is going to be a very delicate business to speak of his diplomatic career. I must steer between the rocks as I best may.

When a man of note in literature dies, the critics and reviewers, and the swarm of paragraphers who write the little "notices" for the newspapers, come by their chance, and are wont to use it with such discretion and intelligence as economical Nature has thought it worth while to bestow upon them. They contribute to the cairn, often too truly by the casting of stones, until the poor silent form beneath groans under their clumsy attentions. What protests would not Dr. Holmes have uttered against those obituary writers who said that he was profoundly influenced by the writings of Emerson, and that the effect of the Emersonian philosophy can be plainly traced throughout his work! Not that he would have desired to come under the sway of a nobler teacher; but he would have wished the truth to be told, and the truth was that he never came beneath any influence whatsoever, either of any individual or of any school. George William Curtis truly says that neither "the storm of agitation nor the transcendental mist that . . . overhung intellectual New England greatly affected" the Doctor. It was certainly the case that he never showed the slightest inclination to enter the circle of the so-called "Emersonians." He understood Emerson with his intellectual intelligence; but he did not appreciate him sympathetically to any considerable degree, and was very far indeed from "sitting at his feet." Emerson wrote of religions, Holmes wrote of creeds; Emerson dealt with Man, Holmes concerned himself with men; Emerson found his topics in idealities, Holmes found his in things concrete; Emerson was mystical, sometimes incomprehensible, but no reader could close his intelligence against the lucidity of every sentence of Holmes.

The truth was that it was interesting to see two men, bred from like stock, belonging in the same generation, living amid the same surroundings, both engaged in knocking off the fetters of old thought and belief, yet doing their work along lines so widely apart, in methods so utterly diverse, reaching such different kinds of men through such different influences, and never moving even tentatively towards any alliance in effort.   The real curiosity is that under such circumstances these two neighbors, fellow-laborers, friends, wrote, each as if he had never heard of the other nor read a line from his pen.   This really was odd, — not that Holmes was influenced by Emerson, but that he did not seem to have been influenced by him in the very slightest degree.

If evidence of this independence were needed, it is abundantly supplied by the Life of Emerson which the Doctor wrote for the American Men of Letters Series.   In point of fact, so well was the Doctor's relationship towards "Emersonianism" known that, when it was learned that he had been invited to write this volume, the selection was generally regarded as far from fortunate.   There was curiosity to hear what Holmes would say about Emerson, but there was no very great expectation of a biography which would gratify the admirers of the philosopher.   It was the Holmes element, not the Emerson element, which was looked forward to.   These anticipations were substantially fulfilled.   The book has many brilliant suggestive passages in the vein of the writer, but the critic must declare that it achieves a limited success in depicting its subject, and therefore, as a biography, it is entitled only to moderate praise.   Yet it may be conceded that the task of writing the life of a philosopher is intrinsically of extreme if not insuperable difficulty; and it is true that the reading public has set the stamp of its approval upon the Doctor's volume by buying it, and presumably also reading it with much avidity.

Probably the inducement to the invitation to write it was found in the remarks which the Doctor delivered before the Massachusetts Historical Society, in May, 1882; for he was never excelled in uttering a graceful tribute, and on this occasion he was equal to his best, as witness this one among many admirable paragraphs: —

"What could we do with this unexpected, unprovided for, unclassified, half unwelcome newcomer, who had been for a while potted, as it were, in our Unitarian cold green-house, but had taken to growing so fast that he was lifting off its glass roof and letting in the hailstorms? Here was a protest that outflanked the extreme left of liberalism, yet so calm and serene that its radicalism had the accents of the gospel of peace. Here was an iconoclast without a hammer, who took down our idols from their pedestals so tenderly that it seemed like an act of worship."

But despite the skill of such happy words, it may be safely believed that the misgivings of the Emersonians were shared by the Doctor himself, and that he undertook his task by no means without anxiety. He wrote his friend John O. Sargent, August 11, 1883: "I took it up very reluctantly, having been a late comer as an admirer of the Concord poet and philosopher. But I have got interested in it, and am reading and studying to get at the true inwardness of this remarkable being and his world. I hope I shall come to be as familiar with him as you are with Horace." This is certainly not a promising attitude for a biog-

rapher to occupy towards his subject, — resolution to
attempt, by study, to get at him.   But if the circumstances called for hard and thorough work, the Doctor
gave it; and in time he was able to write to James
Russell Lowell: "I find the study of Emerson curiously interesting, — few, I think, can bear study into
all his mental, moral, personal conditions as he does." [1]
Thus closely was he conducting his research, rather, it
should be said, his inspection into his subject.   Not
altogether differently in times past he had studied in
Paris; but he had found it easier to get at the cra-
nial bones and the brain-cells than at thoughts and
mental processes.

He exhausted all resources, sought all assistance,
and devoted a long period to the close investigation
of the writings of Mr. Emerson.   The man himself,
as a man, he had known well, and he had felt, with
a sentiment of warm admiration, the rare personal
charm of that gentle and most lovable nature.   He
saw, too, with delighted appreciation, that fine humor
which ran like a delicate, luminous, golden thread
through the subtle braid of Emerson's expression, and
which quite escaped the notice of many of the seri-
ous-minded and high-souled idolaters at the Concord
shrine.   These were great and fortunate aids to the
Doctor, yet in spite of all that he could do, I think
that he never felt entirely easy with his work.   Writing to Mr. Alexander Ireland, he begs to be allowed
to borrow from that gentleman's "very interesting
volume of Recollections;" he "hopes, with some def-
erence," that he "may be able to add something to
what has already been written;" and he consoles himself with the reflection that "the idea of this Series is
rather, I think, to meet the need of that class of read-

[1] August 29, 1883.

ers which dreads a surfeit, though it wants to be fed to a moderate amount, and may be made hungry for more, if we do not begin by cramming too hard." [1]

In the course of his work he writes : —

TO JAMES FREEMAN CLARKE.

February 9, 1884.

MY DEAR JAMES, — Will you please mention to me anything and everything you have printed about Mr. Emerson ?

Where is the letter you brought to the meeting of the Massachusetts Historical Society ?

Is it possible for you to write out for me any reminiscences of Emerson, — of the " Transcendental " people and times, of E.'s relations with yourself — with Margaret Fuller ? — *anything* not already before the public ?

I find myself somewhat in the position of Carlyle's editor — threshing the thrice-beaten straw; and I can do nothing but — let me change the metaphor — pump once more at the old wells.

My dear, blessed, old friend, it is too bad to put so busy a man as you to the torture, but I am myself not unused to the thumbscrew and the bootikins, and have now and then helped out a friend, nay, a stranger, with a blank page before him and a Publisher's demon behind him. But if my request comes inopportunely and distresses or overburdens you, as a straw too much sometimes does, say that your time and hands are too full, or in a single word that you are busy or tired, and forget my request. Not the less shall I remain

Always affectionately yours,

O. W. HOLMES.

[1] January 4, 1884.

October 9, 1884.

My dear Miss Emerson, — You are too kind! Your letter is so full and precise in its answer to my questions that I feel very grateful for the pains you have taken with it. . . . Everybody wishes to know from the original sources of intimate knowledge those conditions of an extraordinary life which it shares with ordinary lives, — with their own.

Dr. Johnson's cups of tea and his hoarded orange-peel make him real to us, and we are thankful to Boswell for telling us about them. In a generation or two your father will be an ideal, tending to become as mystical as Buddha but for these human circumstances, which remind us that he was a man, " subject to like passions as we are," as well as Elias, of whom the Apostle speaks. It will delight so many people to know these lesser circumstances of a great life that I can hardly bear to lose sight of any of them, except the infirmities which time brought with it; and even these were very much less painful to tell of than such as have fallen to the lot of many famous men.

He thanked Mr. Warner,[1] the editor of the Series, for pointing out sundry repetitions. He says : —

" I am afraid there may be others, for I have often picked up the same facts from different sources ; and, writing at intervals, had forgotten the ground I had covered. The truth is that Emerson's life and writings have been so *darned over* by biographers and critics that a new hand can hardly tell his own yarn from that of his predecessors, or one of theirs from

[1] July 11, 1884.

another's. I wish you would point out anything that specially needs correction, and I will do what I can to make it right, if I have to break up stereotype plates to do it. . . . Don't think I am sensitive to corrections, but suggest anything that you, as editor, think will help make the Memoir better."

How deeply the anxiety to do well sank into his mind, and how difficult he found his task, may be inferred from the fact that afterward, in writing the introduction to *A Mortal Antipathy*, he lugged in the matter, and disburthened himself, as from an over-laden recollection of his past labor, of these reflections: —

"And now for many months I have been living in daily relations of intimacy with one who seems nearer to me since he has left us than while he was here in living form and feature. I did not know how difficult a task I had undertaken in venturing upon a memoir of a man whom all, or almost all, agree upon as one of the great lights of the New World, and whom very many regard as an unpredicted Messiah. Never before was I so forcibly reminded of Carlyle's description of the work of a newspaper editor, — that threshing of straw already thrice-beaten by the flails of other laborers in the same field. What could be said that had not been said of 'transcendentalism' and of him who was regarded as its prophet; of the poet whom some admired without understanding, a few understood, or thought they did, without admiring, and many both understood and admired, — among these there being not a small number who went far beyond admiration, and lost themselves in devout worship? While one exalted him as 'the greatest man that ever lived,' another, a friend, famous in the world of letters, wrote expressly to caution me against the danger of overrating a writer whom he is content to recognize as an American Montaigne, and nothing more."

One thing is noteworthy: the biographer got to the end of his work without once telling to his reader any of his own secrets; what he himself held for truth or probability as to the matters dealt with by Emerson, what faith or what feeling he himself had towards mysticism and transcendentalism, toward God and man and the universe and all the points of religion interwoven therewith, he had managed to keep carefully to himself. The curiosity to get at some definite notion of the Doctor's actual beliefs remained unsatisfied, to the great disappointment of many a reader, who made his way through the volume, not in order to find out what Dr. Holmes thought that Emerson thought, but to find out what Dr. Holmes himself thought; and who was no wiser on this point when he closed than when he opened the book. The astute biographer had evaded even this trap and extreme temptation. He would never take his recipes and his formulas out of the province of medicine into that of religion.

When the book was at last on the booksellers' counters, the delivered author wrote to Mr. Ireland,[1] with relief as obvious as if one could hear the sigh: —

" I am taking the opportunity to send you the last book I have written. I doubt whether you will care to read it; I doubt whether you will like it, if you do. I wish that, if it reaches you in safety, you could sit down at once and acknowledge its receipt. You may add, if you choose, that you 'hope in the near future to have the pleasure of reading it,' — the 'near future'

[1] January 15, 1885.

standing for the Greek Kalends. This I say in all sincerity. A volume like this carries dismay with it, when the recipient supposes he is expected to read it from title to Finis, and it is only as a friendly token that I send it."

His brother John read the volume and sent to him a humorous compliment on not having written more: "You have achieved a wonder, it seems to me, in getting your work into so small compass, and I think it no small evidence of ability; people are so apt to swell and become dropsical with biographic autopsies. . . . Now do take a turn at novel-reading and have a blow-out on tea, if you won't go anything stronger."

Perhaps the foregoing remarks on the *Emerson* may seem unduly severe; let the scales, then, be balanced by a critic, who was exceptionally able to form, and was sure to express, a just conclusion in this case, who lived at Concord, knew and fondly cared for Emerson, and never was charged with making truthfulness subordinate to amenities.

EBENEZER ROCKWOOD HOAR TO OLIVER WENDELL HOLMES.

CONCORD, *December* 28, 1884.

MY DEAR DR. HOLMES, — Permit me to formally return my acknowledgment and thanks for your gift of the *Memoir of Emerson*, which will be a valued possession for its own merits, and very precious as a souvenir of your constant friendship.

I was very much astonished, when you made your address on Emerson before the Historical Society, to find how much you knew and understood about him.

This is no disparagement, but merely the result of a strong impression that there were, in the mental activities of each of you, departments (or I might say apartments) which the other had never visited. You will perhaps understand me better when I say that I felt the same kind of wonder at Mr. Emerson's own marvellous discourse on Burns, whose qualities I should have thought to be rather " out of his line " — though very much in mine.

I do not yet believe that you have got hold of all there was in Emerson, any more than I thought in his lifetime that he understood all there was in you. Indeed, "much meditating these things," I incline to think that a perfect sympathy is only possible in a disciple and admirer — pure and simple — who has no separate gift or quality of his own.

But I think the book is admirably done, and will be of great value in making Emerson's public and your public — so far as they are not the same — better acquainted. I have heard two or three very competent persons say that they were sorry there was not more in it of Dr. Holmes ; a double-headed compliment, at once to your faithfulness as a biographer and charm as a writer on your own account.

The memoir of Motley was finished in 1878; that of Emerson in the autumn of 1884. They were the only efforts which Dr. Holmes made in historical or biographical literature, and it cannot be denied that they showed no very high or rare degree of aptitude for that kind of work. There were too many fences in such fields, and he could not move discursively enough.

I saw him once before
As he passed by the door,
    And again
The pavement stones resound,
As he totters o'er the ground
    With his cane.

They say that in his prime,
Ere the pruning-knife of Time
    Cut him down,
Not a better man was found
By the Crier on his round
    Through the town.

But now he walks the streets,
And he looks at all he meets,
    Sad and wan,
And he shakes his feeble head,
That it seems as if he said
    "They are gone!"

Dr. Holmes' Farewell Address, Ha...

edical School. November 28. 1882

J.M. Lowell.

CHAPTER XV

In April, 1886, Dr. Holmes started, with his daughter, Mrs. Sargent, upon a trip to Europe. He had not been abroad since he was a medical student, yet it was only a brief visit that he made now, — four months, including the two voyages, and he passed the time almost wholly in England. He had greatly changed his feelings and opinions concerning England and Englishmen since the days of his golden youth in Paris. Community of language and of blood had done its work; moreover, the Englishmen had appreciated and liberally praised his books, and it would have been unnatural and ungrateful if he had not rendered to them a handsome return in kind. So, now, although it was his last chance to see the world, their little island seemed to bound his desires and his curiosity. His stay was in reality a triumphal tour; he was overwhelmed with attentions, so that it was only by extreme care that he extricated himself alive from the hospitalities of his British friends. But if it was fatiguing it was exceedingly flattering; and it was a novel and interesting experience for the quiet townsman from Boston to find himself in the torrent of London society in "the season." "He is enjoying himself immensely," wrote James Russell Lowell, "and takes as keen an interest in everything as he would have done at twenty. I almost envy him this freshness of genius. Everybody is charmed with him, as it is natural they should be." One regrets a little that the Englishmen did not see him at his best. Of course they appreciated the inroads of age, and made allowances for them; but making allowances is not a vivid transaction, and the visions of fancy fall sadly short of the realism of actual encounter. We must all wish that he had made that trip thirty years earlier.

There is no need to say much of this incident in his life, because the history of the journey was written by the Doctor himself, under the title of *Our Hundred Days in Europe*, a book pleasant enough to glance through, bearing in mind that the chief object of its writing was to make acknowledgment for the courtesies of the reception which had been extended to the author.

It had happened that, after Dr. Holmes had succeeded in outliving the allotted term of human existence, Harvard University became aware that he was a man of somewhat more than average note. The consequence of this discovery had been that, in 1880, he was able to write to James Russell Lowell: "I bought me a new silk gown and went to Commencement, and they made me an LL. D." Now, during his stay in England, the British seats of learning seized the opportunity to do likewise; Cambridge made him a Doctor of Letters, Edinburgh gave him another LL. D., and Oxford made him D. C. L. He was naturally gratified with these honors, and was not at all annoyed when the Cambridge undergraduates burst into an uproarious song of "Holmes, sweet Holmes." At Oxford he was let off with unwonted courtesy on the part of the galleries, for the only chaffing aimed at him personally was from one young gentleman, who expressed a pardonable curiosity to know whether he came in the "One-Hoss Shay." But the like moderation was not shown towards the other participants in the ceremony, according to this account by a gentleman who wrote to *The Outlook*, over the signature of "Christ Church," and spoke as an eye-witness: —

"This 'Commem' of 1886 was a famous one. Honest John Bright had reconciled his Quaker conscience to red robes, and stood up to be honored. His grand face was applauded to the echo. But the gallery gods had heartier applause for Dr. Holmes, whose almost boyish countenance told them of the eternal youth in the poet's heart. What a quick response there was from those other hearts up aloft, who knew that the good Doctor would not mind the unbridled license which they enjoy one day in the year! The complimentary address was being read, Dr. Holmes standing in his scarlet finery, but the noise in the gallery was deafening: 'Hurry up your Latin, man.' 'Open your mouth so that the Doctor can hear.' 'Mispronounced again, sir; the Doctor is laughing at you,' and verily the Autocrat could not keep back a broad grin from that face which seemed indeed always kindly smiling. The speaker did finally stumble and stutter. Then how he was reviled! 'Take a deeper breath, sir.' 'Now, one, two, three.' 'Don't prompt him, O Vice-Chancellor.' 'I say, let him go it alone.' 'Lady's looking over your shoulder, sir.' Dr. Holmes's grin was subsiding as the speaker tried to find his place, so we next heard: 'Doctor wants to know where the joke is, sir.' 'Hurry up! don't you see our guest is tired?' And when at last the end came, and the Autocrat was enrolled among

the worthies, 'Give the Autocrat a seat,' for the
D. C. L. bench was well crowded. 'Room, room!'
'Seat, seat!' 'Come, show your manners, gentle-
men!' 'No place for Wendell Holmes to sit!'"

In December, 1882, Dr. Holmes wrote to his friend
Mrs. Kellogg: "You know I have given up my Professorship. I had a pleasant opening offered me, and
as I had had about enough schoolmastering, I took off
my professor's gown, and now I am in my literary
shirt-sleeves." But literary shirt-sleeves were the garb
for hard work, not for leisure. The biographies afore-
mentioned and the European journal were not up to
the mark of his ambition, which contemplated flights
more like those of the past days. I do not think that
he considered that he could any longer write so well
as he had done in the heyday of his lively genius; but
he thought that he could still write well enough to
justify him in continuing; he believed that many readers would still be interested, chiefly perhaps the older
men and women, who cherished associations with his
earlier work. He knew that, for himself, it was at
once wholesome and pleasurable. So he clung to his
desk and his pen, and there was something at once
pathetic and admirable in the mingling of self-knowledge and resolution which impelled him to it. "The
old man may go below his own mark with impunity,"
he said. He had always been kindly to his fellow-
men, he hoped that they would be kindly also to him;
he set them the example; he extended his native
charity so that it included himself, — dealt out for
his own benefit that which all his life long he had
liberally dispensed for the benefit of others.

Of *A Mortal Antipathy* mention has already been

made in connection with his other novels. It was published in 1885. In March, 1888, he began the series of papers which he happily christened *Over the Teacups*. It would be idle to pretend that they are as good as the talk of the Autocrat; but they make very pleasant reading, with abundant infusion of the old-time wit, wisdom, and humor. Indeed, the display of these qualities, surviving in such freshness and luxuriance after eighty years of life, was an occurrence nearly if not altogether unprecedented in literature. The papers were really a magnificent *tour de force* of a spirited old man, unyielding, holding his own against the column of the hostile years.

The Doctor had been not a little anxious as to the reception which would be accorded to his reappearance in the colloquial vein. He wrote to his friend John Bellows, in England: "I don't suppose I can make my evening teacups as much of a success as my morning coffee-cups were, but I have found an occupation, and my friends encourage me with the assurance that I am not yet in my second childhood." He had modestly "thought that he had something left to say," and he was gratified when he "found listeners." Also he "had occupation and kept himself in relation with his fellow-beings." And although he had "cleared the eight-barred gate" and was not far from the ultimate deadly goal, the gallant old gentleman said: "New sympathies, new sources of encouragement, if not of inspiration, have opened themselves before me, and cheated the least promising season of life of much that seemed to render it dreary and depressing." Of course the way in which the public and the critics took the book was most gratifying; but the Doctor spoke with shrewd though pleased modesty about it. He wrote to Mrs. Dorr: —

"I am glad to know that you liked the *tea* I served you. Those wintry products of my freezing wits have been very kindly received. I was a little doubtful whether it was safe to begin a serial at threescore and twenty, but I found some entertainment in the work, and on the whole have not regretted my audacity. I do not expect to repeat the experiment, but it is not impossible that I may now and then send a paper to *The Atlantic.* Were it not for the continual calls upon me from all quarters, I could hardly help doing a little literary work now and then."

The most remarkable feature in these papers is the poem of "The Broomstick Train," so humorous in conception, so spirited and lilting in execution. It was a marvel, as the production of a man upwards of eighty years of age; if the electric car had not been so recent an invention, we should swear that these dashing stanzas had been written by the Doctor in the flower of his days, and laid away, to be brought forth as the prodigy of those years which it was absurd to call declining, in the face of this ballad. The old gentleman was pleased, and had reason to be, with the compliments which friends lavished upon this wonderful outburst of an octogenarian muse. He wrote: —

TO CHARLES DUDLEY WARNER.

August 13, 1890.

MY DEAR WARNER, — I thank you for the pleasant words you wrote me about "my broomstick poem." It made me feel young to write it, and I am glad you thought it had something of the elasticity of youth in it. An old tree can put forth a leaf as green as that of a young one, and looks at it with a pleasant sort of surprise, I suppose, as I do at my saucily juvenile production. Thank you once more.

A sad occurrence made an hiatus of many months' duration between the first and the second numbers of *The Teacups*. Dr. Holmes had been singularly fortunate in escaping bereavement, but it was impossible to tempt fate through so many years and pass without loss to the end of life. It was in 1884 that his son Edward had died. Now in the winter of 1887–88 his wife followed. To dwell upon what this meant is needless, and I prefer to pass over that grief in silence. His daughter, Mrs. Sargent, at once came to live with him, and after a short while he made courageous efforts to rally, to escape a despairing decadence and come back to a system of life which might still have value and interest. But in April, 1889, the daughter followed the mother. Then Mr. Justice Holmes, with his wife, came to the charge of the Doctor's old age, and they stayed with him during the remainder of his days.

In 1888 also died his classmate, Rev. James Freeman Clarke. This, though of course an entirely different blow, was likewise a grievous one ; I do not know to what extent the two men met from day to day, but certain it is that the Doctor had a warmth of feeling and an admiration for the clergyman such as he entertained for few others, if indeed for any other in these later years. He wrote as follows to another brother of the Class of '29 : —

TO REV. SAMUEL MAY.

June 20, 1888.

MY DEAR MAY, — Do not wish you had spoken more, or less, or otherwise than you did speak at the funeral of our dearly beloved brother Clarke. I was struck with the deep feeling, yet entire self-mastery, which showed itself in your every word and tone.

We cannot disguise the fact, — the keystone of our arch has slid and fallen, and all we can do is to lean against each other until the last stone is left standing alone.

But we must not come together — such of us as are left to meet — for tears and lamentations. If the meetings [1] are not cheerful and hopeful they will be looked forward to with pain instead of pleasure. I think it well, therefore, that the farewell letter, which would sadden us to tears, should, as you propose, be sent in some form to every member of the class. I know, as you do, that if James could have ordered the next meeting and the very few that may be granted to the poor remnant of our threescore brothers, he would have wished it to be as free from sadness as a meeting of old men, bereft of so much that made life bright and beautiful, infirm, dim-eyed, slow of hearing, with halting intelligences and dulled sensibilities, can possibly be.

A precious memory has taken the place of a beloved and noble presence. We must be thankful that we have enjoyed so large a share of a life which belonged to the world as one of its most cherished and rarest possessions. We know not who among us will be the last survivor, but whoever he is, he will be the heir of a great wealth of memories, among which none will be sweeter, none freer from blemish or shortcoming.

I could not do myself or my subject any justice in the remarks which I dictated for the *Christian Register*. At the Historical Society I found I could not see to read my notes, and therefore spoke extempore, in great measure, with more effect, they said, than if I had read what I had written.

[1] Of the class of 1829.

"I could not see to read my notes," says Dr. Holmes. It was not only tears, perhaps, but physical infirmity which caused this inability. He had a cataract gradually forming. With characteristic keenness of self-observation he had himself discovered this, as he told Mrs. Priestley, one of his English friends: "It is now some years since I gave up using the microscope, having found *by the reflection from my lenses* that there was an opacity somewhere in the field of vision of my working eye." To lose the amusement of the microscope was no longer of much account, but the serious question was whether this new menace would be fulfilled to the point of blindness. Fortunately it never was; the Doctor's sight grew very dim; still his handwriting was always legible, with only moderate difficulty, and he could manage to read somewhat so long as he lived. Yet during his last years he had to use the services of a secretary for nearly all his work, and the black cloud ever hovered threateningly in the horizon. It is needless to dilate upon what a misfortune loss of eyesight would have been to him; but one would like to dilate, and eloquently too, upon the serene and cheerful courage with which he faced the dread prospect. He spoke of the condition often, but not once, so far as I have seen, with a moan. He admitted that he rather preferred "eyes *au naturel*." In October, 1887, he wrote to Dr. Weir Mitchell: "I have got to stop writing letters on account of my eyes, which are, I fear, in serious difficulty, though they look well enough." In December of the same year he wrote to Mrs. Priestley: "I do not expect to write many more such letters, for my eyes are getting very bad, and I am afraid I have a prospect of a staff and a little dog before

me, if I live long enough. I enclose one of my formulæ, which I use more and more, often writing or
dictating a few words to be added on the next page.
I have a very bright young secretary, who will do most
of my writing for me, — who does much of it now.
This letter shows you I am by no means blind, for I
am writing it all *propriâ manu*, and though not
elegant, it is far from illegible." And a few days
later the irresistible tendency of his youth for the
making of puns reasserted itself in the following sentence in another letter to the same lady : " My eyes
are getting dreadfully dim, and I should hardly know
your beautiful face across the street. One of them
has, I fear, though I don't quite know — a *cat*aract
in the *kitten* state of development. Well, I can write
still, as you see, but I am getting my pretty secretary
to do more and more of my writing for me." It was
a question, he said, very philosophically, whether he
should outlast his eyes, or his eyes would outlast him.
Very narrowly it may be said that the latter event
fell out, and most happily so.

For a few years after giving up his place at Pittsfield Dr. Holmes passed his summers in various places
and ways, as chance dictated, but after a while, as he
grew older, the element of uncertainty became annoy-
ing, and he established his permanent residence for
the hot weather at Beverly Farms, on the North Shore
of Massachusetts Bay. He had a pleasant little cottage in the village, hard by the railway station, and
when the occupants of the neighboring town of Man-
chester saw fit to christen that place " Manchester-by-
the-Sea," he used to date his letters " Beverly-by-the
Dépot ; " but later he had to abandon this little sar-
casm, for he moved into another house more agreeably

situated. This seaside region is a gay one during the summer months; the shore is very beautiful, and for several miles on each side of the Doctor's residence the summer houses of the city people crowd each other almost too closely, and the ceaseless stream of their gay equipages makes the road lively. The Doctor found much entertainment in the life and bustle of the place, which moreover held many of his and his wife's relatives and friends. He never acquired for it such an affection as he had felt for Pittsfield, yet in the public mind he became closely associated with it, because during the later years of his life his birth-day, falling in the midsummer, came to be celebrated as an anniversary upon which friends sought to demonstrate affection and esteem. The school-children at Beverly Farms came in their holiday clothes to present their greetings, and to take away, each of them, some trifling souvenir. All the neighbors, also, the festal host of the "summer residents," came; flowers and fruit filled the house, often sent from long distances; letters and telegrams descended like a summer shower; sometimes there were very handsome presents: there was, for instance, an elaborate silver cup, inscribed as given by some ladies from whom any token of liking would have had value; poems were addressed to him; and let not the dread reporter be forgotten! for he invariably lent the sanction of his benign presence to the occasion, so that the cup of glory was filled quite to overflowing! The celebration became rather exhausting for the Doctor during the last few years, but his courteous soul would not permit him to say "not at home" to any one who showed to him the kindness of calling. Then, for days afterwards, he struggled to make due acknowledgment for all the tokens sent to him, sometimes trying to write briefly, and always insisting upon at least signing whatever had been written by his secretary after his own tired eyes had given out. Naturally these notes are not worth reproduction, save, perhaps, this one, written " in answer to a little note of birthday greeting sent from Ashfield by " James Russell Lowell, George William Curtis, and Charles Eliot Norton.

BEVERLY FARMS, MASS., *September 2, 1885.*

MY DEAR FRIENDS, — I cannot make phrases in thanking you for your kind remembrance. I wish you could all have been with me on the 29th; every flower of garden and green-house, and fruits that Paradise would not have been ashamed of, embowered and emblazoned our wayside dwelling.

Grow old, my dear Boys, grow old! Your failings are forgotten, your virtues are overrated, there is just enough of pity in the love that is borne you to give it a tenderness all its own. The horizon line of age moves forward by decades. At sixty, seventy seems to bound the landscape; at seventy, the eye rests on the line of eighty; at eighty, we can see through the mist and still in the distance a ruin or two of ninety; and if we reach ninety, the mirage of our possible centennial bounds our prospect.

The interviewers pressed me hard, as you may have learned if you happened to see Monday's *Advertiser.* I surrendered at discretion, and answered all their questions. It looks a little foolish, perhaps, to be paraded as I have been in the *Advertiser* and the *Globe* (which reproduced a felonious old wood-cut of my countenance), but I could not avoid it without something like brutality after all the pains the interviewers had taken to get at me.

My dear
       James,
       George,
       Charles,
I thank you from my heart for remembering me.
                Affectionately yours,
                      WENDELL.

Litera scripta manet. If this scrap of paper should last a century, somebody might think it was another and more famous Wendell's, so I will sign my name in full as

          OLIVER WENDELL HOLMES.

As it has been the practice in this Memoir to insert such letters and notes as fell naturally into the course of the narrative, and such as were hardly of sufficient importance to find a place among the formal "Letters," let me add here what may be called the correspondence of Dr. Holmes's old age.

TO JOHN G. WHITTIER.

                October 18, 1881.

MY DEAR WHITTIER, — It is a pleasure to follow any suggestion of yours, for it is sure to be a good and kind one. I will request Messrs. Houghton & Mifflin to forward a set of my books to Swarthmore College, happy to find myself in such good company as yourself and Longfellow. I have passed a very pleasant summer at Beverly Farms, having nothing to complain of except rather more work of one kind and another than I wanted. I wish I could be utterly idle for a while, but I do not think I could be except on board ship. My peculiar pleasure, besides reading and driving, has been in making diagrams for my anatomical lectures, and this was, after all, work, however agreeable.

I think I do not feel any considerable change in my general condition, — my sight grows dimmer, of course, — but very slowly. I have worn the same glasses for twenty years. I am getting somewhat hard of hearing, — "slightly deaf" the newspapers inform me, with that polite attention to a personal infirmity which is characteristic of the newspaper press. The dismantling of the human organism is a gentle process, more obvious to those who look on than to those who are the subjects of it. It brings some solaces with it: deafness is a shield; infirmity makes those around us helpful; incapacity unloads our shoulders; and imbecility, if it must come, is always preceded by the administration of one of Nature's opiates. It is a good deal that we older writers, whose names are often mentioned together, should have passed the Psalmist's limit of active life, and yet have an audience when we speak or sing.

I wish you all the blessings you have asked for me — how much better you deserve them!

TO JAMES RUSSELL LOWELL.

BOSTON, *April* 29, 1885.

MY DEAR JAMES, — I got yours of the 17th April day before yesterday. I need not say that it touched me deeply. It seems to me that I have been living with sorrow of late — grief of my own and that of others. The loss of my son Edward comes back to me every day, as I think of all that life promised him if he could but have had the health to enjoy it, and that we had hoped was returning to him when he was suddenly taken away.

Only a week or two ago occurred the funerals of two of my oldest friends, — Dr. Hooper and Dr. Cabot. They were buried on the same day. It is as if an autumn wind were tearing away the last leaves all around me. How can I help mourning with you in your separation from one with whom you have lived so long and happily? All that friendship can do to lighten your burden you can be sure of. What public recognition of your services, what civic honors, may await you, I cannot say; but surely no career could have been more brilliantly and deservedly successful than your whole course as a diplomatist. You will come home to be admired and caressed — you will find the friends who are still left you as attached as ever.

I can of course know nothing of your plans, but whether for public or private life, you have a record behind you and a store of memories, which will glorify and render beautiful your coming decades. I do not believe any son of Harvard ever received such a welcome as awaits you. I do not believe any foreign minister ever brought back such a reputation. You may be sure that the country is proud of you, and longs to get you back as much as England longs to keep you.

TO REV. FREDERIC H. HEDGE, D. D.

January 10, 1886.

MY DEAR OLD FRIEND, — You please me much by reminding me that there was one more old schoolmate, townsman, companion, almost coeval, always friend, who could without effort, as if we were boys again, call me Wendell. I can but think of four others, my wife of course excepted, who indulge me in the luxury of my boyish name. . . . The *rari nantes* come very near to each other, as they cling to the few planks left together of the raft they set out upon, three or four score years ago. . . .

TO PROF. THOMAS DWIGHT.

September 4, 1887.

DEAR DR. DWIGHT, — I have never thanked you, I fear, for your kind message. If I were a score or two years younger than I am I might be tempted to envy you, remembering my quarters at the old college, and being reminded of your comfortable and convenient arrangements in the new building. But I do not envy — I congratulate you; and I only hope I did not keep you waiting too long for the place which you fill so ably.

TO JOHN O. SARGENT.

February 10, 1889.

MY DEAR JOHN, — Whether I answered your letter of January 25th, a month almost ago, or not, I cannot swear; but this I know, that I read it with great delight, took down my Horace, found that you had got him neatly and accurately, and envied you for the moment your vital familiarity with that Roman gentleman, who said so many wise and charming things with such *concinnity* as is to be found nowhere else that I know of. Perhaps I answered you at once, but if so, I forgot to mark your letter with the red cross X which alone prevents my answering the same letter three or four times.

I am always delighted to hear from you — there is not a living person, except my brother John, who recalls my college life to me as you do. My friends — contemporary ones — are all gone pretty much.

James Clarke was the one I miss most. William Amory I saw a good deal of in these last years. Asa Gray I liked exceedingly, though I did not see him very often. Herman Inches I go to see pretty often, but he is gradually wearing out, after outliving almost everybody who expected to go to his funeral.

You make some fun of our Class meeting. It was not very exhilarating, but we got through it pretty well. Two who were there last year were missing. . . . There were six of us. . . . Stickney and Smith were both stone deaf, and kept up some kind of telephony with each other. I read them a poem in which were two lines that I remember: "So ends 'The Boys,' a life-long play;" and "Farewell; I let the curtain fall." The drama was really carried out very well. All kinds of character were represented, and we appeared on the stage in larger numbers for a longer time than any class of our generation. . . .

How strange it is to see the sons of our contemporaries getting gray, and their grandchildren getting engaged and married. I take the *labuntur anni* without many *eheus*. The truth is, Nature has her anodynes, and Old Age carries one of them in his pocket. It is some kind of narcotic, — it dulls our sensibility; it tends to make us sleepy and indifferent; and, in lightening our responsibilities (which President Walker spoke of as one of its chief blessings), rids us of many of our worries. I don't think *you* grow old, and in many ways I do not feel as if I did. But sight and hearing won't listen to any nonsense; they both insist upon it: —

'Ανακρέων γέρων εἰ.

I wish I could get my courage up to do a little more writing; perhaps I shall; you would read what I wrote, it may be, and think of the old days of the *Collegian*, where we first wrote side by side.

Good-by; I find it hard to keep up with my cor-respondence, but your letter was a refreshment.

TO JOHN G. WHITTIER.

September 2, 1889.

MY DEAR WHITTIER, — Here I am at your side among the octogenarians. At seventy we are objects of veneration, at eighty of curiosity, at ninety of wonder; and if we reach a hundred we are candidates for a side-show attached to Barnum's great exhibition. . . .

To Dr. Fordyce Barker he wrote in January, 1890: "The Harvard Club of New York have urged me to come to their annual meeting, but I tell them that my *habitat* is the hearth-rug, where I sit and repose like an old tabby cat."

TO JOHN O. SARGENT.

March 15, 1890.

MY DEAR JOHN, — You may be tempted for the moment to say sometimes, "What an insensible creature that old friend of mine is! Here am I, one of the two or three living persons whom he loves to have still calling him Wendell (Lowell is almost the only other one), and I have twice written him within these last weeks, and not heard a word from him in reply." Well, the reason is, I have been overworked with letters and writing for *The Atlantic*, and I had perfect *faith* in you, that you would not say or think anything hard about me because I was not as punctual as I ought to be. Your letters were and are full of inter-

est to me. There was and is that fine-spirited ode
with the life and glow of Horace in it, which I read
with great delight; then there was that kind, friendly
allusion to our old friend, Isaac McLellan. I don't
believe I ever thanked him for his tribute to me on
my threescore-and-twentieth birthday, but I will, you
may be sure. The truth is, I received such a number
of flattering letters, poems, etc. (including a prema-
ture obituary in a Plattsburg newspaper), that I have
to " buck" like a Mexican pony to get rid of my load
of gratitude. Otherwise I could n't have forgotten
dear good old Isaac. How his name recalls those old
days when you and Epes and Isaac and Durivage
were cheeping round with the egg-shells on our callow
shoulders! I ought not to include you, I know, for
you were more matured in style and far more master
of your weapons than most of the rest of us. I had
a copy of *The Harbinger* given me a little while ago
by somebody, and it brought back that whole time to
me. There is a Park Benjamin now, who writes, I
find, and one of whose stories, *The Bombardment of
New York by an Iron-Clad*, I thought mighty good
when I read it. But now my *quasi* contemporaries,
besides yourself, are Lowell, nine years younger, and
just now ailing in a way that makes me somewhat
anxious, and Whittier, two years older. All the rest
of my Boston and Saturday Club cronies are gone. I
miss James Freeman Clarke sadly; he had grown
to be a great power in our community, and was a
favorite in society, as well as active in every good
work. The worst of him was that his incessant industry made everybody else seem lazy. I used to
scold him for working so hard, but it did no good;
he had to work himself to death. At the Saturday

Club, where we used to have those brilliant gatherings, there is hardly a face of the old times except Judge Hoar, and now and then John Dwight, the musical critic.

I am living cheerfully enough with my son and his wife, go to concerts, to small gatherings, but in the main live very quietly. It was a bold, perhaps a rash thing to pledge myself (virtually) to a series of papers, but I found I must either take a vow of silence or begin writing at once, and so I determined to risk it.

My eyes are giving me more and more trouble, yet you see I *can* write legibly; but I have much of my writing done for me by a young woman secretary.

Good-by, dear John, I always love to hear from you.

TO ELIZABETH STUART PHELPS WARD.

BOSTON, *May* 30, 1890.

MY DEAR MRS. WARD, — I really do not know whether I have thanked you for your new story or not, but to make sure, I thank you now. The truth is, I am in arrears with my correspondents; my table is crowded with books unthanked for, unacknowledged even, and of course unread. My secretary, who, in addition to her work at the Athenæum, has been working between two and three hours a day for me, looked so tired yesterday that I told her not to come again until Monday. So I let everything else go until she comes. I am sometimes almost in despair between my wish to make some due acknowledgment to the friends who send me their books and write me their warm-hearted letters, and the difficulty of doing them any kind of justice. I shall have to carry many which I have but half read, and some which I have not read at all, to the country with me, and try to find time to read what I have only looked rapidly through or sometimes only glanced at here. I hate to say that I have not properly read your story, but there is so much study in it, — it suggests so many historical notes which one wishes to make as he goes along, or have a better scholar than himself make for him, that it is not enough to *skim* it for the story like a common romance.

I write with effort, as I am afraid you perceive. I see no peace or rest for me without giving up this everlasting paying of tribute to strangers, who crowd upon me until I am worn out with their questions, their demands, their appeals, and feel like Christian with his burden on his back, with hardly spirit enough left to throw it off. I must tell *you* this, for you were always sympathetic, and will understand that, with so many years as I have to carry, the grasshopper is beginning to be a burden. More and more I am trying to reduce my correspondence to formulæ, and my secretary — a very intelligent and well-trained young lady —

(At this point two colored persons came in and took a piece of my time and a trifling contribution in money.)

Well, I am doing my best to keep my head level in the midst of the strain that is put upon me, and not to let some articles I am writing for *The Atlantic* betray my fatigue and lassitude. A letter from you would do me good, for I take very deep interest in all that relates to you and your affairs. It rejoices my heart to think that you are happy. You are worth loving, and are blessed in loving and being loved.

There is enough of you left over to provide for friendship, and I am proud to count myself one of your friends.

BOSTON, *February* 7, 1891.

MY DEAR MRS. KELLOGG, — Among all the young girls of my acquaintance you are conspicuous as one of the best correspondents that ever warmed my old heart with her lively letters. You are so good, too, not to expect long replies. The truth is, my eyes and my hand get tired with the scribbling I have to do, and it is a charity the good angels take cognizance of when a distant friend bestows three or four pages on me, knowing he or she will only get one in return, and perhaps not as much as that.

I do so love to hear about dear old Pittsfield and what is done there, and who does it, and how the new *city* gets on, and all the rest. What have I got to tell you? Nothing but what the Boston papers report — if you ever see them. I know very little of what is going on. I go to the Symphony Rehearsals and to a five o'clock tea once in a while. I dine out at long intervals, everybody of my generation being dead, pretty much, and the two generations that have come up since my day having their own circles, their own notions, their own habits. My two young people go to the theatre together, and I am glad to have them amuse themselves; but I rarely accompany them. Once in a while we all dine at some public table — Young's or Parker's — just for the fun of it and by way of change. Mrs. Judge knows how to make me comfortable, and does it wonderfully well. But I grow lazy, as I ought to. I would make a business of studying the science of doing nothing, if it did not come to me naturally enough. Yet, when I talk about laziness, I am really kept very busy. Here am I writing to you at 4.30 P.M. this Saturday; ten to one the door-bell will ring in the course of the next fifteen minutes, and a schoolma'am from Oshkosh, or an author from Dakota, or a poetess from Belchertown, will come in and interrupt me, and punch my brain and weary my flesh, so that I cannot get to the bottom of this page. I did n't believe I should get so far as this, when I began. I make my secretary do as much of my letter-writing as possible, and get off with as few words as I possibly can. You are good — you won't call me to account if I do not answer your delightful letters as they deserve. Supposing I should say, next time I get one from you, "Yours received, and contents noted. Blessings on you, *blonde cherub*, for your charming note of ten pages — not one too many." I may have to come to that; but do you write, just the same.

Good-by, dear Mrs. Kellogg, brightest of your sex. Remember me to all that care for me.

TO JOHN G. WHITTIER.

September 3, 1891.

MY DEAR WHITTIER, — I have received both your kind letter and your welcome telegram. I need not apologize for this brief response, — you know all about it. I can only say that the avalanche of letters and other tokens of regard has fallen — nay, is still falling — and I have survived it.[1]

I am longing to see you, and if you are coming to Danvers you must expect me to drive over for an hour's

[1] This refers, of course, to the birthday celebrations.

talk with you. As I have often said, we — that is, you and I, now — are no longer on a raft, but we are on a spar.

I have been well in general health, but have had a good deal of asthma. This climate is too cold and rough for me, but I have found much that is delightful about my residence here. Perhaps the fault is not so much in latitude 42° as in *æt.* 82.

I trust you are coming to Danvers, and that you will tell me as soon as you are there.

TO MRS. PRIESTLEY.

Boston, *November* 1, 1891.

MY DEAR MRS. PRIESTLEY, — Reading and writing letters becomes more and more difficult, but I am not blind by any means, as you see by this specimen of my handwriting. Much of my correspondence is attended to by an intelligent secretary, who could in reality answer most of my letters just as well as I myself. But I was and am so much pleased with your letter of Oct. 11th that I took the pen from the pretty lady who writes for me, determined that you should have a few words direct from me, not filtered through another agency. It is not strange that at threescore and twenty, and two over, one should find his eyes more or less dim, and his ears more or less dull. I like to write out the figures of my age in good Roman characters, thus: LXXXII. It gives them a patriarchal look and adds to what Wordsworth calls " the monumental pomp of age." I would not have said so much about myself if I did not know that you and your husband took and take a kindly interest in me and my conditions. I am living just as when you were here, but the loss of my daughter is not one to be made good in this life. . . . The way in which *The Teacups* was received was very gratifying, — but oh, if only those whom I have lost could have shared my satisfaction! I do not expect to write any more books, but I may possibly publish a magazine article now and then. I am so glad that you and your husband liked my last book. I was taken by surprise when my publishers told me that twenty thousand copies had been disposed of in the course of a few months since its publication. The pleasure of the *pocket* is very well in its way, but the pleasure of the *heart*, when your friends tell you they like what you have done, is of a better quality, and I have had both; your letter was one of the most welcome evidences of my having succeeded with the few whose approval is so much more to be preserved than that of the many. . . .

Thanking you most cordially for your very kind letter, I am, dear Mrs. Priestley,

Always affectionately yours,

OLIVER WENDELL HOLMES.

TO DR. S. WEIR MITCHELL.

October 2, 1893.

MY DEAR MITCHELL, — I was exceedingly sorry to miss your visit the day before yesterday. I value your friendship as highly as I esteem your large and varied gifts and accomplishments, — and I have few friends left whom I can be proud of as well as attached to. Think of it! my last birthday left me threescore and *twenty* with four years added to the ever-growing heap. The parenthesis, which enclosed the year of the century I have already counted, leaves but small margins between 1800 and 1900, and now I find myself almost alone so far as my coevals are concerned. There are, however, two *breakwaters* left between me in my quiet harbor and the great unexplored ocean of eternity: my daughter-in-law's father, Mr. Dixwell, who graduated two years before I did, and that dear old nonagenarian, Dr. Furness, who, I think, will be kept alive by the skill of you Philadelphian doctors until he becomes a centenarian.

I have been riding the high horse — let me get out of the saddle. My birthday found me very well in body and I think in mind. If I am in the twilight of dementia I have not found it out. I am only reasonably deaf; my two promising cataracts are so slow about their work that I begin to laugh at them. I discovered one and studied it, as it was reflected in my microscope, more than a dozen years ago, and I can see with both eyes and read with one; and my writer's cramp is very considerate, and is letting me write without any interference, as you can see.

I wrote a hymn a few months ago, which I will send you if I can find a copy — I don't believe you will say it " smacks of apoplexy," like the archbishop's sermon. If it does, no matter;— I have had some fair work out of those old shrivelled cerebral convolutions.

TO MRS. CAROLINE L. KELLOGG.

BEVERLY FARMS, *July* 24, 1894.

MY DEAR MRS. KELLOGG, — Many thanks for your good long letter. *I* do not write such as that nowadays, but when I write at all, I say the little I have to say in as few words as possible. What with eyes, and fingers that get crampy, and general indisposition to any kind of work — the laziness of slow convalescence, let us call it, — I am but a poor correspondent as a writer, though very good as a reader — of letters like yours.

If I had a million or so of dollars, and forty years instead of threescore and twenty-four, and could take my old place just as I left it, I should like to be your summer neighbor. But my habits are formed, my ways are established, and I am a pendulum with a very short range of oscillation. I send you one of my very best photographs, with all kindest regards.

TO CHARLES DUDLEY WARNER.

BEVERLY FARMS, MASS., *September* 13, 1894.

MY DEAR WARNER, — I am scattering thanks right and left — *manibus plenis* — from hands as full as they can hold; and now I take up yours, and should like to answer it as it deserves to be answered. Your kind expressions are very grateful to me, and I feel more obliged to you, who must have enough writing to do to tire you out, for taking the trouble to say those agreeable and most welcome words. They do me good, — old age at best is lonely, and the process of changing one's whole suit of friends and acquaintances has its moments when one feels naked and shivers.

I have this forenoon answered a letter from the grandson of a classmate, and received a visit from the daughter of another classmate, the "Sweet Singer" of the class of '29. So you see I have been contemplating the leafless boughs and the brown turf in the garden of my memory.

Not less do I prize my newer friendships, and it delights me to sign myself —

Always affectionately yours,

OLIVER WENDELL HOLMES.

CHAPTER XVI

DEATH

DEATH drew near to Dr. Holmes with steps so slow, so gently graded, that the approach was hardly perceptible. Body and mind could be seen to be losing something in vigor, if one measured by intervals of months, but hardly by shorter periods. He was out of doors, taking his usual walks, a few days before the end came; he was up and about the house actually to the last day, and he died in his chair, — painlessly, as so humane a man well deserved to make his escape out of life, — on October 7, 1894. Two days later he was buried from King's Chapel.

The expression of feeling which was called forth by the event was very striking. It was true that the Doctor had outlived his own generation, and had stood before men's eyes for several years past at a point much below his highest excellence. Yet these facts did not seem in any degree to weaken the sentiments of admiration and affection towards him; the world remembered him in his prime, and thought of him at his best. It was singular to note how strong a *personal* feeling there was in all the utterances of regret. I sent to a "press-cutting agency" for the newspaper notices, and thus gathered and glanced over, more or less carefully, probably not less than three or four thousand "clippings," which must have represented not only a very large percentage of the cities and towns, but a goodly proportion of the villages, of the United States, with a great number from England and some from France and Germany. I doubt whether in all this number fifty could have been found which did not call the Doctor either "genial" or "kindly." A verdict from so numerous a jury was conclusive. It was noteworthy how the world had become so profoundly penetrated by the impression. It could not be explained by saying that the Doctor had attacked the inhumanity of the religious creeds, for others had done this; or by saying that he gave constant utterance to amiable sentiments in his writings, for this also had been done by others, even to the point of mawkishness. But in some way or another his writings were so impregnated by an atmosphere of humaneness that it rose from them like a moral fragrance, and the gracious exhalation permeated the consciousness of every reader. His writings had been full of sympathy with his fellows, — his shipmates on board this vessel of the earth, as he once expressed it; and it was commonly felt that this was no comradeship of words only, but a genuine expression of his true nature. He said what all felt, when he wrote: "I have told my story. I do not know what special gifts have been granted or denied me; but this I know, that I am like so many others of my fellow-creatures, that when I smile, I feel as if they must; when I cry, I think their eyes fill; and it always seems to me that when I am most truly myself I come nearest to them, and am surest of being listened to by the brothers and sisters of the larger family into which I was born so long ago." Yet, withal, he had been a strenuous and earnest writer, trenchant when occasion demanded, and had led many a gallant assault on entrenched prejudice. Remembering this, it is interesting to observe how the clergymen now spoke of him, showing a liberal feeling, a Christian charity, which was fully as creditable to those who gave as to him who received the generous laudation. Even the Catholics forgot that he had said that it was "Rome or Reason," the "three-hilled city against the seven-hilled city;" they ignored for a moment the "irrepressible conflict" which he had proclaimed, and gave him fair words of praise. So, too, did some of the Orthodox persuasion. How different this from what would have been the case had he died some thirty years before, with *The Autocrat* and *The Professor* and *Elsie Venner* still fresh productions. Then the religious world would have thought that a very dangerous writer had been timely and wisely removed from his work of mischief.

Of course it was not, in fact, Dr. Holmes who had worked the general change of feeling, of which this good-will, extended to himself, was only a striking manifestation. There had been going on a great tidal movement, which would have advanced without him, without Emerson, without any individual. But he, being a man of strong intellect and sympathetic temperament, had been one of the first to feel the new impulse; he had been among the few who formed the aggressive apex of the advance; he had shocked cherished beliefs, and had taken the consequences in the shape of abuse of himself and misrepresentation of his position; thus he had earned a right to receive that sort of praise and recognition which is accorded to all the so-called leaders of reform, — leaders but rarely *creators* of public sentiment. History indicates that the present age is instinct with such a spirit of humaneness as has never been known in any other civilization, or in any previous stage of our own civilization. There is not found in contemporary literature any other writer reaching so wide a circle of readers as Dr. Holmes did, who was quite equal to him as an exponent or preacher of this development. Like Abou Ben Adhem, he *loved his fellow-men ;* and when I was young all the school-children knew, what I hope all school-children of the present day likewise know, that in the final competition "Ben Adhem's name led all the rest."

Other reflections also are aroused by the words which were spoken and written of Dr. Holmes after his death. There were interesting and appreciative articles in some of the American magazines; but the perfunctory notices of the newspaper press of the country were for the most part discreditable to our journalism. In England his fame received more adequate recognition, and several weekly and daily papers had carefully written articles, expressing generous praise, which was the more valuable because it was critical and discriminating. The high estimation in which the Doctor was held in England deserves mention, alike in justice to him and to the Englishmen. Among the many complaints which we register against the Briton, a prominent one has been a disregard or contempt upon his part for our literary productions. But though Dr. Holmes uttered so exclusively the thought, the sentiment, and the life of New England, and presented the scenery, the characters, the humor of that small region so conspicuously that the soundest criticism to which he was open was that of excessive localism, yet the Englishmen held him in very great popularity, and now showed for his memory as much feeling and honor as his own countrymen did, if not even more. This truly indicated that he had succeeded in drawing the real humankind; it indicated, too, that when we send to England first-rate books they will be read with appreciation.

Punch had some lines so admirable that this volume would be incomplete without them.

"THE AUTOCRAT."

OLIVER WENDELL HOLMES. BORN 1809, DIED OCTOBER 7, 1894.

"The Last Leaf!" Can it be true,
We have turned it, and on you,
    Friend of all?
That the years at last have power?
That life's foliage and its flower
    Fade and fall?

Was there one who ever took
From its shelf, by chance, a book
    Penned by you,
But was fast your friend for life,
With one refuge from its strife
    Safe and true?

Even gentle Elia's self
Might be proud to share that shelf,
    Leaf to leaf,
With a soul of kindred sort,
Who could bind strong sense and sport
    In one sheaf.

From that Boston breakfast-table,
Wit and wisdom, fun and fable,
    Radiated
Through all English-speaking places.
When were Science and the Graces
    So well mated?

Of sweet singers the most sane,
Of keen wits the most humane,
    Wide, yet clear.

Like the blue, above us bent,
Giving sense and sentiment
    Each its sphere ;

With a manly breadth of soul,
And a fancy quaint and droll,
    Ripe and mellow.
With a virile power of " hit,"
Finished scholar, poet, wit,
    And good fellow !

Sturdy patriot, and yet
True world's citizen ! Regret
    Dims our eyes
As we turn each well-thumbed leaf ;
Yet a glory 'midst our grief
    Will arise.

Years your spirit could not tame,
And they will not dim your fame ;
    England joys
In your songs, all strength and ease,
And the " dreams " you " wrote to please
    Gray-haired boys."

And of such were you not one ?
Age chilled not your fire of fun.
    Heart alive
Makes a boy of a gray bard,
Though his years be, " by the card,"
    Eighty-five !

Even the French press forgot, or forgave — or possibly, let us admit, did not know — the expressions of
repulsion which Dr. Holmes had uttered against their
modern nasty literature, and they praised him very
handsomely. It is difficult to imagine that the Frenchmen could really have made much out of his writings,
yet *L'Echo de la Semaine* had a long, a very appreciative, even sympathetic, article about him. From

another sheet I must cut two paragraphs, the one
because it is amusing, the other because it shows such
a fine ranking of much-abused New England:—

"Il se distinguait par un heureux mélange d'humeur
et de sentiment. Il a trouvé bien des mots qui reste-
ront. C'est lui qui, plaisamment, baptisa Boston
l'essieu du monde. Il appelait les tramways à con-
ducteur électrique le train du manche à balai — nous
dirions, je crois, de la queue de rat — jeu de mots un
peu difficile à transporter en français."

"La mort de Holmes marque la fin d'une brillante
période d'écrivains à laquelle appartenaient, à côté
de Longfellow et de Lowell, Whittier, le poète quaker
de l'émancipation des noirs, le philosophe Emerson,
et tant d'autres noms éminents que nous pourrions
citer sans sortir de la Nouvelle-Angleterre, cet étroit
berceau de la civilisation et du génie américain, ce
petit point sur le littoral de l'Atlantique qui est comme
l'âme de la nation."

At the same time a French translation of "The
Last Leaf" appeared, not in rhyme, but preserving
the measure and music of the original with great skill,
and altogether seeming so clever and interesting that
I venture to preserve it here:—

LA DERNIERE FEUILLE.

Je l'ai vu, une fois déjà,
comme il passait devant la porte;
        et de nouveau
les pierres du pavé résonnent,
quand il frappe, en chancelant, le sol
        de sa canne.

On dit que, dans son printemps,
avant que la faucille du Temps
        l'eût ébranché,

c'était le plus bel homme que vit
le Crieur dans sa ronde
   par la ville.

Mais maintenant il marche dans les rues,
jetant sur tout ce qu'il rencontre un coup d'œil
   triste et morne ;
et il secoue sa tête débile
avec un air qui semble dire :
   " Elles sont parties ! "

Les marbres moussus reposent
sur les lèvres qu'il pressa
   dans leur fleur;
et les noms qu'il aimait à entendre
sont, depuis mainte année, gravés
   sur la tombe.

Ma grand'maman disait
(pauvre vieille dame ! elle est morte
   il y a longtemps . . .)
qu'il avait le nez aquilin,
et que sa joue était comme une rose
   dans la neige.

Mais maintenant son nez s'est aminci
et s'appuie sur son menton,
   comme une béquille;
et une bosse courbe son dos,
et une fêlure mélancolique
   est dans son rire.

Je sais que c'est un péché
de ma part d'être ici à ricaner
   de lui sur ma chaise ;
mais le vieux chapeau à trois cornes,
et les culottes, et tout le reste,
   sont si baroques !

Et si je vivais assez pour être
la dernière feuille restée à l'arbre
   au printemps,

qu'à leur tour les gens sourient
du vieux rameau délaissé
où je m'attache !

It used to be the duty of the biographer who wrote of a person whom he had known well to close his memoir by giving some guidance concerning portraits. But photography has nearly or quite done away with all occasion for this. Dr. Holmes's face has certainly become familiar; and every one knows also that he was of short stature, and only in his later years somewhat inclined to be stout. I should say to any inquirer: Get the photograph which pleases you best, and you can't go far wrong; the photographs are almost by necessity good. But distrust the engravings which decorate (?) sundry volumes; I have seen some which were not so bad as one would expect them to be; but it is safe to rule them out of competition with the sun-pictures. The Doctor took a great deal of interest in his own personal aspect, both of face and figure, and, having a passion for physical perfection, he was not altogether satisfied with what Nature had done for him. "Very ugly, but horribly true," he remarked of one of the likenesses; and once, when his publishers wanted a frontispiece, he said: "Take out the wrinkles! Every man, who is going to show his face to people who don't know him, has a right to show it at its best." Unfortunately, when the photographer or engraver takes out wrinkles, he takes out character and expression with them. It may be suspected that the Doctor had himself in mind when he made the Poet at the Breakfast-Table remark: "His personal appearance was not singularly prepossessing; inconspicuous in stature and unattractive in features," etc. But this would have been an unduly severe judg-

ment, which no one else would have passed upon him.
His singular animation was such that one hardly carried away any distinct impression of the lines of his
face; and there was an activity in his movements
which prevented one from thinking of him as at all
physically insignificant, nor in truth was he so.   He
said some things of himself, so good-tempered and
amusing, that I yield to the temptation to print them.

TO DR. FORDYCE BARKER.

BOSTON, *February* 27, 1871.

MY DEAR DR. BARKER, — I have got both your
kind letters, and my mind is at ease about what I am
to do when I arrive at New York.   Country folks
are so bewildered, you know!

My plan is to start on Wednesday morning, as I
told you, and to return on Saturday, if you will keep
me so long.

. . . .

If your son comes to the station, please tell him to
look about until he sets his eyes on the most anxious,
inquisitive, puzzled-looking passenger of the whole
crew, very likely seated on the end of a valise (containing a manuscript and a change or two of linen),
or hanging on to a carpet-bag, and rolling his eyes
about in all directions to find the one who is finding
him.   Five feet *five* (not four as some have pretended)
in height.   Not so far from the grand climacteric as
he was ten years ago.   If there is any question about
his identity, a slight scar on his left arm . . . will at
once satisfy the young gentleman.   On being recognized, I shall rush into his arms, and attend him any
whither in perfect confidence.

TO PAUL H. HAYNE.

BOSTON, *January* 24, 1873.

MY DEAR MR. HAYNE, — I am very happy to help you in your pleasant project of getting your friends' pictures about you in place of their presence, as you cannot have that. I had a photograph taken a few months ago by one of our best artists, which on the whole I consider more satisfactory than any that has been taken of late. At the same time it is only fair to say that I do not pride myself particularly on any show that my portraits make. That is not my fault, however, and I look the camera in the face as good-naturedly as if it were going to make an Adonis of me.

TO DR. S. WEIR MITCHELL.

December 23, 1874.

MY DEAR DR. MITCHELL, —

. . . .

"Please find," as those horrid business letters say, the last photograph, or one of the last, that I have had taken. The photograph is a fair portrait enough; but I do not think my face is a flattering likeness of myself. Such as it is, however, you are most welcome to the picture, and if you do not like it, you can shut it up in Paley's *Natural Theology* or Sam Jackson's *Principles of Organic Medicine*, if you happen to have a copy of either of these books, and it will be safe from inspection for one generation at least.

TO JAMES RUSSELL LOWELL.

BOSTON, *March* 18, 1882.

MY DEAR JAMES, — I do not see why I should be writing to you just as if you were at a distance from me. *Here* you are on my table in the shape of Underwood's *Memoir*, embalmed, living, in fragrant adjectives as sweet as the spices that were wrapped up with the mummy of the grandest of the Pharaohs. *There* you are in a large reproduction of Mrs. M——'s painting. There you are again, in plain sight as I sit, in the group where I, too, have the honor of figuring. I have been constantly reminded of you of late by the daily presence of that same lady, Mrs. M——, who had a fancy for painting me, too, to which I felt bound to yield, although I have always considered my face a convenience rather than an ornament. I found her a very pleasant little lady, and I think she has made a picture which looks very much like you. The effect is very Titian-like, and you might pass for a Doge — (do not read it Dodge) — of Venice — (not Salem).[1]

TO MRS. E. S. SINCLAIR.

September 23, 1882.

MY DEAR MRS. SINCLAIR, —

. . . .

I am very glad you liked my photograph; it is certainly less disagreeable than some I have seen — but Nature did not ask my advice about my features, and I take what was given me and am glad it is no worse. . . .

"A good caricature, which seizes the prominent features and gives them the character Nature hinted, but did not fully carry out, is a work of genius." Thus Dr. Holmes wrote in the *Hundred Days*, re-

[1] A local jest ; the Dodge family is almost a clan at Salem, Massachusetts.

membering doubtless that he himself had once served as an inspiration to some sketcher gifted with genius of this kind; for *Vanity Fair* (London) had once published a full-page caricature of him, — one of its famous series of caricatures. It was grotesque, and yet it certainly was extremely clever, with so singular a life-likeness that many of his acquaintance declared that it brought him before them better than the graver portraits. He was not less amused and pleased by it than were his friends, for after all one is often philosophical in paying a fine which is based on one's own fame. In this light he regarded the drollery, and laughed good-naturedly.

When Dr. Holmes was about starting upon his trip to England, in 1886, his friend Rev. James Freeman Clarke, D. D., addressed to him some stanzas of farewell. The Doctor's expression concerning them, in his note of thanks, makes it appropriate to close these volumes with them.

TO JAMES FREEMAN CLARKE.

April 26, 1886.

MY DEAR JAMES, — I cannot tell how sweetly this sounded to me and now reads — *dim*, a little, with those half-formed "natural drops" that Milton speaks of.

Do you know what I want to ask? Will you not print these dear lines as my *envoi?*

The lines were : —

"May all good thoughts go with thee from this shore,
All kindly greetings meet thee on the other ;
Bring all they can they will not give thee more
Than we send with thee, Poet, Friend, and Brother.

" While thou art absent we will say, ' How often
The gloom from off our hearts his smile has lifted ;
How well he knew our harder mood to soften,
With gleams of sunlight where the storm clouds drifted !

" ' And how, when that o'erwhelming weight of duty
Pressed upon Lincoln's weary hand and brain,
Our Holmes's song of tenderness and beauty
Gave that worn heart a moment's rest again !

" ' Go, then, dear friend, by all good hopes attended ;
To mother-England go, our carrier-dove,
Saying that this great race, from hers descended,
Sends in its Holmes an Easter-gift of love.' "

LETTERS

I. TO JAMES RUSSELL LOWELL

BOSTON, *November* 10, 1848.

MY DEAR SIR, — I am not a fair judge — because
I have some fair words among my betters whom you
speak of. I attribute not the least value to my opinion. But I think it [1] is capital — crammed full and
rammed down hard — powder (lots of it) — shot —
slugs — bullets — very little wadding, and that is gun-
cotton — all crowded into a rusty looking sort of a
blunderbuss barrel as it were — capped with a percus-
sion preface — and cocked with a title-page as apropos
as a wink to a joke.

I did of course what everybody else does — looked
to see if my own name was in the volume for good or
evil, — but in doing so I saw enough to make me
begin and go straight through it, — a thing I am not
prone to. There is a vast deal of fun in it — plenty
of good jokes, — but better than that, there is a force
and delicacy of mental diagnosis (to speak profession-
ally) that really surprised me. Carlyle & Emerson,
for instance — the distinctions are subtile enough for
Duns Scotus, yet not fantastic. I thought I could see
meaning in every little scintilla of a trait you pointed
out; but it would have been a blank had not that
wonderful comet-seeker of yours — your fine achro-

[1] The reference is to *The Fable for Critics*.

matic apprehension — directed my poor intellectual lenses to it.

Miranda is too good. I don't know these people much, but I supposed she *posed* for our old towns-woman, that used to be, — in the eocene period, when I was young. I have heard of a peg to hang a thought on, but if I want a thought to hang a Peg on I shall know where to go in future. . . .

I shall send you my little book — which you may have seen advertised — in a few days. I liked a let-ter you once wrote me, very much, but I am afraid it is of no use to bother yourself with me. I can't be one of the "earnest" folks if I try ever so hard. I see so many bright facets in this crystalline order of things that I should like to set the whole of it, if I could, in a ring of verse, and play it on my finger in the sunshine of the " Infinite Soul " forever and ever. But you come in with your pumice and rub the polish off of one surface after another, — first the convivial facet with the temperance sand and scrubbing-cloths ; then the patriotic facet with the abolition grit; and so of the rest. However, I am thinking of what you said ever so long ago, and perhaps you would agree with me now, that it is easier to beget a new poet, or adopt one at the House of Industry, than it is to put new viscera — heart, brain, nerves, etc. — into the organization of an old one.[1]

I think I understand you, and I know you under-stand me. There are a thousand things I admire in your intellect, and I am only too well pleased that such an old-fashioned versifying squaretoes as myself has done anything which pleased you. In the little book I spoke of I have not been very squeamish. I

[1] Referring to letter to Lowell, *ante,* i. 295.

have printed my jolly verses, — on second thought I don't feel afraid they will hurt anybody, and I know they will please some.

As for your poem, to come back to it, it speaks for itself that you will not let yourself be snuffed out as Keats did, if the American Dick—— and the rest should abuse you for it. It is fun, after all, to see a man that is not afraid of this or that little squibbing blackguard, —and I do think — excuse the expression — but I do think you have given them *beans*.

Hoping that you will live a great many years to whack pretension, to praise without jealousy, to separate the sham from the real, but above all to throw your own manly and gentle nature into the graceful forms of art,

I am yours most truly.

8 MONTGOMERY PLACE, *January* 14, 1849.

I thank you, my dear sir, very sincerely for the *Vision.* It is a little book, it is thin ; there is not much more thickness to it than to a consecrated wafer, but one may get more out of it than from many a whole loaf. Many parts of it are eminently poetical, and the whole story is a pure, beautiful, entire conception. To my ear it wants finish in some portions, and is marred by certain incongruities, one or two of which I will mention. Thus, the picture part of the poem is Yankee in its effect, and so far out of keeping. The *dandelion,* for instance, is an excellent herb, poetically and gastronomically, but has no particular business in a poem which means to carry you as far from Cambridge and 1849 as may be.

Again —

"As the hang-bird is to the elm-tree bough."

What propriety in introducing the Baltimore oriole in the tableau of that old feudal castle? There are "objective" instances, as the Rev. Homer Wilbur's critic would say, of a want of unity, which shows itself "subjectively" in various other passages, where the old story, which should have been brocaded throughout with old-world and old-time imagery, is overlaid with fire-new philanthropizing and philosophizing generalities.

You laugh at the old square-toed heroic sometimes, and I must retort upon the rattlety-bang sort of verse in which you have indulged. I read a good deal of it as I used to go over the kittle-y-benders when a boy, horribly afraid of a slump every time I cross one of its up-and-down hump-backed lines. I don't mean that it cannot be done, or that you have not often done it so as to be readable and musical; but think of having to read a mouthful of such lines as this : —

"For the frost's [?] swift shuttles its shroud had spun."

There is only one man that can read such lines, and that is my quondam student Mr. George Cheyne Shattuck Choate, whose apprenticeship in learning to pronounce his own name has made him a match for all sorts of cacoepy.

Now as to what pleases me most, — for one likes to know how each different taste is affected.

Not the picture of June — it has great beauties but some of the discords I have spoken of — not the departing knight (paragraph III. p. 11) — it is bold, spirited, eminently picturesque, but exaggerated; not the leper's speech (p. 13), which reminds me too much of some of our "transcendental" friends.

The *brook* is the most ingenious and exquisitely finished piece of pen fancy work I have seen for a long time.

"Builds out its *piers* of ruddy light" struck me as a fine expression. But paragraph III. of part second is eminently beautiful, — the thought is natural and striking, the painting vivid, and the personification of the little spring altogether charming. Paragraph VI. of the same part is very striking, and the moral finely enucleated, only as it seems to me the knight is a little *too* good to allow Giles and Hodge to come into his dressing-room at all times without knocking.

You will not find fault with me for the freedom of my criticisms, I am quite sure, but feel assured that a few blemishes, as they seem to me, do not lead me to overlook the many beauties in which the poem abounds.

164 Charles Street, *November* 26, 1868.
(*Thanksgiving Day.*)

My dear James, — I have been reading your poems — those I knew so well over again — those I did not know, to find them worthy of their companionship.

The world is with you now, and I can add very little to the welcome and the honors with which your new volume will be received. I cannot help, however, saying how much I am impressed by the lusty manhood of your nature as shown in the heroic vigor of your verse; by the reach and compass of your thought; by the affluence, the felicity, and the subtilty of your illustrations, which weave with the thoughts they belong to as golden threads through the tissue of which they form part; and perhaps most of all by that *humanity* in its larger sense, which belongs to you beyond any of those with whom your name is often joined. While I have been reading these grave and noble poems I have forgotten that you were a wit and a humorist, — that you were a critic and an essayist, to say nothing of your being a scholar such as we breed, if at all, only as the phœnix is bred.

But your genius and your radiant panoply of accomplishments do not make you insensible to the congratulations and the good wishes of your friends — especially of your old friends; and I, though not one of the very oldest — the pre-Adamite Company, — have seen my hair whiten since my life was richer for your friendship, and, if I mistake not, a silver arrow or two — perhaps from the head of one of those Dandelions you sung of in the springtime — lodge in the brown magnificence of your kingly beard.

Take my thanks, then, for the beautiful volume of noble verse, and my love and best wishes that you may live long to adorn and honor the literature of your country and your language.

164 CHARLES STREET, *January* 29, 1868.

MY DEAR JAMES, — The two beautiful volumes came yesterday, — not less welcome because they have been long looked for.

It is too late to praise the *Biglow Papers*, since the world has put the broad seal upon them. Besides, their qualities so contend for the mastery that if one gets only its due the others will seem unfairly dealt with. I must not say they are alive with wit and

humor, for these are used with a purpose which lends
dignity to their most sportive words. I think of the
retiarius every time you step out on the sand, — you
hold a net of fun in one hand and a trident of sense,
wisdom, and honesty in the other.

But if I say too much of these qualities I am in
danger of forgetting all there is of feeling, of eloquence, of subtlety, of learning, of observation, and,
best of all, of true human nature in these full-blooded
poems. So I will stop short in my praises, lest I
should pile them so high that I should become envious
of the monument I had reared, and grudge you some
of the many gifts the gods have so freely granted you.

It has been one of the great privileges of my last
decade to enjoy your friendship, and these volumes
will always make me richer, not merely by what their
pages hold, but by constantly reminding me of the
many delightful hours I have passed in the sunshine
of your companionship.

296 BEACON STREET, *March* 22, 1871.

MY DEAR JAMES, — I got the other day your rich
volume of criticisms and essays, which I blushed to
set against the pauper Essay I sent you. . . .

.   .   .   .

I have read much of your book in the *North
American* and a little at odd minutes since it came,
and I find wherever I open it so much scholarship,
such acuteness of criticism, such overflowing exuberance of happy illustration, such continual sparkle of
wit and humor, that I am afraid it makes me feel as
Thackeray did when he read something of Dickens's
— What is the use of trying against such a man as

this? But again I think that my study lamp burns just as well as if there were no Fresnel illumination in the light-house, and comfort myself with the thought that, in a region where there is so much darkness, it is worth while for each and all of us to let his light shine as it can, were it only a match he scratches on his boot-sole.

I have not welcomed you to my new house yet, where I hope to see you whenever you can stretch your legs so far or take a seat in the cars which leave the Tremont House every twenty minutes. They are driving me out of my library at this minute, to be dispossessed for the rest of the week — the ceiling having to be re-frescoed by Guido Reni (Macpherson) in consequence of a pipe's bursting in the cold snap.

So, hoping to meet you before long, I am as always.

296 BEACON STREET, *September* 28, 1875.

MY DEAR JAMES,[1] — Two faculty meetings on Thursday of this week (Dental and Medical) which I cannot miss, and my lectures on the following Thursdays, keep me in Boston in despite of all temptations. I never go to any shows nowadays — formerly they were *autre chose* — but if I did go to any, cattle-shows would be my favorite resort — especially in Spain, where I understand they have very fine ones. At our native exhibitions I have a wonderful liking for looking at prize pumpkins and squashes — great fellows marked 100 lb., 120 lb., 127 lb.! and so on — the rivalry excites me like a horse-race. As for fatted calves and the like, I am as eager for them as the prodigal son. The Great Cheese commonly shown

---

[1] Replying to an invitation to a cattle-show.

comes in for a share of my admiration. The sampler worked by a little girl aged five years and three months, and the patchwork quilt wrought by the old lady of eighty-seven years, four months, and six days, receive alike my respectful attention. I lift the dasher of the new patent churn with the proud feeling that I, too, am a contriver and see my unpatented gimcrack[1] in every window. And the ploughing-match, too — not quite so actively exciting as Epsom (I don't mean the salts, of course, but the race), but still equal to bringing on a mild glow of excitement. Yes, I miss a good deal in not going to the cattle-shows.

But we missed you sadly, my dear fellow, on Saturday. Good and great men are getting scarce, my James, and you must not be trifling in this way with your gouts and gastralgias.

Do thank your son-in-law —(I met him the other day and he showed me a photograph of one of his children, which was a credit to all concerned) — for complimenting me with a wish for my presence.

I have been having a very pleasant vacation at Beverly, Nahant, and Mattapoisett, and am beginning my seven months' lecture course feeling quite juvenile for an elderly gentleman — however, the *elders* always had a good deal of real pith in them, I remember, in my boyish days! and I suppose it is so now.

BOSTON, *March* 21, 1876.

MY DEAR JAMES, — Your book, " From the author," has been lying with a heap of others, sometimes on top, sometimes underneath, for weeks and weeks, and I have never yet thanked you for it.

[1] The hand-stereoscope.

I was quite right. It was not written in a hurry, must not be read in a hurry, and need not be thanked for in a hurry. I have read one of the papers from time to time just when I felt like it, and it is only a day or two since I finished reading the Dante, which was the last I took up, and having read laid down with a sigh of regret that I could not earlier in my life have come under those influences (perhaps I ought to say could not have inherited those gifts) which would have fitted me to read such an Essay as a scholar and not as a school-boy.

There is no need of my praising such a piece of criticism as this, — and I speak of this especially as the most elaborate, the most profound, the most learned, and the most subtile, where all are remarkable for these qualities in various degree, — I say there is no need of my praising a masterpiece like this. It serves a great purpose, quite independently of its value with reference to Dante and his readers; it shows our young American scholars that they need not be provincial in their way of thought or their scholarship because they happen to be born or bred in an outlying district of the great world of letters. We Boston people are so bright and wide-awake, and have been really so much in advance of our fellow-barbarians with our *Monthly Anthologies*, and *Atlantic Monthlies*, and *North American Reviews*, that we have been in danger of thinking our local scale was the absolute one of excellence — forgetting that 212 Fahrenheit is but 100 Centigrade. That is one way of looking at ourselves; and the other, as you know, is looking on ourselves as intellectual colonial dependents, and accepting that "certain condescension in foreigners," which you have so deliciously exploded, as all that we are entitled to.

These criticisms of yours are more truly authoritative for me than any others that I read, and when I thank you for them it is as a pupil thanks a master. If I have sometimes spoken of criticism as a secondary function of the man of letters, I cannot have been thinking of such criticism as yours, the side-lights of which, if brought together, would make a series of brilliant original essays.

BOSTON, *December* 25, 1877.

MY DEAR JAMES, — What can I do better, this Christmas morning, than sit down and write Your Excellency a few lines or pages, as the case may be? I venture to say that the Boston postmark looks pleasantly on the back of a letter — for you have paid your debts before sailing, I do not question, and I am sure that any letter from your own country will bring nothing but kind messages to one of its few representatives whom it has any special reason to be proud of. Of course you are very fresh in all our memories just now, for it is only a week yesterday since we were celebrating Whittier's seventieth birthday, and on that occasion, as you know, I trust, before this, no one was more fully and warmly remembered than yourself. I please myself with thinking that you have had the *Daily Advertiser* with the account of the Dinner at the Brunswick, and the following number of the same paper, in which Norton's response to a toast in your honor is given at length. It was very happy and full of feeling, and received by the audience in a way that would have pleased you. But you ought to have been there yourself to have been welcomed as you would have been, not merely for a thousand reasons which you know so well, but more especially as the first Editor of *The Atlantic*, who set it on its legs — (why not? You have often heard of an *arm* of the sea) — and in the words of Byron, bade it "roll on," which it has done so stoutly ever since. That dinner is almost all I have to tell you about, for at the November Club I could not be, because Eliot called a Faculty meeting which prevented my going, and I was out of town during the summer months, so that I have really seen almost nothing of our mutual friends since I bade you good-by on board the Parthia. Even John I have not seen for weeks. My daily lecture, my visits to poor Edward Clarke, who died a few weeks ago, answering letters and looking over the books that are sent me — it is a lean life, isn't it? But I am getting notes together for my *Memoir of Motley*, and now and then writing a little something, for instance, a piece called "My Aviary" for the January *Atlantic*, and some verses for the Whittier dinner. *You* have something to tell, but what can I say to interest you? The migrations of the Vicar and his wife from the blue bed to the brown were hardly more monotonous than the pendulum-swing of my existence, so far as all outward occurrences go. Yet life is never monotonous, absolutely, to me. I am a series of surprises to myself in the changes that years and ripening, and it may be a still further process which I need not name, bring about. The movement onward is like changing place in a picture gallery — the light fades from this picture and falls on that, so that you wonder where the first has gone to and see all at once the meaning of the other. Not that I am so different from other people — there may be a dozen of me, *minus* my accidents, for aught I know — say rather ten thousand. But what a strange thing life is when you have waded in up to your neck and remember the shelving sands you have trodden!

I have often asked and now and then heard from you. You were said to have had some trouble, rheumatic or other, but at last accounts to be rid of it. You were quoted as saying that your office was one that required a good deal of work, or more work than some of the other diplomatic stations. I hope you are well and used to your labors by this time, but I will say to you as I used to say to Motley, that I would on no account lay any burden upon you in the shape of answering this or any future letter of mine except at your convenience and as briefly as you will. With kindest regards to Mrs. Lowell,

I am as always.

BEVERLY FARMS, *September* 22, 1878.

MY DEAR JAMES, — Love me, love my — poems is not the way in which it is generally put. Love my poems, love you, would come nearer the truth. It did me good to get those pleasant words about my *Atlantic* verses, which I read, by the way, at the Φ B K dinner, of which society they chose me President. So you see I have the honor of being your successor. I feel oldish for such places, but I think, generally speaking, the higher the place one holds, the more work others do for him, so that logically the supreme position in the universe would be one of absolute repose. Sixty-*eight* quotha! I shall never couple those two figures again after my name — sixty-*nine*, by'r Lady — and so few good old men left! When a man says to himself, I am now in my seventieth year — still more when he *writes* it, as I do now, he feels as if he were talking about somebody else, or reading in the obituary column of a newspaper, or scraping the moss from an old gravestone and spelling it out; but the idea that he is himself the subject of the malady called threescore years and ten — or like soon to be — the age at which King David (the brother poet, I mean) was advertising for a dry-nurse —

I leave that sentence unfinished, expressly, intentionally, for what can I say to match the absurdity of the thought which presents itself as a fact and sounds so like a lie! — Ah well; age is well enough — but just now —

. . . .

I almost blush to write with so very little beyond the changes from the blue bed to the brown to tell you.   Next Monday — the 30th, that is — we expect to return to Boston, having passed a delightful but exceedingly quiet summer here at Beverly Farms. . . . We are at a small wayside house, where we make ourselves comfortable, my wife, my daughter, and myself, with books, walks, drives, and as much laziness as we can bring ourselves to, which is quite too little, for none of us has a real genius for the *far niente*. All round us are the most beautiful and expensive residences, some close to the sea beaches, some on heights farther back in the midst of the woods, some perched on the edge of precipices; one has a net spread out which she calls a baby-catcher, over the abyss, on the verge of which her piazza hangs shuddering.   We go to most of these fine places once during the season.   We see the fine equipages roll by (the constable does *not* take off his hat), and we carry as contented faces as most of them do. . . . I wonder

if you have ever found time to write your notice of
Edmund Quincy? My *Memoir of Motley* is essentially done, and I have tied it up to carry to town with
me. It is long for a Hist. Soc. memoir — nearly two
hundred pages of my manuscript, which is square and
pretty well filled. It cost me some trouble and may
possibly provoke some antagonism, but the disputes
are so nearly burned out (those about the Vienna
resignation and the London recall) that my poking in
the ashes may not burn my fingers. It is no great
matter whether it does or not; I shall say my say in
decent and, I think, very moderate language. — Evening before last I ran up to town to dine with Phillips
Brooks, who had Dean Stanley as his guest. The
Dean's face reminded me most oddly of that of my
classmate, the late Judge Bigelow. I had some interesting talk with him, especially about the Motleys.
Motley was a very warm admirer of yours, as you
must know. He was one of the two you referred to, I
feel sure, as making up a large part of the world which
it was a pleasure to please by your writings — in one
of your last poems, I mean, which I have not by me to
refer to. Whenever my Memoir is printed I will
send you an early copy. I do not suppose you have
much time to read, but you can turn the pages over,
and get your Sancho to cut them if they are not cut
already.

I am at the bottom of my page, and ask myself:
why did I write? What had I to tell? Nothing, almost, but my letter tells you that you are remembered
in the quiet little place I write from, and I am but
one of the many who often think of you and long to
see you back again.

BOSTON, *May* 13, 1879.

MY DEAR JAMES, — Three or four months ago I
sent you a copy of a *Memoir of Motley*, in which I
thought you might find a few pages to interest you.
Yes, sent it, but it never went, as I have recently
learned. I left the care of it to the publishers,
Houghton & Osgood, who sent it, as they thought, to
the right people — Putnam, I think, in New York —
at any rate, it was too heavy for the post, it seemed
— (too heavy! ominous) — and so it lay quietly in
their dungeon, week after week and month after
month, and I am afraid has not gone yet, but I will
find out very soon. I was provoked. Not that you
want the book so much, not that you have got to read
it and write a letter to me about it — *Dii prohibete* —
but I wanted you to know that you are in the memories of many you have left behind you, mine especially.
Think what the Club, where we oftenest met, now is.
Emerson is afraid to trust himself in society much,
on account of the failure of his memory and the great
difficulty he finds in getting the word he wants. It is
painful to witness his embarrassment at times, — still
he has made out to lecture at Concord lately. I hope
you saw that touching note of his, declining some invitation, in which he spoke of his memory as " hiding
itself." Longfellow never comes; I think he has not
been since you left us, though I meet him once in a
while at a private dinner-party. Charles Norton
comes, it is true, and now and then another Canta-
brigian or two, but the *club* is reduced to little more
than the dimensions of a *walking-stick*. I went last
time and had some talk with C. N., who is greatly
interested in an archæological association, of which he
is the moving spirit. It is going to dig up some gods

in Greece, if it can get money enough — I suppose they may be required in some quarters to supply an apparent want.

I am busy, as usual. I wish I could bring more to pass, for I am hardly ever idle. A fortnight ago I went to New York, and had a fine time, being break-fasted, lunched, dined, and made much of. Of course I had to say something for myself, and so I did. These occasional *autos-da-fé*, at which I am a kind of asbestos victim, are almost wearing the life out of me. It is as bad as habitual drunkenness, this habit I have been led into. Now comes the Moore centennial — it is worse than the seventeen-year locust plague — this centennial epidemic. " What do I write for?" Because they cajole, and flatter, and tease, and I have got into the way of yielding. Why can't you get a furlough and drop in at the Φ B K meeting? they have made me President, because I am over-ripe, I sup-pose. Backward the course of empire takes its way. You were President when your hair was — brown? Mine is white.

I write to tell you about the book you ought to have and have not got — you shall have it, whether you want it or not. Don't forget us all. Kindest regards to Mrs. Lowell.

BOSTON, *December* 4, 1879.

MY DEAR JAMES, — At half-past six P. M. yesterday I got up from a " breakfast " given to me at the Brunswick by the publishers of *The Atlantic*. My friends were there in great force, except Longfel-low, who sends me an affectionate note this morn-ing, telling me how he was prevented by a sharp and sudden attack of influenza from coming. Of course, a banquet from which the two L's are absent is shorn of its brightest ornaments, but we did — they did, I should say — as well as possible under the circumstances, and this morning I look back on all the fine things that were said and sung about me, and feel like a royal mummy just embalmed. The only thing is, that in hearing so much about one's self it makes him think he is dead and reading his obituary notices. My table is covered with letters, some of which are shrieking for answers, but I sit down to write to you first for a special reason. If you should see a copy of the *Advertiser* — and I suppose you may look at a Boston paper now and then — you will see in that of December 4th a report of this festival, and you will find your own name mentioned by me. I spoke of you as having been the cause of my writing *The Autocrat* by what you said to me when *The Atlantic* was started, and that any pleasure my writings had given, and my own enjoyment of the immediate occasion, they owed to you in addition to your own *noble* contribution to our literature. The wretches printed "noble" *notable!* The idea of my applying that lukewarm word to the grand poems which so largely merit the adjective I gave them! I was so vexed that, if I had not slept off my breakfast, I should have had an indigestion. It is perfectly true that but for these kind and *confident* words of yours I might not have taken up my pen in serious earnest, and so have missed the chance of saying some things I am glad to have said and which others have been willing to listen to.

BOSTON, *February* 25, 1880.

MY DEAR JAMES, — It is six weeks since I received
your letter (of December 27th). When I think, as I
return to it, of all you have been through within the
past year, I reproach myself for not having sent at
least a few words of reply before this. In spite of all
you told me, I do not think I can bring home to myself in imagination the terrible strain it must have
been to watch one so dear to you through a long period
of danger and distress, — unconscious, too, of all the
affectionate care bestowed upon her, — and this in a
strange land and with duties, I suppose, which were
peremptory in their demands upon you. Most fer-
vently I hope — what if I said I pray? — not to Almighty "Protoplasm," surely, — that the precious life
so interwoven with your own may be spared to you and
restored to its former health, so that she, with whom
you have been through the valley of the shadow, —
almost that of death, — may be your companion during the brilliant years which lie before you.

You have forgotten how many pleasant things you
said to me in your last letter. It is my turn now.
Ever since you dined at my table in company with
Motley, I have thought of you as a Diplomatist in the
making. I believe everybody is pleased with your
appointment, here at home. Leland (Hans Breit-
mann), who has been living in London some years,
says you will be the most popular American Minister
we have ever sent. I cannot help thinking "J. B."
will take to you all the more heartily because you
have lashed him pretty well in the poems which everybody in England (who reads) read at the time (if
Rutledge's statistics are an index), and which will be
re-read now with renewed delight for the neatness with

which the licks were laid on. It won't hurt you to have won your spurs from Oxford and Cambridge before you showed yourself to the Dons as an official personage. All things considered, I think nobody has appeared at the British Court from this side of the Atlantic since John Adams, who had a right to a sense of inward satisfaction quite up to your own. And what a place to fill! Do you remember what I myself said once?

> I would *perhaps* be Plenipo,
> But only near St. James.

Of course, all of us knew you ought to be there, and many of us hardly doubted that you would be. You know what creatures we have sometimes sent abroad as ministers, of any one of whom, if we should say that our realm contained

> Five hundred as good as he,

it would be considered as a libel by implication. On the contrary, we consider you to be a regular *e pluribus Unum* (I mean *The One* out of a great many). You may get as much European epidermis as you like, the strigil will always show you to be at heart an unchanged and unchangeable New Englander. You are anchored here, and though your cable is three thousand miles long, it will pull you home again by and by; at least, so I believe, so I think all who know you believe. That is just what we like, — a man who can be at his ease in Court or cloister, and yet has a bit of Yankee backbone that won't soften in spite of his knee-breeches, his having to be " with high consideration," and the rest. All this I could n't help saying, for I feel it to be true as you know it to be.

If I write you a letter from time to time, pray do

not let it weigh upon you that it must be *answered*. I think you can have very little leisure for any private correspondence.

BOSTON, *January* 17, 1881.

MY DEAR JAMES, — Whether you have time to *read* a letter is the question with me, not whether you have time to *write* one in answer. You must have more to do, to see, to say, to think about, than we quiet people at home can dream of. But I do not feel quite happy without reminding you once or twice a year, or even a little oftener than that, that there is such a place as New England, and that you have some friends there who have not forgotten you, and who will be very glad to see you back again — that is, whenever you have got enough of it and come of your own accord. . . .

Perhaps you would like a word or two about the Club. No meeting the last Saturday of December, that being the 25th. The last of November we had a very good meeting for these degenerate days — Emerson *hors de combat*, mainly, Agassiz dead, Longfellow an absentee, Lowell representing — the Club — at Her Imperial Majesty's Court. I feel like old Nestor talking of his companions of earlier days — divine Polyphemus, godlike Theseus, and the rest, — " men like these I have not seen and shall never look on their like " — at least until you come back and we have Longfellow and all that is left of Emerson to meet you. I say " all that is left." It is the machinery of thought that moves with difficulty, especially the memory, but we can hardly hope that the other mental powers will not gradually fade as that has faded.

It is your business to outlive all of the group with

which, though ten years younger than the youngest, you are commonly named. If, as may be hoped, you should pass the later years of a long life in the old town you know and love so well, what a position you will hold — what homage will surround you! And what memories you will have to live upon! I am very much struck with the effect a few additional years have in adding to the respect and the tender regard with which one is treated. Of course I see this in the way in which Emerson and Whittier and Longfellow are looked upon and spoken of; but I myself experience some of the same kindliness in the way in which I am received and spoken of, and am finding out that every age has its own privileges and pleasures.

You ought to have been at the Cambridge semi-centennial, when your delightful and most welcome note was read. I only attended the school-gathering in the forenoon, at which Longfellow said a few words, and sat in the chair the children presented him a year or two ago, and I read a few verses. You must see our papers and must have seen the account — unless you are more thoroughly weaned from bathycolpian Cambridge than I believe you ever will be.

Also you ought to see yourself embalmed in *Harper's Magazine*. Underwood is potting our (literary) interiors, and doing us up in spices like so many dead Pharaohs.

With loving remembrance,
Always faithfully yours.

Don't think I expect answers.

My little calendar reads thus : —

JULY

25

Wut 's best to think may n't puzzle me nor you,
The pinch comes in decidin' wut to do.

J. R. LOWELL.

MY DEAR JAMES, — I wonder if you find time to
read anything besides official papers? As for writing,
you must have enough of that to do *per alium* if not
per teipsum. Still, I told you I should write you from
time to time, and now I am here at the seaside, and
there is a little lull in my labors, and I am going to
remind you that there is a Western hemisphere where
you have a few friends left yet — I hope you may find
them all when you come back. I think Longfellow
shows his added years very plainly. I went a year or
so ago with him to be photographed, and the picture
showed less life than any I had seen of him. This
may have been temporary, but I own that he appears
to me more languid in his air and movements — it is
not strange at seventy-four. But I have often noticed
that there are unexplained movements in health at
different ages, especially in later years, both downward
and upward, towards Avernus and back again, so that
one who seems to be failing will grow younger again
next year, and begin quite fresh after his episode of
depression. Emerson is gently fading out like a photograph — the outlines are all there, but the details
are getting fainter. He keeps his Egeria always near
him to hint the right word to him — his faithful
daughter Ellen. Whittier is pretty well, I believe, —
but I have seen none of our old friends for some
weeks, since I have been quietly living at my old

quarters at Beverly Farms.   The last Club I went to
was at the end of May.   The "Saturday" is not what
it was when you were with us.   We do our best to
keep it alive.   I, and a number of others, always pay
two dollars whether we are there or not; which makes
it easier for the financial infirmities. . . . The little
block almanac or calendar, from which I took the text
for this 25th of July, 1881, is one of several of a
similar aspect which have been published here lately.
Many of the mottoes are from your poems, others from
the friends with whom your name is often coupled, of
whom I have the honor to be one now and then.   There
has been a great deal done of late, especially in the
West, to popularize American writers, especially poets.
They have Brown, Jones, and Robinson "days" in
Cincinnati and other cities — B. J. & R. being one or
another of a very limited group of living writers, all
of New England birth.   When the school-children
learn your verses they are good for another half century at any rate.   But we are getting smothered with
readable verse, like that girl in a novel I was reading
the other day, who smothered herself with roses and
other flowers instead of a pan of charcoal.   I wish the
women that send me their manuscripts would do as
much!   I will not ask you a question, because you
might feel as if you ought to answer it, but I cannot
help wondering if you see the inside of any printed
books nowadays, except those you must consult.   I
have probably mentioned Edward Everett's story of
Lord Palmerston to you every time I have written —
namely, that he said, on being asked if he had read
so and so: that he did not read any printed books.
I have no doubt that, if I write again, I shall tell this
over again.

I begin to wonder whether you will ever come back to your (college) perch after so high and long a flight. What an oracle you will be, if you do! I can imagine you sitting at John's table with your old village cronies around, and discoursing to them on the small amount of wisdom with which the world is governed, and the great amount of talk that covers it. . . . All possibilities, however, are open to you, and your old friends may have to live chiefly on the memories of the time when you were among us, unless they live to be nonagenarians, when you will perhaps find yourself once more in the shade of your elms — and laurels.

BEVERLY FARMS, MASS., *August* 29, 1883.

MY DEAR JAMES, — What can I do better on this, my seventy-fourth birthday, than sit down and remind you of my protracted existence? It seems so long since I said good-by to you on board the steamer — so long to me, and how much longer to you! You would have a great deal to tell me, and I have next to nothing to tell you, yet you know I claim this one-sided correspondence as my specialty. I should really feel ashamed if I thought I entailed any sense of obligation on you by my occasional letters. I have told you all along that I should write from time to time, and I mean to do it. But when I sit down and think of myself looking over at my old neighbor digging his potatoes, taking my daily walks (with my wife) to the beach, to the woods, or to the garden (Mr. F. Haven's), driving to Smith's Point, Essex Woods, Chebacco Pond, seeing no company except now and then a distinguished visitor, — Mr. Evarts, Mr. Bayard, or estrays from Washington, — when, I say, I think of

myself slowly oxydating in my quiet village life, and
of you in the centre of everything, yourself a centre,
I smile at the contrast, and wonder whether you still
remember there is such a corner of the universe as
that from which I am writing. I hear of you through
various channels. I saw you in *Punch* the other day,
— a very pretty compliment it was he paid your
speech at the Lord Mayor's something or other. I
wonder if anybody sent you the Cambridge paper in
which your name was mentioned (with Gaston's and
another) as a good candidate for Governor. How
would you like, I wonder, the old shoes in which His
Excellency, General Butler, stands to-day. I always
thought you might turn up as the "dark horse" in
some of the great handicap races. In the mean time
you are greatly missed in our world of letters. We
have had a promise of a Life of Hawthorne which you
were to do for the series of American Men of Letters.
I hope you will not give that up, for no one can fill
your place. I should like mightily to see your name
on the list, — it *is* announced, — but also to know that
you were to find or make the time to write the Memoir
in the intervals of diplomatic and social occupations,
if such a thing is conceivable. I myself am at work
on Emerson. I remember your early characterization
of him, and of Carlyle, in the *Fable for Critics*, but
when I get back to Boston I shall look out for all you
have said about him and his followers in your various
Essays, expecting to find my best conclusions anticipated. I find the study of Emerson curiously interesting; few, I think, can bear study into all their
mental, moral, personal conditions as he does. I wish
you were here, that I could talk him over with you.

You must be what our people call " a great success "

in England; now come home (when you are ready) and you shall be Sir Oracle — not Magnus but Maximus Apollo, among your own admiring fellow-citizens.

Boston, May 20, 1885.

My DEAR JAMES, — I have just been reading your fine address at the unveiling of the bust of Coleridge. I read it not only with admiration of its masterly criticism, but with many incidental thoughts and recollections which it brought up, my own first reading of "The Ancient Mariner," and the strange kind of intoxication it produced, a feeling as if I had been stunned and was left bewildered. What must I needs do but read the poem over again; and, being somewhat light-headed from a cause which I will mention, I got a fair reminiscence of the old *stunning* sensation. The cause I refer to is the fact that I have been shut up for nearly a fortnight with the worst attack of illness I have had for many a year. Until to-day the fever has been constant and prostrating, and I have been as worthless an invalid as you would desire to see — or rather, not see. " Give me some drink, Titinius," has been my favorite quotation. But I have followed you to the Abbey, to Windsor Castle, to Eton with Mr. Gladstone, and am thinking how soon you are to be back among innumerable admirers and a multitude of friends — missing, alas! how many faces of those who would have made your welcome sweet. You have two paths open before you now in your splendid maturity, a career of ambition with its excitements and possible rewards, and an age of well-won and honored retirement from toilsome duties, with leisure for the studies and labors which you love best.

Old friends will return to you, if you want them, — new friends will cluster thickly about you; all that can be done to make the old Cambridge life worth living for you will be at your call. But I do not forget the sacred ground I am approaching; I may be able to say things I cannot write, at least not now, after these many days of heated blood and throbbing pulses, in which time has been unreal and dream-like, and I find myself at length like one just waking from a trance. Your return must be an experiment to yourself. You come back a new man to old scenes which have been filling up with new life and leaving many a blank space where you will look for a face that was familiar. But your welcome will be without a parallel, and you can choose your own companionships. If you are tired of your old Cambridge surroundings, — and they must seem very limited after the wide life you have been living, — you have the latch-keys of *two* Universities in your pocket, and can suit yourself in the matter of localities. Of course we all hope you will come and make Elmwood classical again.

I am afraid that my words as well as my handwriting betray the strain through which my nervous system has been passing — but I hope to be all right before your return.

BEVERLY FARMS, *July* 19, 1888.

MY DEAR JAMES, — The enclosed printed paper, sent to me to send to you, must be my apology for writing when I have nothing to tell you of interest outside of my own affairs — which I love to think are not wholly without some interest for you. Here I

am, then, in a really pleasant country house, living
with my daughter, seeing little company of course,
but now and then a pilgrim in the shape of an inter-
viewer or a sight-seer, who fancies that I am worth a
visit. I am writing nothing at present — I feel that
sat prata biberunt from my cistern, at least until the
springs have filled it up, which it is rather late in life to
look for. I have taken some interest in other people's
projects lately, — in some tree-portraits which Mr.
Henry Brooks is getting up, and for which I have
written an introduction, — in a Slang, etc., Dictionary which Leland is going to publish, — I referred
him to you for Yankee phrases, which you know better than anybody else, — in a new *Library of Amer-
can Literature* in ten volumes, large octavo, edited
by E. C. Stedman and Ellen M. Hutchinson, of which
I received four volumes yesterday, with a promise of
the others, as they are issued. You will, no doubt,
receive a complimentary copy in due season. Much
good may it do you ! I have often referred to Duyck-
inck's *Cyclopædia of American Literature*, not always without interest. I have barely looked into this
work, which begins with Captain John Smith, and in
its fourth volume reaches Buckminster and William
Tudor. How is he — are they — going to fill six more
volumes after 1820 ? I think you will have to come
in for a good large contribution.

I am living as agreeably as is possible under my
conditions. . . . But in the mean time my sight grows
dimmer, my hearing grows harder, and I don't doubt
my mind grows duller. But you remember what Lan-
dor said : that he was losing his *mind*, but he did n't
mind that, — he was losing or had lost his *teeth* —
that was his chief affliction. Between nature and art

I get on very well in the dental way, — as for the mental, I will not answer. The last years of a protracted life are made tolerable by a series of natural anodynes, which blunt the sensibilities to some extent at sixty or seventy, and after that go on benumbing one nerve-tip after another until, if we live long enough, we come to a state of passive apathy. It is hardly right for me to say this, for I am pretty thoroughly alive yet. But just now I feel no inclination to write, — perhaps when autumn comes I may feel more like it. *You* have many bright years before you, but next month brings me to the beginning of my 80th year (how those figures look!), and not much can be looked for after that. No matter — I have said most of what I had to say.

I told you I had nothing to write about. You have, and when you have nothing better to do I shall be delighted to hear from you.

(I send one of my encyclicals, cut from a note of proper form and dimensions.)

January 2, 1891.

MY DEAR JAMES, — Your beautiful present of your collected works lies on my table in my reception-room, or lesser library, waiting for me to make a place of honor for it on the shelves near my hand in my library proper. I shall have to ask certain great authors, whom if I named you might accuse me of flattery, to lie a little closer, or to go up a shelf higher, to give your volumes place. I hope you will add two or three or more volumes to the noble collection, before you lay down your pen. It is such a comfort, when one gets a shining New Year's or Christmas gift, to read upon it the word *sterling*. I might say that of your literary work, only we do not have to look to find the hall-mark.

You and I meet in a work which has greatly taken my fancy, — Mr. Henry Brooks's account of some of our great Massachusetts elms and other trees. I suggested the work thirty years ago, and gave him the hint of the five-feet-long rod, or wand, to give an idea of the size of the trees. I wrote the Introduction, and I found you were ahead of me after all. For Mr. Brooks found his leading [?] poetical motto in your verse. I am glad we come together, even if I get the worst of it.

Our poor old raft of eighteen-twenty-niners is going to pieces ; for the first time no class meeting is called for the 8th of January. I shall try to get the poor remnant of the class together at my house ; but it is doubtful whether there is life enough left for a gathering of half a dozen. I have a very tender feeling to my coevals. You are not old enough to have a right to my octogenarian sensibilities and sentimentalism ; but for want of older friends you must share in these clinging and lingering affections which the penultimate sometimes if rarely indulges toward the antepenultimate of a decade younger date. The honest truth is, that the eighth decade is so loaded with bodily and mental infirmities in a great majority of cases, that the survivors, who find themselves in it, have a sympathy with each other which the lusty septuagenarian can hardly share. Your temporary ailment has brought you nearer to us for a while, but when you get all right and have been so for a time, you will heartily [?] realize the difference between

your vital conditions and those of Whittier and myself. Among other octogenarian weaknesses the habit
of prosing, as you see, is very noticeable; so I will say
no more, but thank you again most warmly for your
beautiful gift, and assure you of my long-cherished
admiring affection.

II. TO JAMES WILLIAM KIMBALL

December 10, 1858.

MY DEAR SIR, — I write to thank you for your kind and truly Christian letter. The only regret I have felt was, that you seemed too fearful of giving offence. There is no need of further debate — we understand each other pretty well — kind souls both; and both, I believe, after the truth.

It is well for me to have corresponded with you in one way, because it will make me more cautious of giving offence; bad in another way, for the goodness of men holding to ancient beliefs is the greatest obstacle to new truths — and as no past century has failed to bequeath us new views in religion, *somebody* must give us new light in this. I should like to help, if I might; but though I have been sometimes rudely and (even of late) needlessly attacked on erroneous [representations] of what I have said, I do not like to offend good people; and if I err in this way it is as Saul did, thinking he was doing God service. But if somebody had not been offended a century ago, we should now have been hanging each other's grandmothers for witches.

I hope to send you a copy of my book in a few days, when I get some that are to my taste. I should like a copy of your little book, referred to. I have not finished the other yet, but shall do it soon.

March 8, 1860.

MY DEAR SIR, — Lectures being over, I am going to fulfil my promise, or threat, and send you a few thoughts on the subjects of your letter.

Let me begin with two remarks.

First, I have great pleasure in hearing you, or hearing from you, because I am entirely convinced of your kind spirit and sincerity, and that your Christianity has its true seat — in the heart.

Secondly, I have not the least personal desire to change *any* other person's faith, who lives in peace with God and man, except just so far as he is an aggressive spiritual neighbor. One of my women goes to Mr. Kirk's, a very good young woman, I think. Two others are Roman Catholics; both of them are models. I have no disposition to meddle with the belief of either. Heaven has more gates than Thebes ever had, I believe, and I cannot suppose that these people, or any others, must borrow my key. But though I do not wish to make proselytes to my creeds, positive or negative, I like to state my beliefs to those who are inquiring; and these of course are principally young persons, and especially of the intellectual classes. I have less hesitation, as the old traditional Westminster Catechism system has shown itself, in my experience, a dead failure, as I explained to you the other day. I will now touch your principal points briefly, to show how they strike my apprehension. 1. "Gaining" by truth — "comfort" from adopting this or that view. I accept such ideas and language as appropriate to the "Retreat for aged and infirm women," but not for you or me. Truth is often very *un*comfortable. If that has anything to do with your accepting it, I shall have to say: "Good-morning, Mr. Kimball, — we had better not waste each other's time in talking about these matters." I can't help it whether I gain or lose by a truth; I *must* accept it. "But, Doctor, your *views* are [not] necessarily *truth*." "Very possibly, Mr. Kimball. But if you begin by saying that your personal interest — your profit — your comfort are to enter into an astronomical, geological, ethnological, or other scientific question you and I are to discuss, as an element for the solution of it, I say again: 'Good-morning, Mr. Kimball.'"

2. If you choose to accept that hypothesis I mentioned, and which seems to have struck you, viz., that the world was created with mock skeletons of almost innumerable mock genera and species, many of them holding the remains of mock food in their mock interiors, and with their teeth ground down as if by long use; in other words, if you choose to believe the Creator the prototype of charlatans and jugglers, I shall have to say again, always with perfect respect and courtesy: 'Good-morning, Mr. Kimball.'"

3. My statistics of clergymen, schoolmasters, children, showing the average results of the technical "evangelical" culture, must not be made too much of. So far as they go, they prove that a very large percentage of very bad men are formed under these influences; but everybody knows that a great many good men grow up in this as in every form of faith. I have full confidence that in your own case your articles of belief are entirely consistent with love and good-will to all men; though what you mean by "freedom from solicitude of all kinds," and "equanimity" in the prospect that the vast majority of these fellow-creatures, whom you love, are to wallow in fire

forever, I cannot understand. Perhaps you do *not*
believe this; then you take the liberty to exercise
your reason in accepting, or rejecting, or explaining
away, a scriptural doctrine; which is all that I do,—
or am supposed to do.

4. The Fall of Man. If the book of Genesis is a
mere collection of beliefs and traditions, most of which
God hath in these last days flatly contradicted out of
his own authentic bibles of the firmament and the
planetary strata, why of course the story of the Fall
of Man must share the fate of Deucalion's deluge.

I don't, therefore, enter upon the discussion of your
questions of the origin of evil, etc., and your difficulties about it. All our present concern is, whether
we have an authentic Divine communication in the
book of Genesis. The most influential priesthood the
world ever saw, more than half of them bound hand
and foot in Romanism, are bribed by everything this
world can offer — money, place, prejudice, fear, hope
— to maintain Genesis to be literally the word of
God, — and yet the belief is weakening every day,
and bids fair in a generation or two to belong only
to the ignorant and the hirelings of ecclesiasticism.
Very uncomfortable, no doubt, to Galileo, to Dean
Buckland, who went crazy, to Hugh Miller, who blew
his brains out — some say *because* they were uncomfortable!

Perhaps you will say nothing of *importance* has been
disproved in Genesis. Please to mark this: every
statement in that book has always been defended as
important until the advance of knowledge has rendered it utterly untenable; *then* it becomes *unimportant;* and yet every commentator is seizing every
external fact in corroboration of these early books,

while he rejects all that invalidate their authority, first as faults, and, as I have said, when science has annihilated that ground, as *unimportant!* Examples: *Astronomy :* 1. It is a lie that the earth moves round the sun. 2. Science proves the lie is true. 3. Of no importance whether the earth moves round the sun or not. *Cosmogony :* The world was made six thousand years ago. Deluge all over the earth four thousand years ago. Geology proves a universal deluge. Wonderful confirmation of Genesis. (See Buckland's old book, *Reliquiæ Diluvianæ.*) Science moves on a generation. Universal deluge not a fact, not possible. World million of ages old. Some shut their eyes and hoot at Geology. Some say it is *unimportant.* Some invent nonsensical tricks, like the *make believe* system already referred to. So of the history of the race, etc.

If any of the distinct statements of Genesis are proved erroneous, of course the "Fall of Man" and the old dogma,

> "In Adam's fall
> We sinned all,"

become a mere legend.

If the truth of the statements in Genesis about creation is an open question, then the Fall of Man is an open question also, and no open question is to be *assumed* as a truth of Divine Revelation.

5. *Re-generation. Re-creation. Re-formation.* All figurative terms. Sometimes there is a sudden and great change of character, — a slaver sea-captain becomes a saint (John Newton). In such a case it is as proper to say a man is re-generated as to say that an overworked minister is "another man" after six months of *re-creation.* But in most cases of even

distinct conversion the change of character is very partial, and it is never total. Every sensible Deacon knows that his church members continue to love money, power, place, pretty faces, good dinners, etc. Perhaps not as much as before re-generation or re-formation, but so as to be easily managed by one or the other of these influences.

The fatal effect of misinterpreting this figurative expression is seen in education. It poisons the train-ing of children from the cradle to treat them as nat-ural haters of God. I know no other way to account for the shocking effects I have seen, and everybody has constantly seen, from these doctrines in families. You remember a striking series I gave you in detail. I grant, however, that with a certain number of chil-dren, especially the feeble, the scrofulous, the con-sumptive, they produce a sickly saintliness which is often interesting, though in the larger sense abnormal. I much prefer persons who have been *trained* to spir-itual life — (Train up a child, etc.) — to those who have been *changed* to it. That is just exactly the advantage of our Christian civilization : that the new birth is, as it were, hereditary in the better races, so that a good proportion of children will grow up spiritually-minded, if they are treated as Christ would have treated them (Of such is the K. of H.), and not cut down to the roots, as fast as they sprout, by a soul-withering dogma. At the same time I wish you distinctly to observe that I recognize sudden changes of character as one of the means by which the Spirit of God reclaims those who have wandered from the path in which they have been or should have been trained.

I know some persons I should be very glad to see

"converted." But the finest characters and noblest souls I have met have never been through any such technical process. Its frequency and phenomena appear to depend very much on the grade of intelligence and social position.

Holy affections are what we want, I suppose. The great majority of "converted" persons I have met with could not be distinguished from other people by any outward evidence of possessing them. On the other hand, I have seen abundant evidence of them in many persons to whom the very phraseology of "conversion" would sound strange and unfamiliar. "Ah, but, Doctor, they had not the supreme love of God. They did not love Him with all their soul, with all their mind, strength, etc." I answer, *Nobody does.* The command is a mere figure and hyperbole. If for instance, a man loved God with *all his mind,* he could not spare a part of his mind to give attention to any earthly object. But we are commanded to love our neighbors, our wives, our husbands, even our enemies, each of whom will require a portion of our mind to be either loved or hated. Therefore, if we obey this command, we cannot love God with *all* our mind. If we love God with *all* our mind we cannot obey this command.

The only way I can judge whether a man loves God is the apostle John's way, — to see whether he loves his brother. Applying this, I do not think the technical "converts" have compared favorably with the best persons, not technical "converts," I have known, or with the Roman Catholic holy men and women.

In short, I consider that conversion of a Jew or a heathen to a new religion — from formalities to spir-

itual beliefs and affections — was one thing ; and that
education in a Christian community and family ought
to be a kind of congenital conversion, and very commonly is, especially in the cultivated classes; so that
with them "conversion" is the exception and Christian nurture the rule, while, as you pass downward in
the social scale, "conversion" is the rule and natural
Christian development the exception. The moral and
religious standard is most elevated, I think, in the
higher social ranks, where development is the rule.
Observe that I say the "higher," not the highest, for
these last have some special temptations. I have
written more than I meant to. I don't know that I
shall want to take the trouble to write another letter,
but I shall be very happy to hear from you. I repeat
it, I have no doubt your creed agrees with you, and
that under it your Christian affections grow and flourish. I have not the least desire to change it, if you
are really satisfied with it. Like all other good and
kind men, you do not practically carry out some of its
legitimate conclusions. If it makes you happy I am
glad, but I cannot forget that it left William Cowper
on his death-bed in "unutterable despair;" and I
have seen enough of it in practice to feel sure that
it has yet something to gain and a good deal to be
rid of.

March 18, 1860.

MY DEAR SIR, — I return the extract, which I
have read with pleasure, and the paper, which has
furnished me amusement. I reciprocate all your
kindly feelings most cordially, and I have no doubt
that if all the "evangelicals" I have known had had
hearts and tempers like yours, I should have looked

less critically at some of their beliefs. Let me repeat it, — I have no wish to change your belief in anything, so far as it is adapted to your spiritual nature and necessities. Much of it I share with you: a supreme and absolute faith in one great Father; a revelation of Himself, "at sundry times and in divers manners," — infallibly in creation, more or less fallibly in all that has been committed to human tradition, preeminently in the life of one of the "sons of God" known on earth as the Anointed, of whom we have some imperfect records. That religion consists in holy affections, the evidence of which is in righteous life. If you believe that man is born under a curse derived from Adam, I do not. If you believe that a finite being is allowed to ruin himself forever, I do not. At any rate I am sure you *hope not*. If you accept the whole collection of tracts called "the Bible" — the canon of which represents a *majority vote*, nothing more or less, — as infallible, I think your ground is *demonstrably* untenable.

You and I may like to exchange opinions sometimes on special points, without going into protracted general discussions. It may not be important to your "salvation" to hold correct opinions on many points, where truth can be easily reached by any fair inquirer; but to your rational nature, to your dignity as a being entrusted with the sacred franchise of thought, it may be very important. Heaven will not be the same to the saint who has slumbered on the pillow of tradition as to him who has kept his mind open to all truth. Whenever we can fix upon any single definite point in which we are interested, I shall always be pleased to compare our beliefs and their grounds.

May 12, 1876.

Many thanks for your kind letter, dear Mr. Kimball, which I have read with the same feeling of respect and sympathetic assent to much of it as I have often listened to your conversation. The logic of the heart is too strong with you to let you be a quite faultless standard of dogmatic theology; but I think the mild, vaccinated form of that complaint is not so far removed from health by any means as the old natural disease of Calvinism. I shall not tell you just how much I agree with you, and just when I differ or dispute, but content myself with renewing my expression of thanks for the interest you take in my spiritual condition, and assuring you that your faith includes what I hold to be the essentials — love of man and love of goodness — to the latter of which you may give what name you choose, but which I think many of your fellow-creatures have loved and still love under a different one.

January 24, 1879.

My dear Mr. Kimball, — It is very difficult to carry away the exact meaning of a somewhat rambling conversation. I find that I agree with most of what you say in your letter, and, so far as I can see, you have somewhat misinterpreted my expressions. King David was, like Burns, much given to women, but he had the finest emotional religious nature that has recorded itself, and we are all too glad to use his words, dearer on the whole to us than any other except those of Christ himself. The fact that Burns drank and lived in license does not prevent our recognizing the human element, which makes the " Cotter's

Saturday Night " and " Auld Lang Syne " go to our hearts.

You misunderstand my notions of government in this world. I only repeat the scriptural doctrine, that the physical laws to which all are submitted have no moral discrimination. If you do not like my statement of the proposition, you can take that in the thirteenth chapter of Luke, second and fourth verses. I mean just that and no more. Gravity & Co. do not trouble themselves about moral distinctions — a snow-slide will smash a saint as willingly as a sinner — so these verses imply — so we feel practically. The rain falls on just and unjust — the sun rises on the evil and the good.

Therefore the sense of justice demands a rectification of these conditions in a future state — in other words, that a strictly moral government shall take the place of the present, which is so largely physical. This is what the New Testament promises — as do other and older religions — that of Egypt, for instance.

I, like you, am an optimist — not quite so confident, perhaps, but still living in the habitual trust that this life is a school, the seemingly harsh discipline of which will be explained when we get into one of the upper classes. I dare not say that we are sure of this; but it is the only belief which makes life worth living. Some, I think, will say they are as sure of a future life as of this — but many good people speak more modestly and hesitatingly. They hope; they trust; they encourage the belief; live in it and die in it.

So, too, I agree with you about the practical effect of the doctrine of Retribution. In one point I might not stand on exactly the same ground with yourself.

I consider the traditional beliefs so firmly grounded, especially in the Roman Catholic Church, — which is the only one logically safe, as it seems to me, though I am far from a Romanist, — I consider these traditional beliefs, I say, so firmly grounded that the effects of such truths as "rationalists" have charge of and proclaim are very slow and gradual, and far less dangerous to the order of society than if they were easily and at once accepted. There are some beliefs I myself have which I should expect and rather hope to see antagonized, as many might not be ready to accept them without injury.

I suppose you know how many of the great Dutch Biblical scholars deal with the Hebrew traditions. If not, you should get hold of *The Bible for Learners*, translated not long ago and republished in this country. I am afraid our Sunday-school teachers would have hard work with their learners, if these learners got hold of the teachings of these learned divines; but whatever there is of truth in them will work its way *slowly* into general currency, — *slowly;* that is the safeguard. In that way the belief in witchcraft went out, without making all men Sadducees, as it was feared its disappearance certainly would.

As to the terrible disadvantages — bad blood — neglected education, evil example, etc., to which so large a fraction of mankind are submitted, all that is a reason to demand, as well as expect, a future state, if the world has a moral Governor.

Even as to the being "born again" I am not so sure that we might not partially agree. Love and obedience must be formed in the character somehow, before it is fit for the *best company*. Who reported that private midnight conversation, whether it was correctly reported, just what it meant, is not quite clear to me. It should seem there was nothing in it that a "master in Israel" should not have been already acquainted with.

I do not want, and I have not the time, to discuss the points on which we differ; but I am happy to point out some on which we agree.

With the highest regard and esteem, I am, dear Mr. Kimball,

Very sincerely yours.

January 20, 1883.

MY DEAR MR. KIMBALL, — Many thanks for your letter and the little book, which I read immediately on receiving it. All spiritual experiences are interesting, but their character depends greatly on temperament, cheering and hopeful in a man like yourself, despairing and suicidal in melancholic persons like Cowper.

Your Bible is my Bible; but you have only to look at the Biblical literature of to-day and you will see that the collection of separate treatises known under that name, many of them by unknown authors, is studied in a very different way from that in which our parents looked at it. You must not find fault with me for belonging to the present, when you see the changes that have shown themselves in the Church of Scotland, the Church of England, the theological schools of New Haven and Andover, and in the whole drift of opinion on the subject of eschatology, the Fall of Man, and the other doctrines dependent on this last conception of the relation of the race to its Creator. We cannot go back to the mother's womb of old beliefs.

Are you not rejoiced beyond all expression to see that there is a growing disbelief in the doctrine that a great part of mankind are doomed to everlasting torture with fire and brimstone, as expressly stated in certain too familiar texts?

Are you not glad that against any such belief is arrayed that other statement: "God is love"? I know you must be; and so you need not take the trouble to answer my questions.

III. TO JOHN LOTHROP MOTLEY

BOSTON, *February* 16, 1861.[1]

MY DEAR MOTLEY, — It is a pleasing coincidence
for me, that the same papers which are just announc-
ing your great work, are telling our little world that
it can also purchase, if so disposed, my modest two-
volume story. You must be having a respite from
labor. You will smile when I tell you that I have
my first vacation since you were with us, — when was
it? in '57? — but so it is. It scares me to look on
your labors, when I remember that I have thought
it something to write an article once a month for *The
Atlantic Monthly;* that is all I have to show, or
nearly all, for three and a half years; and in the mean
time you have erected your monument more perennial
than bronze in these two volumes of *alto rilievo.* I
will not be envious, but I must wonder, — wonder at
the mighty toils undergone to quarry the ore before
the mould could be shaped and the metal cast. I
know you must meet your signal and unchallenged
success with little excitement, for you know too well
the price that has been paid for it. A man does not
give away the best years of a manhood like yours,
without knowing that his planet has got to pay for
his outlay. You have won the name and fame you
must have foreseen were to be the accidents of your
career. I hope, as you partake the gale with your

---

[1] This letter has been already printed in the *Motley Correspondence*

illustrious brethren, you are well ballasted with those other accidents of successful authorship.

I am thankful, for your sake, that you are out of this wretched country. There was never anything, in our experience, that gave any idea of it before. Not that we have had any material suffering as yet. Our factories have been at work, and our dividends have been paid. Society — in Boston, at least — has been nearly as gay as usual. I had a few thousand dollars to raise to pay for my house in Charles Street, and sold my stocks for more than they cost me. We have had predictions, to be sure, that New England was to be left out in the cold if a new confederacy was formed, and that the grass was to grow in the streets of Boston. But prophets are at a terrible discount in these times, and, in spite of their predictions, Merrimac sells at $1125. It is the terrible uncertainty of everything — most of all, the uncertainty of opinion of men, I had almost said of principles. From the impracticable Abolitionist, as bent on total separation from the South as Carolina is on secession from the North, to the Hunker, or Submissionist, or whatever you choose to call the wretch who would sacrifice everything and beg the South's pardon for offending it, you find all shades of opinion in our streets. If Mr. Seward or Mr. Adams moves in favor of compromise, the whole Republican party sways, like a field of grain, before the breath of either of them. If Mr. Lincoln says he shall execute the laws and collect the revenue, though the heavens cave in, the backs of the Republicans stiffen again, and they take down the old Revolutionary king's arms, and begin to ask whether they can be altered to carry minié bullets.

In the mean time, as you know very well, a monstrous conspiracy has been hatching for nobody knows how long, barely defeated, in its first great move, by two occurrences, — Major Anderson's retreat to Fort Sumter, and the exposure of the great defalcations. The expressions of popular opinion in Virginia and Tennessee have encouraged greatly those who hope for union on the basis of a compromise; but this evening's news seems to throw doubt on the possibility of the North and the Border States ever coming to terms; and I see, in this same evening's paper, the threat thrown out that, if the Southern ports are blockaded, fifty regiments will be set in motion for Washington! Nobody knows; everybody guesses. Seward seems to be hopeful. I had a long talk with Banks; he fears the formation of a powerful Southern military empire, which will give us trouble. Mr. Adams predicts that the Southern Confederacy will be an ignominious failure.

A Cincinnati pamphleteer, very sharp and knowing, shows how pretty a quarrel they will soon get up among themselves. There is no end to the shades of opinion. Nobody knows where he stands but Wendell Phillips and his out-and-outers. Before this political cataclysm, we were all sailing on as quietly and harmoniously as a crew of your good Dutchmen in a *treckschuyt*. The Club has flourished greatly, and proved to all of us a source of the greatest delight. I do not believe there ever were such agreeable periodical meetings in Boston as these we have had at Parker's. We have missed you, of course, but your memory and your reputation were with us. The magazine which you helped to give a start to has prospered, since its transfer to Ticknor & Fields. I suppose they may make something directly by it, and,

as an advertising medium, it is a source of great
indirect benefit to them. No doubt you will like to
hear, in a few words, about its small affairs. I don't
believe that all the Oxfords and Institutes can get the
local recollections out of you. I suppose I have made
more money and reputation out of it than anybody
else, on the whole. I have written more than anybody
else, at any rate. Miss Prescott's stories have made
her quite a name. Wentworth Higginson's articles
have also been very popular. Lowell's critical articles
and political ones are always full of point, but he has
been too busy as editor to write a great deal. As for
the reputations that were *toutes faites*, I don't know
that they have gained or lost a great deal by what
their owners have done for *The Atlantic*. But, oh!
such a belaboring as I have had from the so-called
"evangelical" press, for the last two or three years,
almost without intermission! There must be a great
deal of weakness and rottenness, when such extreme
bitterness is called out by such a good-natured person
as I can claim to be in print. It is a new experience
to me, but is made up for by a great amount of sympathy from men and women, old and young, and such
confidences and such sentimental *épanchements*, that,
if my private correspondence is ever aired, I shall pass
for a more questionable personage than my domestic
record can show me to have been.

Come now, why should I talk to you of anything
but yourself and that wonderful career of well-de-
served and hardly-won success which you have been
passing through since I waved my handkerchief to
you as you slid away from the wharf at East Boston?
When you write to me, as you will one of these days,
I want to know how you feel about your new posses-

sion, a European name. I should like very much, too, to hear something of your every-day experiences of English life, — how you like the different classes of English people you meet, — the scholars, the upper class, and the average folk that you may have to deal with. You know that, to a Bostonian, there is nothing like a Bostonian's impression of a new people or mode of life. We all carry the Common in our heads as the unit of space, the State House as the standard of architecture, and measure off men in Edward Everetts as with a yard-stick. I am ashamed to remember how many scrolls of half-an-hour's scribblings we might have exchanged with pleasure on one side, and very possibly with something of it on the other. I have heard so much of Miss Lily's praises, that I should be almost afraid of her if I did not feel sure that she would inherit a kindly feeling to her father's and mother's old friend. Do remember me to your children ; and as for your wife, who used to be Mary once, and whom I have always found it terribly hard work to make anything else of, tell her how we all long to see her good, kind face again.

Give me some stray half hour, and believe me
                              Always your friend.

                         BOSTON, *November* 29, 1861.[1]

MY DEAR MOTLEY, — I know you will let me begin with my personal story, for you have heard before this time about Ball's Bluff and its disasters, and among them that my boy came in for his honorable wounds. Wendell's experience was pretty well for a youngster

[1] This letter has been already printed in the *Motley Correspondence.*

of twenty. He was standing in front of his men when a spent ball struck him in the stomach and knocked him flat, taking his wind out of him at the same time. He made shift to crawl off a little, the colonel, at whose side he was standing, telling him to go to the rear. Presently he began to come right, and found he was not seriously injured. By the help of a sergeant he got up, and went to the front again. He had hardly been there two or three minutes when he was struck by a second ball, knocked down, and carried off. His shirt was torn from him, and he was found to be shot through the heart, — it was supposed through the lungs. The ball had entered exactly over the heart on the left side, and come out on the right side, where it was found, — a minié ball. The surgeon thought he was mortally wounded ; and he supposed so, too. Next day, better ; next after that, wrote me a letter. He had no bad symptoms, and it became evident that the ball had passed outside the cavities containing the heart and lungs. He got on to Philadelphia, where he stayed a week, and a fortnight ago yesterday I brought him to Boston on a bed in the cars. He is now thriving well, able to walk, but has a considerable open wound, which, if the bone has to exfoliate, will keep him from camp for many weeks at the least. A most narrow escape from instant death ! Wendell is a great pet in his character of young hero with wounds in the heart, and receives visits *en grand seigneur*. I envy my white Othello, with a semicircle of young Desdemonas about him listening to the often told story which they will have over again.

You know how well all our boys behaved. In fact, the defeat at Ball's Bluff, disgraceful as it was to the planners of the stupid sacrifice, is one as much to be remembered and to be proud of as that of Bunker Hill. They did all that men could be expected to do, and the courage and energy of some of the young captains saved a large number of men by getting them across the river a few at a time, at the imminent risk on their own part of being captured or shot while crossing.

I can tell you nothing, I fear, of public matters that you do not know already. How often I thought of your account of the Great Armada, when our own naval expedition was off, and we were hearing news from all along the coast of the greatest gale which had blown for years! It seemed a fatality, and the fears we felt were unutterable. Imagine what delight it was when we heard that the expedition had weathered the gale, and met with entire success in its most important object.

February 3, 1862.

My DEAR MOTLEY, — I got your letter of January 14th day before yesterday, Saturday. I was a little out of spirits yesterday, on account of ugly rumors as to the tone of the English press, etc., which had the effect of knocking down stocks somewhat in New York, and dashing our sanguine anticipations a little for the time. This morning the papers tell us that many of these representations are thought to be mere secession contrivances, and we hear from Washington that the advices from foreign Governments were never so friendly as at this time. They begin to talk about the *entente cordiale* between this country and England as like to be reëstablished — so may it prove! Not that England can ever be to us what she has been. Those sad words from John Bright's letter have expressed the feelings that have sunk deep into the hearts of all (who have hearts to be reached) among us. "There has been shown [us] no generosity, such as became a friendly nation, and no sympathy with [us] in [our] great calamity." Those beautiful breasts of our "mother" country, from which it seemed that nothing could wean us, have shrivelled into the wolf's dugs, and there is no more milk in them for us henceforth evermore. The West end is right. Not by aggression, but by the naked fact of existence, we are an eternal danger and an unsleeping threat to every government that founds itself on anything but the will of the governed. We begin to understand ourselves and what we represent, now that we find who are our enemies, and why, and how they would garrote us now that our hands are on these felons' throats, if they could paint a lie over so that its bones would not show through. I do believe Hell is empty of Devils for the last year, this planet has been so full of them helping the secession liars.

You don't want my rhetoric, but plain talk about what is going on. We are generally hopeful, so far as I hear talk around me. The Mason and Slidell matter has long been in the silurian strata of the past. The events that are more than six weeks old all go with pre-adamite creations. All the world seemed to think Pilot Seward was drifting on to a lee shore, and that he would never double that terrible Cape Fear in the distance. Presently he heaves in sight, canvas all spread, and lo! it seems the wind is blowing *off* the shore, as it has been any time these fifty years.

Confidence holds good in McClellan, I feel well assured. The *Tribune* attacks him; some grumble at delays; but I believe the wisest heads are as yet reasonably patient. They know that the Virginian roads are impracticable at this particular time. They know the enlistment period of many of the rebel troops is about to expire — *before this very month is out.* It is perfectly plain from the rebel organs that the delay is telling immensely on them; that they begin to feel the pressure of the *cordon sanitaire* which is drawing its ring of fire around them.

The financial business seems now to be the immediate subject of doubts and differences of opinion. I talked with Frank Lowell this morning about it. He did not profess to be an expert in finance (though he must have a good deal of acquaintance with it). He thought the difficulty was in Chase's inexperience, not providing long enough beforehand for the inevitable want of the Treasury. About the taxation schemes, you may find out from the papers, — I have n't found out what the scheme is which is likely to be adopted. I believe our people are worked up to the *paying* point, which, I take it, is to the fighting point as boiling heat (212°) to blood heat (98°).

When I write you letters you must take my ignorance with my knowledge, and I know rather less of finance than you do of medicine. I have always thought that if I had passed a year or two in a counting-room it would have gone far towards making a sensible man of me. But I have no doubt you have other friends who can tell you what there is to be told, not found in the papers, on this matter of finance and currency. I only know there is a great split about making government paper legal tender, and if I could see Bill Gray five minutes just at this point, could find out where the pinch is, and what *kept him awake* a week or two ago, as I hear something did, thinking about it.

I have told you I am hopeful, and always have been. Hands off, and we'll lick these fellows out of their insolent adjectives. We did lick 'em well at Mill Spring the other day, and at Drainsville a little before this, and, I myself entertain no manner of doubt, can whip them man for man at any time, in a fair field, picked against picked, average against average. We are the conquerors of Nature, they of Nature's weaker children. We thrive on reverses and disappointments. I have never believed they could endure them. Like Prince Rupert's drops, the unannealed fabric of rebellion shuts an explosive element in its resisting shell that will rend it in pieces as soon as its tail, not its head, is broken fairly off. That is what I think, — I, safe prophet of a private correspondence, free to be convinced of my own ignorance and presumption by events as they happen, and to prophesy again — for what else do we live for but to guess the future in small things or great, that we may help to shape it, or ourselves to it.

Your last letter was so full of interest, by the expression of your own thought and the transcripts of those of your English friends — especially the words of John Bright, one of the two foreigners that I want to see and thank — the other being Count Gasparin — that I feel entirely inadequate to make any fitting return for it. I meet a few wise persons, who for the most part know little — some who know a good deal, but are not wise. I was at a dinner at Parker's the other day where Governor Andrew and Emerson, and various unknown dingy-linened friends of progress, met to hear Mr. Conway, the not unfamous Unitarian minister of Washington, Virginia-born, with seventeen secesh cousins, fathers, and other relatives, tell of his late experience at the seat of Government. He had talked awhile with father Abraham, who, as he thinks, is honest enough, but simply incompetent and without a plan. I don't know that his opinion is good for much. He is an out-and-out immediate emancipationist, — believes that is the only way to break the strength of the South; that the black man is the life of the South; that they dread work above all things, and cling to the slave as the drudge that makes life tolerable to them. He believes that the blacks know all that is said and done with reference to them in the North; their longing for freedom is unalterable; that once assured of it under Northern protection, the institution would be doomed. I don't know whether you remember Conway's famous " One Path " sermon of six or eight years ago. It brought him immediately into notice. I think it was Judge Curtis (Ben) who commended it to my attention. He talked with a good deal of spirit. I know you would have gone with him in his leading ideas. Speaking of the communication of knowledge among the slaves, he said if he stood on the upper Mississippi and proclaimed emancipation, it would be told in New Orleans before the *telegraph* would carry the news there!

I am busy with my lectures at the college, and don't see much of the world. But I will tell you what I see and hear from time to time, if you like to have me. I gave your message to the Club, who always listen with enthusiasm when your name is mentioned. My boy is here — still detailed on recruiting duty — quite well. I hope you are all well and free from all endemic visitations, such as Sir Thomas Browne refers to when he says that "cholical persons will find little comfort in Austria or *Vienna*."

P. S. Our last accounts from the Burnside expedition, which had such a hard time getting to its destination, are all very encouraging.

BOSTON, 21 CHARLES STREET,
August 29, 1862.[1]

MY DEAR MOTLEY, — I don't know how I can employ the evening of my birthday better than by sitting down and beginning a letter to you. I have heard of your receiving my last, and that you meant to reply to it soon. But this was not in the bond, and whether you write or not, I must let you hear from me from time to time. I know what you must endure with a non-conductor of a thousand leagues between you and this great battery, which is sending its thrill through us every night and morning. I know that every different handwriting on an envelope, if it comes from a friend, has its special interest, for it will give an impression in some way differing from that of all others. My own thoughts have been turned aside for a while from those lesser occurrences of the day, which would occupy them at other times, by a domestic sorrow, which, though coming in the course of nature, and at a period when it must have been very soon inevitable, has yet left sadness in mine and other households. My mother died on the 19th of this month at the age of ninety-three, keeping her lively sensibilities and sweet intelligence to the last. My brother John had long cared for her in the most tender way, and it

[1] This letter has been already printed in the *Motley Correspondence.*

almost broke his heart to part with her. She was a daughter to him, she said, and he had fondly thought that love and care could keep her frail life to the filling up of a century or beyond it. It was a pity to look on him in his first grief; but Time, the great consoler, is busy with his anodyne, and he is coming back to himself. My mother remembered the Revolution well, and she was scared by the story of the redcoats coming along and killing everybody as they went — she having been carried from Boston to Newburyport. Why should I tell you this? Our hearts lie between two forces, — the near ones of home and family, and those that belong to the rest of the universe. A little magnet holds its armature against the dragging of our own planet and all the spheres.

I had hoped that my mother might have lived through this second national convulsion. It was ordered otherwise, and with the present prospects I can hardly lament that she was spared the period of trial that remains. How long that is to be no one can predict with confidence. There is a class of men one meets with who seem to consider it due to their antecedents to make the worst of everything. I suppose —— —— may be one of these. I met him a day or two since, and lost ten minutes in talk with him on the sidewalk; lost them, because I do not wish to talk with any man who looks at this matter empirically as an unlucky accident, which a little prudence might have avoided, and not a theoretical necessity. However, he said to me that the wisest man he knew — somebody whose name I did not know — said to him long ago that this war would outlast him, an old man, and his companion also, very probably. You meet another man, and he begins cursing the Government as the most tyrannical one that ever existed. "That is not the question," I answer. "How much money have you given for this war? How many of your boys have gone to it? How much of your own body and soul have you given to it?" I think Mr. —— —— is the most forlorn of all the Jeremiahs I meet with. *Faith*, faith is the only thing that keeps a man up in times like these; and those persons who, by temperament or under-feeding of the soul, are in a state of spiritual anæmia, are the persons I like least to meet, and try hardest not to talk with.

For myself, I do not profess to have any political wisdom. I read, I listen, I judge to the best of my ability. The best talk I have heard from any of our home politicians was that of Banks, more than a year and a half ago. In a conversation I had with him, he foreshadowed more clearly the plans and prospects, and estimated more truly the resources, of the South than any one else with whom I had met. But prophets in America and Europe have been at a very heavy discount of late. Count Gasparin seems to me to have the broadest and keenest understanding of the aims and ends of this armed controversy. If we could be sure of no intermeddling, I should have no anxiety except for individuals and for temporary interests. If we have grown unmanly and degenerate in the north wind, I am willing that the sirocco should sweep us off from the soil. If the course of nature must be reversed for us, and the Southern Goths must march to the "beggarly land of ice" to overrun and recolonize us, I have nothing to object. But I have a most solid and robust faith in the sterling manhood of the North, in its endurance, its capacity for a military training, its plasticity for every

need, in education, in political equality, in respect for
man as man in peaceful development, which is our
law, in distinction from aggressive colonization; in
human qualities as against bestial and diabolical
ones; in the Lord as against the Devil. If I never
see peace and freedom in this land, I shall have faith
that my children will see it. If they do not live long
enough to see it, I believe their children will. The
revelations we have had from the Old World have
shed a new light for us on feudal barbarism. We
know now where we are not to look for sympathy.
But oh! it would have done your heart good to see the
processions of day before yesterday and to-day, the air
all aflame with flags, the streets shaking with the tramp
of long-stretched lines, and only one feeling showing
itself, the passion of the first great uprising, only the
full flower of which that was the opening bud.

There is a defence of blubber about the arctic
creatures through which the harpoon must be driven
before the vital parts are touched. Perhaps the
Northern sensibility is protected by some such encas-
ing shield. The harpoon is, I think, at last through
the blubber. In the mean while I feel no doubt in my
own mind that the spirit of hostility to slavery as the
cause of this war is speedily and certainly increasing.
They were talking in the cars to-day of Fremont's
speech at the Tremont Temple last evening. His allusions to slavery — you know what they must have
been — were received with an applause which they
would never have gained a little while ago. Nay, I
think a miscellaneous Boston audience would be more
like to cheer any denunciation of slavery now than
almost any other sentiment.

Wednesday evening, September 3d. I have

waited long enough. We get the most confused and
unsatisfactory yet agitating rumors. Pope seems to
be falling back on the capital after having got the
worst of it in a battle on the 30th. Since that there
has been little fighting so far as we know, but this
noon we get a story that Stonewall Jackson is march-
ing by Leesburg on Baltimore, and yesterday we
learned that Cincinnati is in imminent danger of a
rebel invasion. How well I remember the confidence
that you expressed in General Scott, — a confidence
which we all shared ! The old General had to give
up, and then it was nothing but McClellan. But do
not think that the pluck or determination of the
North has begun to yield. There never was such a
universal enthusiasm for the defence of the Union
and the trampling out of rebellion as at this perilous
hour. I am willing to believe that many of the
rumors we hear are mere fabrications. I won't say
to you: "Be of good courage," because men of ideas
are not put down by the accidents of a day or a year.

December 15, 1862.

MY DEAR MOTLEY, —

.   .   .   .

As I am in the vein of saying things that ought to
please you, let me say that my heart always swells
with pride, and a glitter comes over my eyes, when I
read or hear your denunciations of the enemies of
liberty at home and abroad, and your noble pleas for
the great system of self-government now on its trial
in a certain sense — say rather, now putting our people on trial, to see whether they are worthy of it.
There were many reasons why you should have lost

your passion for a republican government. The old civilizations welcome you as an ornament to their highest circle. At home you of course meet in the upper political spheres much that is not to your taste — untaught men, uncouth women, plebeian aspects. But you remain an idealist, as all generous natures do and must. I sometimes think it is the only absolute line of division between men, — that which separates the men who hug the actual from those who stretch their arms to embrace the possible. I reduce my points of contact with the first class to a minimum. When I meet them, I let them talk, for the most part, for there is no profit in discussing any living question with men who have no *sentiments*, and the non-idealists have none. We don't talk music to those who have no ear; why talk of the great human interests to men who have lost all their moral sensibilities, or who never had any? One thinks of these same abstractions as practical matters in times like these and places like this. You know quite as well as I do that accursed undercurrent of mercantile materialism, which is trying all the time to poison the fountains of the national conscience. You know better than I do the contrivances of that detested horde of mercenary partisans who would in a moment accept Jeff Davis, the slave-trade, and a Southern garrison in Boston, to get back their post-offices and their custom-houses, where the bread they have so long eaten was covered with slime, like that of their brother serpents, before it was swallowed. The mean sympathizers with the traitors are about in the streets under many aspects. You can generally tell the more doubtful ones by the circumstance that they have a great budget of complaints against the government,

that their memory is exceedingly retentive of every
reverse and misfortune, and that they have the small
end of their opera-glasses towards everything that
looks encouraging. I do not think strange of this in
old men; they wear their old opinions like their old
clothes, until they are threadbare, and we need them
as standards of past thought which we may reckon our
progress by, as the ship wants her stationary log to
tell her headway. But to meet *young* men who have
breathed this American air without taking the conta-
gious fever of liberty, whose hands lie as cold and
flabby in yours as the fins of a fish, on the morning of
a victory — this is the hardest thing to bear. Oh, if
the bullets would only go to the hearts that have no
warm human blood in them! But the most generous
of our youth are the price that we must pay for the
new heaven and the new earth which are to be born of
this fiery upheaval. I think one of the most trying
things of a struggle like this is the painful revelation
of the meanness which lies about us unsuspected.
Perhaps I am harder than you would be in my judgment, but it does seem to me that the essential elements of the armed debate now going on are so evident, that it is a shame for any man, woman, or child
in the land of school-houses and colleges not to know
which is the civilized side — though the youth at
Cambridge, in England, may settle it in their debat-
ing society that God and all his holy angels are with
the slave-breeders.

Thomas Starr King, who has been the apostle of
liberal religion and political freedom in California,
wrote me two or three weeks ago that he was to deliver some lectures on American Poets, among whom
he was good enough to include me. He wanted some

verses to finish off the lecture he had devoted to me, and I wrote him a dozen, of which one or two may prove readable to you. They are not to be printed as yet, but by and by perhaps will come out in *The Atlantic* (which by the way is thriving, I understand, in these times). . . .

[Written in margin of the letter.] The title of this Poem is " Choose you this Day whom you will serve." How absurd! I have written the whole piece out in full. I do solemnly aver that when I began this letter I had no thought of the above poem; I do conscientiously assert that when I began the poem on the preceding page I had no intention of copying more than three or four of its verses. So help me Phœbus!

Horns to bulls, stings to bees — to poets verses, as weapons of offence and defence. However, if you should write me a letter one of these days, you may criticise them if you like, as they may not be printed for months yet. I think Starr King will speak them so as to put meaning into them, if they have none of their own.

I have said nothing about the military situation. This noon I was saying that I looked for news from the other side of Richmond. This afternoon it comes. I am writing Monday. What news may come to-morrow is quite uncertain, but I myself cannot help thinking that Burnside will be very glad to wait, if he can, until the cannon begin to roar to the east and the south of Richmond. I will leave a little space for anything I may hear before I mail my letter.

Tuesday, December 17th. I could have wished that the mail and my letter had gone yesterday. We get to-day the news that Burnside has withdrawn all his troops over to this side of the Rappahannock, and taken up his pontoon bridges. He failed in his repeated attempts to storm the rebel works, and found it such a desperate undertaking that he seems to have given up for the present. There is no question that this news has exercised a most depressing effect on all but the secession sympathizers, who, grudging every success to the Cabinet and its new general, are secretly comforted, as I guess by certain signs, that the "Onward to Richmond" has again met with a check. It looks to me now as if the movement were a precaution against a possible necessity rather than an immediate necessity. The river was fast rising with the rain which was falling. It would never do to be cut off from supplies and reinforcements by a swollen stream, and so Burnside quietly, and as it seems without loss, without the enemy's being aware of what he was about, last night sent over his artillery, and then followed it by all his infantry. We have become so used to disappointments that we have learned to bear them with a good deal of equanimity. We hope this is only temporary, but it has dashed our spirits, and begun to knock stocks about a little. . . . You will think, I know, of my first-born in the midst of the scenes his regiment has been going through. He is suffering from dysentery, I am afraid pretty sick, but we are impatiently waiting to hear from him. A note of two or three lines, written in pencil to a friend in Philadelphia on the 10th, was the first news we had of his being ill, and is the last thing we have heard from him to the present moment. He cannot have been in the fights, and therefore must have been really "down," as he says in his note. The experience has no doubt brought on with aggravated symptoms the trouble from which he suffered so severely on the Chickahominy, but which did not keep him from being on duty until the last of the battles — Malvern Hill — had been fought.

Let us keep up our courage for our country and ourselves. It is harder for you, I have no doubt, than for me, at home and getting the news two or three times daily. Many things that sound ill do not worry me long, for I am a man of large faith, and though the Devil is a personage of remarkable talents, I think the presiding wisdom is sure to be too much for him in the end. We are nervous just now, and easily put down, but if we are to have a second national birth, it must be purchased by throes and agonies, harder, perhaps, than we have yet endured. I think of you all very often; do remember me and my wife (who is giving all her time to good deeds) most kindly to your wife and daughter.

Yours always in faith and hope.

BOSTON, *October* 10, 1865.[1]

MY DEAR MOTLEY, — When Miss Lily left us last March, we hardly thought she would be so very soon back in America as we hear she is to be. I cannot let the day of her marriage go over without a line to her father and mother as a substitute for the epithalamium with which a century ago I should (if all parties had been extant) have illuminated the *Gentleman's Magazine*. I hear from one of my Providence friends the best accounts of Mr. Ives. I hope that the alliance will prove very happy to her, to you, to

[1] This letter has already been printed in the *Motley Correspondence*.

your wife, and all your connections. It is having a son, a brother, born full grown, to receive a daughter's husband as a member of one's family. With all the felicitations which rise to my lips, for I feel now as if I were talking with you face to face, I cannot help remembering how much there must be of tender regret mingling with the blessings that follow the dear child over the threshold of the home she had brightened with her presence. Even the orange flowers must cast their shadow.

Yet I cannot help thinking that the new attractions which our country will have for you will restore you and your family to those who grudge your possession to an alien capital; and that, having stood picket manfully at one of our European outposts through the four years' campaign, you may wish to be relieved, now that the great danger seems over. So we shall all hope, for our sakes. What a fine thing it would be to see you back at the Saturday Club again! Longfellow has begun to come again. He was at his old place, the end of the table, at our last meeting. We have had a good many of the notabilities here within the last three or four months; and I have been fortunate enough to have some pleasant talks with most of them. Sir Frederick Bruce, the new Minister, pleased us all. You may know him, very probably. White-haired, white-whiskered, red-cheeked, round-cheeked, with rich dark eyes, hearty, convivial, not afraid to use the strengthening monosyllable, for which Englishmen are famous, pretty freely, outspoken for our side as if he were one of us, he produced, on me at least, a very different effect from that of lively Lord Napier or plain and quiet Lord Lyons.

I had a good deal of talk with Grant, whom I met

twice. He is one of the simplest, stillest men I ever saw. He seems torpid at first, and requires a little management to get much talk out of him. Of all the considerable personages I have seen, he appears to me to be the least capable of an emotion of vanity. He can be drawn out, and will tell his habits and feelings. I have been very shy of repeating all he said to me, for every word of his is snapped up with great eagerness, and the most trivial of his sayings, if mentioned in the hearing of a gossip, would run all through the press of the country. His entire sincerity and homely truthfulness of manner and speech struck me greatly. He was not conscious, he said, of ever having acted from any personal motive during his public service. We (of the West), he said, were terribly in earnest. The greatest crisis was the battle of Shiloh; that he would not lose; he would have fought as long as any men were left to fight with. If that had been lost the war would have dragged on for years longer. The North would have lost its *prestige*. Did he enjoy the being followed as he was by the multitude? "It was very painful." This answer is singularly characteristic of the man. They call on him for speeches, which he cannot and will not try to make.

One trait, half physiological, half moral, interested me. He said he was a good sleeper; commonly slept eight hours. He could go to sleep under almost any circumstances; could set a battle going, go to sleep as if nothing were happening, and wake up by and by, when the action had got along somewhat. Grant has the look of a plain business man, which he is. I doubt if we have had any ideal so completely realized as that of the republican soldier in him. I cannot get over the impression he made on me. I have got some-

thing like it from women sometimes, hardly ever
from men, — that of entire loss of selfhood in a great
aim which made all the common influences which
stir up other people as nothing to him. I don't think
you have met Stanton. I found him a very mild,
pleasant person to talk with, though he is an ogre
to rebels and their Northern friends. Short, with
a square head, broad not high, full black beard turning gray; a dark, strong-looking man; he talks in
a very gentle tone, protruding his upper lip in rather
an odd way. Nothing could be more amiable than
the whole man. It was pleasant chat, mainly, we had
together. One thing he said which I could not forget.
Speaking of the campaign of the Wilderness: "It
was the bloodiest swath ever made on this globe."
Perhaps a little *hasardé*, this statement, but coming
from the Secretary of War it has its significance.

Old Farragut, whom I foregathered with several
times, is the lustiest *gaillard* of sixty-something, one
will meet with in the course of a season. It was odd
to contrast him and Major Anderson. I was with
them both on one occasion. The Major — General, I
should say — is a conscientious, somewhat languid,
rather bloodless-looking gentleman, who did his duty
well, but was overtasked in doing it. Nothing would
have supported him but, etc., etc.; but the old Admirable — *bonâ fide* accident — let it stand; is full of
hot red blood, jolly, juicy, abundant, equal to anything, and an extra dividend of life left ready for
payment after the largest expenditure. I don't know
but he is as much the ideal seaman as Grant the ideal
general; but the type is not so rare. He talks with
everybody, merry, twinkling-eyed, up to everything,
fond of telling stories, tells them well; the gayest,

heartiest, shrewdest old boy you ever saw in your life. The young lady (so to speak), whom you would naturally address as his daughter, is Mrs. Farragut, the pretty wife of the old heart-of-oak Admiral.

Mr. Burlingame has come home from China on a visit. It is strange what stories they all bring back from the Celestials. Richard Dana, Burlingame, Sir F. Bruce, all seemed filled with a great admiration of the pigtails. " There are twenty thousand Ralph Waldo Emersons in China," said Mr. B. to me. " We have everything to learn from them in the matter of courtesy. They are an honester people than Europeans. Bayard Taylor's stories about their vices do them great injustice. They are from hasty impressions got in seaport towns." This is the kind of way they talk.

Mr. Howells, from Venice, was here not long ago; tells me he has seen you, who are his *chef*, I suppose, in some sense. This is a young man of no small talent. In fact, his letters from Venice are as good travellers' letters as I remember since " Eothen."

My son, Oliver Wendell H., Jr., now commonly styled Lieutenant-Colonel, thinks of visiting Europe in the course of a few months, and wants me to ask you for a line of introduction to John Stuart Mill and to Hughes. I give his message or request without urging it. He is a presentable youth, with fair antecedents, and is more familiar with Mill's writings than most fellows of his years. If it like your Excellency to send me two brief notes for him, it would please us both, but not if it is a trouble to you.

And now, as I am closing my gossipy letter, full of little matters which I hoped might interest you for a moment, let me end as I began, with the thoughts of you and yours, which this day brings up so freshly before me. Peace and prosperity and happiness to both households, the new and the old! What can I say better than to repeat that old phrase, — the kindly Roman's prayer as a poor Christian would shape it on this "auspicious morning," *quod bonum, faustum, felix, fortunatumque sit!* Love to all.

BOSTON, *July* 18, 1869.

MY DEAR MOTLEY, — It is two months to-day since I dined with you at No. 2 Park Street. You ought to be at home by this time in London, and ready for my little budget of Boston small-talk, which ought to be welcome to you as a change from the great affairs with which you are dealing, or of which you must be thinking. I am only anxious that they should be small enough matters that I write to you about, for I have talked a good deal with Sumner of late, and know what laborious correspondence you have to keep up with him. I have had some talk with Judge Hoar, too, and I know you must be occupied enough for the first weeks or months with your new duties to find little time or thought for the trifles with which I fill up my slight pages.

I believe my staple is commonly myself, a person in whom I am ashamed to take so much interest, but he is so fond of you, and misses you so much, that you can excuse almost anything.

I had been writing continuously for a good while when you went away, in a somewhat new direction, but whether anything will come of it I am not yet quite sure. In the mean time I have been disgracefully good-natured and written several small occasional copies of verses, one or two of which I shall enclose, to remind you of my fatal facility at that kind of good-natured literature.

I think, on the whole, the most interesting thing I have to tell you relates to a piece of literary and personal history, which I trust to your discretion a little prematurely. Singularly enough, I suspect you to be one of a limited number of persons to whom the main facts involved have long been familiar.

At the request of Mrs. Stowe, I looked over the proofs of an article, which is to come out in the September number of *The Atlantic Monthly*, and will consequently startle the world about the *middle of August*, — before which time I consider it as confidentially in my knowledge, and imparted to you (for whom it may possibly have less interest than I suppose) in the exercise of my own discretion.

It relates to the true history of Lord Byron's relations with Lady Byron, as disclosed to Mrs. Stowe by Lady B. The essential point is that incestuous relation which is represented as the true source of the difficulty, and though the name of the relative is not mentioned, it is plain enough who is referred to.

I was not consulted about the matter of publishing Lady Byron's revelations. Mrs. Stowe assured me that she had made up her mind about *that*. All she asked was my literary counsel and supervision, which I very willingly gave her.

This article must create a great sensation in many quarters, — you know better than I, a great deal, how far it will be a surprise in the circles of English society. So, look out, about the middle of August, for the September number of *The Atlantic Monthly.*

We have had the Coliseum fever, and happily recov-

ered. It was a grand affair, I assure you. I doubt
if forty thousand people were ever seen before under
one unbroken continuity of roof, in a single honest
parallelogram. I will give you in little its dimensions,
as compared with the Coliseum at Rome, — which
last building had *velaria*, very probably, for emperors, ambassadors, and
such, but had no proper roof. The
audience was truly a wonderful sight, and the vast
orchestra and chorus, though not deafening, as many
expected, was almost oceanic in the volume of its
surges and billows. I wrote a hymn for it, which
Amory told me, two days ago, I had not been praised
enough for. How I loved him!

And that reminds me to tell you that there was a
very pleasant excursion, two days ago, where I met
him, and he made me happy, as I tell you. Mr.
George Peabody — the Dives who is going to Abraham's bosom, and I fear before a great while — asked
a company of twenty or thereabouts to come to Danvers, — or rather "Peabody," as they call it now, —
to look at the buildings he has given, the library, etc.,
and have a good time and a collation. There was
Mr. Adams and Mr. Sumner — governors, judges, —
Mayor Shurtleff, Bigelow, Warren, Clifford, William
Gray, and so on, and among the rest William Amory
and myself. We had a very pleasant day of it. I
said to myself: It is just possible, not likely, but it
may possibly happen, that they will call on you for
something. So I wrote them a toast, or sentiment.
It was nothing, but it touched them off like a lucifer
match. I wish we had had you there. We would
have squeezed you, as we did Sumner, and got a
speech out of you, which could hardly help being un-

premeditated.   I believe I was the only person there
wary enough to foresee the possibility of a sudden
call, — I know that Dr. Lothrop had to ask an extempore blessing, — which he did so well that we thought
he must have been rehearsing it for a week.   You
shall have my " sentiment," taking it for granted that
you understand the difference between fireworks on
the evening of July Fourth and the look of the frames
the next morning : —

> Bankrupt !   Our pockets inside out !
>   Empty of words to speak his praises !
> Worcester and Webster up the spout !
>   Dead-broke of laudatory phrases !
> Yet why with flowery speeches tease,
>   With vain superlatives distress him ?
> Has language better words than these —
>   " The Friend of all his race — God bless him ! "
>
> A simple prayer, but words more sweet
>   By human lips were never uttered
> Since Adam left the country seat
>   Where angel wings around him fluttered !
> The old look on with tear-dimmed eyes,
>   The children cluster to caress him,
> And every voice unbidden cries —
>   " The Friend of all his race — God bless him ! "

More little matters.   We have got a grand new
equestrian statue of George Washington, "first in
war," etc., in the Public Garden.   It reminds me of
Rauch's statue of Frederic at Berlin, which I never
saw, except in a glass stereograph — almost as good,
however, as the statue itself.   It faces down Commonwealth Avenue, as if he were riding out of Boston.   I
wonder we have not had an epigram, in some New
York paper, to the effect that he is turning his horse's
tail to us.   They can turn it about, however, as they

have done with Everett's. I suppose *you* will be in bronze one of these days, — but I hope they will make you face Boston. This new and first equestrian statue we have seen here is generally admired. I think it is admirable in its effect, and I have not heard any but favorable criticisms so far. So you see, what with her Coliseum, and its thousand instruments and ten thousand singers, and its "man on horseback" (what a wonderfully picturesque generalization that was of Caleb Cushing's!), and its two members of the Cabinet and Minister to England, our little town of Boston feels as good as any place of its size, to say nothing of bigger ones.

We saw in the paper, the other day, that you, with your wife and daughters, were going into society "with a rush," as it was elegantly put. I hope you have strength and patience for the labor that must be connected with all this social expenditure of vitality. You remember I got some quinine pills for you, as you went off, — they did not kill you, that is certain, — whether they did you any good, I am afraid you have forgotten by this time.

. . . .

I am going to enclose you my Halleck poem, written at the request of the New York Committee, and one or two other trifles. They will have a home flavor, I know, and you will get a whiff of Boston and Cambridge associations out of them, if nothing else, — just as Mr. Howells told me, coming in in the cars, yesterday, that the smell of the Back Bay salt water brought back Venice to him. . . .

BOSTON, *September* 26, 1869.

MY DEAR MOTLEY, — You need never excuse yourself for not sending letter for letter — I do not expect
it — I was going to say I do not wish it, for I feel
what a load any letter must be to one overburdened
already with such a mass of correspondence. Even
without this special reason I should never be very
particular. I can say with Lady Montagu: "I am
not so wrong-headed as to quarrel with my friends the
minute they don't write; I'd as soon quarrel at the
sun the minute he did not shine, which he is hindered
from by accidental causes, and is in reality all that
time performing the same courses and doing the same
good offices as ever."

The first thing I naturally recur to is the Byron
article. In your letter of August 4th you say "there
will be a row" about it. Hasn't there been! We
have had three storms this autumn: 1. The great
gale of September 8th, which I recognized while it
was blowing as the greatest for fifty-four years, — for
you remember that I remember *the* September gale.
2d. The Byron whirlwind, which began here and
travelled swiftly across the Atlantic; and 3d, the gold-
storm, as I christened the terrible financial conflict
of the last week. About the Byron article I confess
that, great as I expected the excitement to be, it far
exceeded anything I had anticipated. The prevailing
feeling was that of disbelief of the facts. The general
opinion was strongly adverse to the action of Mrs.
Stowe. My impression is that the belief in the essential fact is growing stronger since the unsatisfactory
statements of the parties most interested. I see that
there is a more decided division of opinion on the main
question in England than here — or than there was

here at first, at any rate. In the mean time the poor woman, who, of course, meant to do what she thought an act of supreme justice, has been abused as a hyena, a ghoul, and by every name and in every form, by the baser sort of papers. The tone of the leading ones has been generally severe, but not brutal. I might have felt very badly about it, if I had had any responsibility in counselling Mrs. S. to publish, but she had made up her mind finally, and had her article in type, before I heard or knew anything of it.

. . . .

This last week we had a Humboldt celebration, or rather two, in Boston. One in which Agassiz was the orator, the other in which a German — Heinzel by name — was the speaker. Agassiz did himself credit by a succinct account of Humboldt's life and labors, and interesting anecdotes of his personal relations with him. He was in great trouble all the time. . . . Curious hint for public speakers who use glasses. I sat next Charles Sumner. " Agassiz has made a mistake," he said, " he has eye-glasses — he ought to have spectacles. In three or four minutes his skin will get moist and they will slip and plague him." They did not in " three or four minutes," but in the last part of his address they gave him a good deal of trouble, keeping one hand busy all the time to replace them as they slid down his nose. Remember this if you have occasion to speak an hour or two before an audience in a warm room. Of course I wrote a poem, which I had the wonderful good sense to positively refuse delivering in Music Hall after the long Address of Agassiz, but read at the *soirée* afterwards. I thought well of it, as I am apt to, and others liked it. Applaud my abstinence in not sending it to you — it will

be in print one of these days, perhaps in *The Atlantic*.
. . . That same day Heinzel, as I said, delivered an
address, to the Germans chiefly, in Boston, in which
he claimed Humboldt as an Atheist, in opposition to
Agassiz, who cited passages in which Humboldt referred to the Deity.

Longfellow has got home, not looking younger, certainly, but luminous with gentle graces as always.
Walking on the bridge two or three weeks ago, I met
a barouche with Miss G—— and a portly mediæval
gentleman at her side. I thought it was a ghost,
almost, when the barouche stopped and out jumped
Tom Appleton in the flesh, and plenty of it, as afore-
time. We embraced — or rather he embraced me and
I partially spanned his goodly circumference. He has
been twice here — the last time he took tea and
stayed till near eleven, pouring out all the time such a
torrent of talk, witty, entertaining, audacious, ingenious, sometimes extravagant, but fringed always with
pleasing fancies as deep as the border of a Queen's
cashmere, that my mind came out of it as my body
would out of a Turkish bath — every joint snapped
and its hard epidermis taken clean off in that four
hours' immersion. Tom was really wonderful, I think.
I never heard such a fusillade in my life. You may
be sure your name came up between us, and if you
had been just outside the door you might have heard
"something to your advantage," as the *Times* adver-
tisements have it; for your oldest friends are among
the warmest, you may be well assured.

.   .   .   .

So you see I have told you of small local and personal matters, not so well as a lively woman would
have done it, but as they came up to my mind. I

read somewhere lately a letter of a great personage
then abroad — I think it was old John Adams —
in which he begs for a letter full of trifling home-
matters. He gets enough that strains him to read,
and he wants undress talk. I can tell you nothing of
the large world you will not get better from other
correspondents, but I can talk to you of places and
persons and topics of limited interest which will
perhaps give you five minutes of Boston, and be
as refreshing as a yawn and stretch after being fixed
an hour in one position. Park Street looks very
dreary since you and your wife and daughters have
left it — I can't help hoping that you will be sated
with honors and labors by and by. I have not said
a word about the race, which was on the whole a
pleasant interlude, notwithstanding our misfortune.

BOSTON, *April* 3, 1870.

MY DEAR MOTLEY, — I feel as if I must have
something or other to say that will interest you, but
what it is, if there is anything, I can hardly guess as
yet. *L'appetit vient en mangeant*, I have no doubt,
and if I can only tell you that I am alive and have not
forgotten you, I shall perhaps feel better for saying it.
I have been rather miserable this winter by reason of
asthmatic tendencies, which, without preventing me
from doing my work, keep me more or less uncomfortable, and tell me to decline my invitations for a while.
I have been well enough, however, of late, and went
to a dinner-party at Mrs. ——'s yesterday, and a kind
of *soirée* she had after it. This good lady (who is a
distant relation of Mrs. Leo Hunter) had bagged Mr.
Fechter, the player, who has been turning the heads

of the Boston women and girls with his Hamlets and
Claude Melnottes.   A pleasant, intelligent man, —
you may have met him or at any rate seen him, —
but Boston *furores* are funny.   The place is just of
the right size for æsthetic endemics, and they spare
neither age nor sex — among the women, that is, for
we have man-women and woman-women here, you
know.   It reminds me of the time we had when Jef-
ferson was here, but Fechter is fêted off the stage as
much as he is applauded on it.   I have only seen him
in Hamlet, in which he interested rather than overwhelmed me.   But his talk about Rachel and the rest
with whom he has played so much was mighty pleasant.

Another sensation in a somewhat different sphere
is our new Harvard College President.   King Log
has made room for King Stork.   Mr. Eliot makes the
Corporation meet *twice* a month instead of once.   He
comes to the meeting of every Faculty, ours among
the rest, and keeps us up to eleven and twelve o'clock
at night discussing new arrangements.   He shows an
extraordinary knowledge of all that relates to every
department of the University, and presides with an
aplomb, a quiet, imperturbable, serious good-humor,
that it is impossible not to admire.   We are, some of
us, disposed to think that he is a little too much in a
hurry with some of his innovations, and take care to
let the Corporation know it.   I saw three of them the
other day and found that they were on their guard, as
they all quoted that valuable precept, *festina lente*,
as applicable in the premises.   I cannot help being
amused at some of the scenes we have in our Medical
Faculty, — this cool, grave young man proposing in
the calmest way to turn everything topsy-turvy, taking
the reins into his hands and driving as if he were the

first man that ever sat on the box. I say amused, because I do not really care much about most of the changes he proposes, and I look on a little as I would at a rather serious comedy.

" How is it? I should like to ask," said one of our number the other evening, " that this Faculty has gone on for eighty years, managing its own affairs and doing it well, — for the Medical School is the most flourishing department connected with the college, — how is it that we have been going on so well in the same orderly path for eighty years, and now within *three or four months* it is proposed to change all our modes of carrying on the school — it seems very extraordinary, and I should like to know how it happens."

" I can answer Dr. —— 's question very easily," said the bland, grave young man: " there is a new President."

The tranquil assurance of this answer had an effect such as I hardly ever knew produced by the most eloquent sentences I ever heard uttered. Eliot has a deep, almost melancholy sounding voice — with a little of that character that people's voices have when there is somebody lying dead in the house, but a placid smile on his face that looks as if it might mean a deal of determination, perhaps of obstinacy. I have great hopes from his energy and devotion to his business, which he studies as I suppose no President ever did before ; but I think the Corporation and Overseers will have to hold him in a little, or he will want to do too many things at once.

I went to the Club last Saturday, and met some of the friends you always like to hear of. I sat by the side of Emerson, who always charms me with his delicious voice, his fine sense and wit, and the delicate way he steps about among the words of his vocabulary, — if you have seen a cat picking her footsteps in wet weather, you have seen the picture of Emerson's exquisite intelligence, feeling for its phrase or epithet, — sometimes I think of an ant-eater singling out his insects, as I see him looking about and at last seizing his noun or adjective, — the best, the only one which would serve the need of his thought.

Longfellow was there, — not in good spirits I thought by his looks. On talking with him I found it was so. He feels the tameness and want of interest of the life he is leading after the excitement of his European experience, and makes no secret of it. I think the work of translating Dante kept him easy, and that he is restless now for want of a task. . . . I hope he will find some pleasant literary labor for his later years, — for his graceful and lovely nature can hardly find expression in any form without giving pleasure to others, and for him to be idle is, I fear, to be the prey of sad memories.

Lowell was not at the Club. I saw him at the February one seeming well and in good spirits.

Agassiz, you know, has been in a condition to cause very grave fears. I am happy to say that he is much improved of late. . . .

I have left no room to talk of your affairs, to sympathize with your spoliation, — to say how grand we all felt when we read of your famous reception of the great folks the other day, nor to tell you how we miss you and your family here in your own little city, which you must not forget because it looks so small in the distance. You like a letter from me every few months, I am sure, though there is not a great deal in it. You know you need not answer.

BOSTON, *December* 22, 1871.

MY DEAR MOTLEY, — It is several months, I think,
since I have put you to the trouble of reading one of
my gossiping letters, telling you all about myself and
my small affairs and the trivialities which I can think
of as possibly like to interest you. I saw your brother
Edward yesterday, and he told me that he had just
written you twelve pages of news, so that it does seem
this time as if I should have hard work to find anything to tell you about that you do not know already.
. . . At this moment, as I write, a flock of a hundred
or more wild ducks are swimming about and diving in
a little pool in the midst of the ice, for the river has
just frozen over again, and the thermometer was at
zero yesterday. I think you would call my library a
pleasant room, even after all the fine residences you
have seen. I do not think the two famous Claudes
of Longford Castle, with the best picture Turner ever
painted between them, would pay me for my three
windows which look out over the estuary of Charles
River. But you know what a faculty I have of being
pleased with anything that is mine. You will indulge
me, I know, in telling you about matters that interest
me, especially as I have to take so much interest in myself lately, because I have a good deal to do and must
put my spirit into it, and that makes one more or less
an egotist. Firstly, then, our new President, Eliot,
has turned the whole University over like a flapjack.
There never was such a *bouleversement* as that in our
Medical Faculty. The Corporation has taken the
whole management of it out of our hands and changed
everything. We are paid salaries, which I rather
like, though I doubt if we gain in pocket by it.
We have, partly in consequence of outside pressure,

remodelled our whole course of instruction. Consequently we have a smaller class, but better students, each of whom pays more than under the old plan of management. It is so curious to see a young man like Eliot, with an organizing brain, a firm will, a grave, calm, dignified presence, taking the ribbons of our classical coach and six, feeling the horses' mouths, putting a check on this one's capers and touching that one with the lash, — turning up everywhere, in every Faculty (I belong to *three*), on every public occasion, at every dinner *orné*, and taking it all as naturally as if he had been born President. I don't know whether I said all this last time and the time before that, but if I did I trust you have forgotten it. In the mean time Yale has chosen a Connecticut country minister, *æt.* 60, as her President, and the experiment of liberal culture with youth at the helm *versus* orthodox repression with a graybeard Palinurus is going on in a way that it is impossible to look at without interest in seeing how the experiment will turn out.

I suppose Edward has told you all about the Grand Duke's visit and the stir it made in our little city. You are so used to great folks that a Grand Duke is not more to you than a Giant or a Dwarf is to Barnum; but we had not had a sensation for some time, and this splendid young man — for he is a superb specimen — produced a great effect. I suppose you get the Boston papers sometimes and read what your fellow-citizens are doing. The dinner the gentlemen [gave] was a handsome one — *thirty-five* dollars a plate ought to pay for what the Californians call a "square meal." Speeches and a poem, of course — blush for me! — the whole affair was a success, with

one or two fiascos. H—— made a sad mess of it;
nobody understands how he can contrive, with so
much taste and experience as he has, to make such a
piece of work as he did the other night, and as he did
at the Burns Centenary Dinner. D—— was as heavy
as a Dutch galleon, — his grandpa was Ambassador
to Russia, and he was thinking too much about that,
perhaps. D—— is able, but somehow he does not
clear the top bar. Winthrop was admirable; Lowell
was very happy. Phillips Brooks was much applauded; and the Russian Minister that was — Cata-
cazy — made a speech which, under the circumstances,
was adroit and felicitous to a wonderful degree.
Winthrop went over its points two or three evenings
ago at a dinner at our friend William Amory's, and
considered it, for a man placed as he was, almost marvellous for what it said and for what it avoided. Well,
en revanche for our dinner, the Grand Duke gave one
at the Revere House to a few guests, *viz.*, the Governor, President Eliot, Longfellow, Lowell, Mr. Fox,
Mr. Winthrop, the Russian Consul, myself, and his
suite. It was very handsome and very pleasant, and
I had some very pretty speeches made to me, as I
don't doubt everybody else did, for it is my belief that
flattering adjectives are the modern substitute for the
broad pieces which princes and nobles used to scatter
so freely in other days. . . .

Just now I am in rather good spirits, because I
have begun a new series of papers for *The Atlantic*,
for which I am to be handsomely paid, and which
people seem to be inclined to accept kindly. I do not
think I am quite contented unless I am doing something besides lecture at the College; but I can never
come within sight of that industry which would have

made you famous for learning, if that was not eclipsed by more brilliant qualities. I hope you are going on with your work to your satisfaction, and I can't help hoping you will get through with it, by and by, and come back to the place that wants you and the friends that miss you. We come together on Saturdays and have good talks and pleasant, rather than jolly, times. Many of your old friends are commonly there, — among the rest Sumner not rarely. . . . There is a great deal of good feeling, I think, in our little circle of literary and scientific people here. I find Longfellow peculiarly sweet in disposition, gentle, soothing to be with, not commonly brilliant in conversation, but at times very agreeable, and saying excellent things with a singular modesty. It is almost impossible to make him speak in public, — he would not say one word when called upon at the dinner to the Grand Duke, — but at the last Club he offered the health of Agassiz, — who was just about to leave on the exploring expedition for the Pacific, — and made a very neat little speech, which was received with much applause. . . .

I ought to have spoken, but I forgot it, of Sumner's attitude to Grant, which, I judge from the papers, is one of uncompromising hostility. Attempts have been made to reconcile them, but it seems without success. He is now going very strongly for the one-term principle, — not to go into effect [till ?] after the next election. You know all about this, very probably, by direct information from Sumner himself.

Well, I have *jasé* to more than your heart's content, I am sure, and I can only send my love and my wife's love to all of you, and assure you all that many friends want to see you all very much, and we as much as any.

BOSTON, *August* 28, 1872.

MY DEAR MOTLEY, — I want to talk to you about matters that interest everybody, but my pen will have its way and begin as usual with my own affairs. I have got through the series of papers I am writing for *The Atlantic* in good season, and they will be published from month to month during the year, and in a volume on the 17th of October.

.   .   .   .

Your niece-in-law, Mrs. Lewis Stackpole, is one of the few civilized persons I have seen on the pavement since I came back. She was in Boston on a flying visit, looking as ruddy and as hearty as rowing and sailing could make her. The children were all well, she said, — little Lewis and I are great friends, and when I lift him up he drops my letters into the iron box with a skill which he and I consider remarkable.

.   .   .   .

A year ago about this time I was staying at Nahant, in the house with Sumner. He talked a good deal with me about public matters, — among other things about the next election. Did I think Grant would be reëlected? — Yes, I did. — You think Grant will be the next President, do you? — Yes, I do. Sumner looked as many volumes as ever did my Lord Burleigh, but said nothing. I have not seen him since the astounding political movements of the last few months. I must say — but you know all about it — a great deal more, probably, than I do — that he does not carry his usual following with him. I think he must have been startled to find that, of all his political associates, General Banks, whose company I fear he would not have elected, is the only one with anything more than a local name, whom he has transferred to the new party, — I mean among our Massachusetts people. You will smile when you see I say " *he* has transferred." I did not mean to put it quite so strongly, but I doubt if he would be greatly shocked, for our friend Charles, who has been and is a great power in the land, is a little prone to think *l'état c'est moi.* I trust you are sensible enough not to consider my opinion as worth two cents. But such as it is I put it on record for my future confusion, if I turn out to be mistaken. I believe the Greeley movement will be a *diminuendo*, and the Grant and Wilson one a *crescendo*. I happened to meet that illustrious swell, Sam O——, this morning, looking as big as if he had just swallowed the Archbishops of York and Canterbury, and I found his talks with New York people of different conditions and interests convinced him of the same thing. I do not suppose you mean to take any part in this contest, but I thought you would like to have my guess to throw into the heap of conjectures. It seems odd to find Garrison and Phillips, Dana and Hoar, all going directly against Sumner.

I see your book is soon promised. How happy you ought to consider yourself that you have a record of noble achievements, which have given you a great and lasting reputation to fall back upon after the disappointments of political life, which not even Sumner's life-long service could secure him against. Love to your wife and children.

November 16, 1872, Saturday.

MY DEAR MOTLEY, — I wrote to you on Michaelmas day, as an Englishman would reckon, September 29th, a couple of sheets of the usual personalities and trivialities, I suppose, for I hardly know what was in them. *Now* I feel as if I had something to write about, and yet I really believe I have very little to tell you in addition to what you must have learned through many channels before this letter reaches you.

The recollection of the Great Fire will always be associated with a kindly thought of yourself in my memory. For on Saturday, the 9th November, your sister, Mrs. S. Rodman, sent me a package of little Dutch story-books, which you had been so good as to procure for me. You have no idea with what a child-like, or if you will childish, interest I looked at those little story-books. I was sitting in my library, my wife opposite, somewhere near nine o'clock, perhaps, when I heard the fire-bells and left the Dutch picture-books, which I was very busy with (trying to make out the stories with the aid of the pictures, which was often quite easy), and went to the north window. Nothing there. We see a good many fires in the northern hemisphere, which our windows command, and always look, when we hear an alarm, towards Charlestown, East Cambridge, Cambridge, and the towns beyond. Seeing nothing in that direction I went to the windows on Beacon Street, and looking out saw a column of light which I thought might come from the neighborhood of the corner of Boylston and Tremont streets, where stands one of the finest edifices in Boston, the "Hotel Boylston," put up by Charles Francis Adams. The fire looked so formidable, I went out, thinking I would go to Commonwealth Avenue and get a clear view of it. As I went in that direction I soon found that I was approaching a great conflagration. There was no getting very near the fire; but that night and the next morning I saw it dissolving the great high buildings, which seemed to melt away in it. My son Wendell made a remark which I found quite true, that great walls would tumble and yet one would hear no crash, — they came down as if they had fallen on a vast feather-bed. Perhaps, as he thought, the air was too full of noises for us to note what would in itself have been a startling crash. I hovered round the Safety Vaults in State Street, where I had a good deal of destructible property of my own and others, but no one was allowed to enter them. So I saw (on Sunday morning) the fire eating its way straight toward my deposits, and millions of others with them, and thought how I should like it to have them wiped out with that red flame that was coming along clearing everything before it. But I knew all was doing that could be done, and so I took it quietly enough, and managed to sleep both Saturday and Sunday night tolerably well, though I got up every now and then to see how far and how fast the flames were spreading northward. Before Sunday night, however, they were tolerably well in hand, so far as I could learn, and on Monday all the world within reach was looking at the wilderness of ruins. To-day, Saturday, I went with my wife to the upper story of Hovey's store on Summer Street, a great establishment, — George Gardner, you remember, owns the building, — which was almost miraculously saved. The scene from the upper windows was wonderful to behold. Right opposite, Trinity Church, its tower standing, its walls partly fallen, more imposing as a ruin than it ever was in its best estate, — everything flat to the water, so that we saw the ships in the harbor as we should have done from the same spot in the days of Blackstone (if there had been ships then and no trees in the way), here and there a tall chimney, — two or three brick piers for safes, one with a safe standing on it as calm as if nothing had happened, — piles of smoking masonry, the burnt stump of the flagstaff in Franklin Street, — groups of people looking to see where their stores were, or hunting for their safes, or round a fire-engine which was playing on the ruins that covered a safe, to cool them, so it could be got out, — cordons military and of the police keeping off the crowds of people who have flocked in from all over the country, etc., etc.

Any reporter for a penny paper could tell you the story, I have no doubt, a great deal better than I can. You will have it in every form, — official, picturesque, sensational, photographic ; we have had great pictorial representations of it in the illustrated papers for two or three days.

I hope you and your friends lose nothing of importance. . . . But everybody seems to bear up cheerfully and hopefully against the disaster, and the only thought seems to be how best and soonest to repair damages.

Things are going on now pretty regularly. Froude is here, lecturing ; I went to hear him Thursday, and was interested. He referred to " your great historian, Motley," in the course of his lecture. After the lecture we had a very pleasant meeting of the Historical Society at Mr. J. A. Lowell's, where Froude was present. Winthrop read a long and really interesting account of the fires which had happened in Boston since its settlement, beginning with Cotton Mather's account of different ones, and coming down to the " Great Fire " of 1760. Much of what

he read I find in Drake's *History of Boston*, from
which also I learn that the " Great Fire " began in
the house of Mrs. Mary *Jackson* and Son at the sign
of the Brazen Head in Cornhill, and that all the
buildings on *Colonel Wendell's* wharf were burned.
My mother used to tell me that her grandfather
(Col. W.) lost forty buildings in that fire, which
always made me feel grand, as being the descendant
of one that hath had losses, — in fact makes me feel a
little grand now, in telling you of it. Most people's
grandfathers in Boston, to say nothing of their great-
grandfathers, got their living working in their shirt-
sleeves, but when a man's g. g. lost forty buildings,
it is almost up to your sixteen quarterings that you
knew so much about in your Austrian experience. . . .

August 26, 1873.

MY DEAR MOTLEY, — You can imagine how sad all
your friends felt when they got that first story of your
illness. It came in such a way that it was hard to
disbelieve, and although we all hoped that it might
be a telegraphic sensational over-statement, the relief
was very great and the rejoicing most hearty when
we received the second message, that your complaint
had been magnified in an "absurdly exaggerated"
story, and that it did not threaten your life or your
continued usefulness and enjoyment. There are few
men better loved by their friends than yourself;
and who are there of whom their country is prouder
as representing its noblest literary attainment and
achievement? Such was the feeling produced by
that first telegram that it seemed almost like a resur-
rection to picture you again in health, and in the full

exercise of all your active powers. But I, who saw Agassiz utterly prostrated by an attack evidently involving the nervous centres, and have since met him again and again in company and at the Club as full of life as ever, and seen him successfully start a new school on his island domain, am ready to believe that great scholars are beyond the reach of those enemies to life which are too much for common people. You know Ben Pierce has shown that good brains make their owners live longer than ordinary ones. Only they must *rest* at intervals from their work. I believe the absolute necessity of this is recognized by our practitioners of to-day as never before, and I trust, if you have been working too hard, they will scare you into a flash of idleness, or, at the most, easy labor.

All the above is said in virtue of my once having been your medical adviser. You may be well enough to laugh at doctors before this reaches you, and I most sincerely hope that your neuralgia, or whatever the trouble may be, has left you, with nothing to remember but the hint that you must not overtax that vast capacity for work and that indomitable spirit, which have already raised such enduring monuments.

May I gossip a few minutes? I write, you see, from Nahant, where I have been during July and August, staying with my wife in the cottage you must remember as Mr. Charles Amory's. . . . So I have been here, as I said, playing cuckoo in the nest, with my wife, who enjoys Nahant much more than I do — having had more or less of asthma to take off from my pleasures. Still, there has been much that is agreeable, and as a change from city life I have found it a kind of refreshment.

Many of your old friends are our neighbors. Longfellow is hard by, with Tom Appleton in the same house, and for a fortnight or so Sumner as his guest. I have enjoyed a great deal in their company. Sumner, who was very nearly killed and buried by the newspapers, seems as well as ever, and gave us famous accounts of what he did and saw in England, among other things a certain christening, where a Very Distinguished Personage officiated as godmother. It sounded like a story out of a picture-book to our ears, unused to such grandeur, and we listened like the three-years child of "The Ancient Mariner." You remember our old friend Pepys; well, I don't believe you made as much of a live queen as he did of a mummied one.

Nearly opposite me is ——, who calls you by your old college name, as Falstaff called the Prince *Hal*, and who with all of us was greatly concerned when we got the false telegram. —— and his wife come in and out of their square box of a house like the little man and woman who emerge from the respective doors of their small residence as the weather is fair or foul. He sits and smokes on the piazza; she waters her plants with the fidelity of a nursing-mother. Time has not darkened his locks or softened the somewhat rigid outlines of his character; he is still "a good hater," and tosses the objects of his contempt with a short, muscular jerk, as a bull tosses a dog. I think he does not touch the world at a great many points — in which particular he differs from the porcupine. There is something likeable if not lovable in hard old ——; everybody likes a rill from a rock better than the water of a stream that runs profusely over sand or mud. A little further on is your long-suffering classmate, I——. I drop in to see him every day or two.

Invalidism is a profitable recreation, but a poor profession. You remember the iron chamber with seven
windows overhead, in the *Blackwood* story. The
captive wakes the second morning and counts but *six;*
the third morning he can count but *five*, and so on,
until the prison walls close on him. Poor I—— has
been going through some such experience; he bears it
as well as might be expected, but his ailments necessarily absorb too much of his thought for his mind to
keep its interest in other matters, as it would were he
not always suffering. Still, I think he likes to have
his friends visit him, and it has been one of my chief
pleasures here to drop in and have a chat with him,
that should make him forget his troubles, if that might
be, for a few minutes, or a good many minutes, not
very rarely.

I have dined since I have been here at Mr. George
Peabody's with Longfellow, Sumner, Appleton, and
William Amory; at Cabot Lodge's with nearly the
same company; at Mr. James's with L. and S., and at
Longfellow's *en famille*, pretty nearly. Very pleasant dinners. I wish you could have been at all of
them. I find a singular charm in the society of Longfellow, — a soft voice, a sweet and cheerful temper, a
receptive rather than an aggressive intelligence, the
agreeable flavor of scholarship without any pedantic
ways, and a perceptible *soupçon* of humor, not enough
to startle or surprise or keep you under the strain of
over-stimulation, which I am apt to feel with very
witty people. Sumner seems to me to have less imagination, less sense of humor or wit, than almost any
man of intellect I ever knew. P. B. said of him in
the Temple Place days, that if you told him the moon
was made of green cheese, he would say, "No! it

cannot be so," and give you solid reasons to the contrary. We had a pleasant little laugh over his unimaginative way of looking at things to-day. But we like to hear him talk, and give him his head whenever he gets into a narrative *quorum pars*, — and you know well in how many large affairs and with how many notable persons he has been concerned in his national and personal career.

I have been twice at your brother Edward's, who seems to have everything charming about him. My wife thinks his two daughters the very pictures of all that is lovely, and I must say it would be hard to find two sweeter specimens of young American womanhood. I was quite surprised at his daughter-in-law's talent for sketching. She catches likenesses in a remarkably happy way.

Nahant is a gossipy Little Pedlington kind of a place. As Alcibiades and his dog are not here, they are prattling and speculating and worrying about the cost of Mr. J——'s new house, which, externally at least, is the *handsomest country house I ever saw*, and is generally allowed to be a great success. The inside is hardly finished, except the hall and dining-room, which are very fine.

On Monday we go back to Boston, after two months' stay. Mr. Sargent sailed for home on the 21st in the Siberia. I have not room for any more gossip, and there is not the least chance for all the kind messages I should send you from the many friends all around me.

Pray do not think of troubling yourself to *answer* this letter, no matter how well you feel.

May 18, 1874.

MY DEAR MOTLEY, — It was a real surprise to me
to get your letter of the 17th April. Much as I was
gratified to receive such a proof that your mind and
your hand were, so far as that showed, in good working order, I had to accept the fact you told me —
that a pen felt like a sledge-hammer in your hand;
and my first impulse was to say you must not make
such an effort again to give me the assurance that you
remember me kindly. I know you do, and if you
remain as silent as your own hero, or the Egyptian
Sphinx, or Harpocrates himself, you never need think
that I shall count you in my debt, or forget to let
you hear from me now and then, whenever I have
anything to tell you.

Let me talk, then, as if you were sitting by me here
in my library, — not forcing myself to speak only of
what is enlivening, but speaking of things as they
have been going on round us lately.

I know you will want to hear something about the
friends we have lost lately, but I hardly remember
what I have already written; I am sure at any rate
that we had not had Schurz's Eulogy. It was a remarkably satisfactory and successful performance,
happy in its delineation of the grand features of Sumner's character, picturesque in its details of scenes in
which he figured, written in miraculously good English for a foreigner, and delivered in a very impressive
way. I dined with him and his wife and daughter
at Mrs. Lodge's after the Eulogy, and passed a very
pleasant evening. Of course, let me say *en passant*,
Mrs. Lodge always has something affectionate to say
about you and your family whenever I meet her.
Your estimate of the loss the nation has sustained in

Sumner's death does not seem in the least an exaggerated one. I should say that the general verdict would concur very nearly with your own opinion.

.   .   .   .

Coming home from ——, William Amory joined me, and wanted to know all I could tell him about you. I always find him good company — in some ways better than anybody else, for he has known Boston on its fairer side longer as well as better than almost any other person I can talk with easily, has a good memory, talks exceedingly well, and has a pleasant, courteous way which is exceptional rather than the rule among the people that make up our New England society.

Yesterday I went out to Cambridge and called on Mrs. Agassiz — the first time I have seen her since her husband's death. She was at work on his correspondence, and talked in a very quiet, interesting way about her married life. What a singular piece of good fortune it was that Agassiz, coming to a strange land, should have happened to find a woman so wonderfully fitted to be his wife that it seems as if he could not have bettered his choice if all womankind had passed before him, as the creatures filed in procession by the father of the race!

I have been, too, to see Hillard, and saw him for the first time. He is quite crippled — cannot move his arm, and walks with a crutch, but talked not without a certain degree of cheerfulness. I was told that he had improved very much within the last few weeks. Another invalid, whom I visit now and then, is old Dr. Bigelow. He is now eighty-seven years old, and I think is rather proud of saying so. He used to be rather shy about his age, I fancied, though the Trien-

nial Catalogue settles the matter pretty closely for all
our graduates. His iron-gray wig was the most admirably managed confession with extenuating circumstances that ever *perruquier* put together. There was
just gray enough to hint that he did not call himself
exactly young, and a good background of dark, to
imply that others were not to call him old. He is
utterly blind, as I think I have told you, and yet is
very cheerful, and talks of old times in a very agreeable and amusing way.

Since I wrote last I have got through my winter
course of lectures, and enjoy my release from almost
daily duties, which I like well enough, and which
probably make me happier than I should be without
them. I begin now, since the new order of things
came in with the new president, in October, and lecture five and four times a week until the beginning of
May. It used to be only four months. But even in
the interval of lectures I do not get free from a good
deal of work of one kind and another. I have done
enough to know what work means, and should think I
had been a hard worker if I did not see what others
have accomplished. I can never look on those great
histories of yours and think what toil they cost, what
dogged perseverance as well as higher qualities they
imply, without feeling almost as if I had been an idler.
But I suppose it is not worth one's while to think too
much about what he might have done or might have
been. Our self-determination is, I suspect, much more
limited than we are in the habit of considering it.
Schopenhauer says that if a cannon-ball in its flight
suddenly became conscious, it would think it was
moving of its own free-will. I must not let my meta-
physics take away the merit of your labors, but still I

think you were in a certain sense predestinated and forced by some mysterious and irresistible impulse to give Holland a history, and make yourself a name in the world of letters.

I have not yet read the *Life of Barneveldt*, and cannot do justice to it until I have finished up some things that have been waiting to be done and will not be put off any longer. But I think I shall have a special enjoyment in it, not merely because it is one of your pieces of historical tapestry, but for a reason I will tell you. I happened to see in a London Catalogue that was sent me the name of a book which you, no doubt, know well enough, and which may be of small account in your valuation — *Meursii Athenæ Batavæ*. It has something more than fifty portraits of Professors in the University, together with plans of Leyden and the manner of its relief, etc., etc. I have become so familiar with the features of Gomarus and Arminius, of William of Orange and "Janus Dousa," of Grotius and Joseph Scaliger and the rest, that I am all ready to read about the times in which they lived. I took down your volume with the siege of Leyden in it, and read it with infinite delight, having the plan of my little quarto volume before me. I began to understand, as I never did before, the delight which must have blended itself with your labors in bringing to the light the old story of that little land of heroes; and my own Dutch blood moved me to a livelier sense of gratitude to you for all you had done to rescue that noble past from oblivion, than I had ever felt before.

I must have told you in my last all the gossip I could think of about the gayeties of the past winter. I have come down — or got up — to dinner-parties as the substantial basis of my social life. They have

slacked off (Novanglice) of late, so that I am now as
domestic as a gallinaceous fowl, in place of chirruping
and flitting from bough to bough.

In the mean time I have my little grandchild to
remind me that I must not think too much of the
pomps and vanities of the world, with two generations
crowding me along.

.   .   .   .

We are all well, and living along in our quiet way
with as much comfort as we have any right to, and
more than most people have to content themselves
with.   I have one trouble I cannot get rid of, namely,
that they tease me to write for every conceivable anniversary.   I wrote a hymn which was sung at the
delivery of Schurz's Eulogy.   Waldo Higginson came
this afternoon to get me to write a hymn for the dedication — no — the opening or completion of the Memorial Hall.   You remember Sydney Smith's John
Bull — how he "blubbers and subscribes," — I scold
and consent.

July 26, 1874.

MY DEAR MOTLEY, — I am in town, that is, if you
will let me call Boston *town* — along with my wife,
never more agreeably alone, except that the middle of
the day is rather hot.   We are both trying very hard
to be lazy, which is next to impossible for her, and
not so easy for me as I could wish.   In the mean time
the world is providing us with sensations of various
kinds, which keep up something like pulsations in the
emotional centres.   First, we had the comet, which
whisked its tail under the nose of the Great Bear for
a few evenings, and which somebody announced in
one of our papers as about to close the human stage

of terrestrial developments by asphyxiating the whole of us with carbonic acid gas or some such unbreathable atmosphere. In your higher latitude you ought to have seen more of "Coggia's" comet, which they pretended was making straight at us and to hit or miss somewhere about the 20th of this month. Then we had the "boy-fiend," — the most remarkable case of demoniacal propensities I ever heard of, — a boy of fourteen years old, who enticed small children into lonely places and cut and mutilated them in various strange, yet *quasi* methodical fashions, ending by cutting the throats of a little girl and afterwards of a little boy. They had a story of pre-natal influences, that reminded me of a heroine of one of my own books, but I believe it was not founded in anything. Then came the most odious, repulsive, miserable, dragging piece of scandal this country has ever known, — of which we have heard a great deal too much already, but for that very reason must now hear the whole, that we may know what to think of it. The Byron business was bad enough, but Byron had been long dead, and nobody took him for a saint, however innocent he may have been of the particular offence Mrs. Stowe charged upon him. But here is the most popular Protestant preacher, I think, that ever lived, a man whose church would be filled, if there was a bullfight in the next street, — who gets a salary of twenty thousand dollars and is worth it to his church, — who, as a lecturer, is handled by his impresario as if he were a prima donna, — who has done more sensible, effective, good-natured talking and writing to the great middle class and the "unknown public" than any man we ever had in this country, — with a good deal of Franklin's sense and humor, with a power of holding great assemblies like Whitfield, — the best known and most popular private citizen, I suppose, we have ever had, — a saint by inheritance and connections of every kind, and yet as human as King David or Robert Burns, so that his inherited theology hangs about him in rags, and shows the flesh of honest manhood in a way to frighten all his co-religionists, — here is this wonderful creature, popular idol, the hope of liberal orthodoxy, accused of reading the seventh commandment according to the version that left out the negative. There is no doubt that he has compromised himself with unsafe persons and brought grave suspicions on himself, but the hope is universal that his defence, yet to come, will show that he has been slandered, and that his own assertions of innocence will be made good by a thorough sifting of the testimony that is brought against him. His accuser, Theodore Tilton, appears as badly as a man can, in every point of view, but it is pretended that other witnesses are to be called, and sick as everybody is of the monster scandal, it is felt that all must be known, since so much has already been made public. I am afraid you will turn away with something like disgust from the pages that I have filled with this matter, but the truth is, nothing ever made such a talk, and if it had been a settled fact that the comet was to hit the earth on the 22d of July, late on the evening of the 21st people would have been talking of the great "Beecher-Tilton scandal."

You may well imagine I have little but these newspaper matters to talk to you about. We are living in a desert. I feel, as I walk down Beacon Street, as if I were Lord Macaulay's New Zealander. I expect to start a fox or a woodchuck as I turn through Clarendon or Dartmouth Street, and to hear the whir of the partridge in Commonwealth Avenue. The truth is I have no country place of my own, and we are so much more comfortable in our house here that we can hardly make up our minds to go to any strange place in the country, or by the seashore. . . .

Yesterday the Saturday Club met, and found ourselves fourteen, or more, in all — Lowell, with his seven L's great and small, being with us for the first time since his return. Except that he has cut his handsome shining locks, I should not notice any change in him. He is just as pleasant and natural as always, and it is hard to believe that he has been away so long. Longfellow is, I suppose, at Nahant, at any rate he was not there; but Emerson was, and Dana and Judge Hoar, and among the rest "Bill Hunt," the artist, who has been a member some time. . . . Bill looked like a St. Peter by Rembrandt, in a brown velvet coat, and I did not see his infelicities depicted on his apostolic countenance. . . .

Don't give me up because I have spoiled these two sheets of note-paper with poor, petty, paltry cackle about matters that should never have been talked of. They have in point of fact taken the place of everything else almost, in common talk. I have only space left to say that you must not think of tiring yourself with holding that pen which weighs so much in your hand, even to acknowledge this letter. I hear you have been improving, though rather slowly, and I shall hope to hear that you keep on so until you are well enough to come back and rejoice all our hearts.

December 21, 1874.

My dear Motley, — I could hardly make up my mind to write until I had something cheerful and pleasant to say, for I knew that the great trouble of your brother Edward's family would sadden everything I should say until you had had time, and all of us had, to turn the leaf on which that sorrow was written.

Now, then, that we have another little S—— boy next door but one to us, now that we have just had a most agreeable reminder of you all in the shape of an English visitor, I feel as if I could write a Christmas letter with something of life in it. . . . As for the beauty of apple-dumplings and plum-puddings and babies' faces, that is a matter I do not go into so confidently; but I *think* this is a very good-looking baby. . . .

Mr. A—— W——, to whom you gave a letter to me, proves to be a very nice young fellow. There is something very pleasing, ingenuous, natural, fresh, and unspoiled about him which pleases us all very much. He came to dine with us once, and made himself very agreeable — quite different from any Englishman I have seen for a good while, but having a quality I have recognized ever since my student-days in Paris belonging to some young Englishmen and almost never found in Americans. It is a certain delightful childlike element — not the emotional mobility of many continental people — not that of Agassiz, for instance, who laughed and cried like a three-year-old boy, and gave one such a hug as a father gives his baby — a child its father, I should have said, — but a kind of simplicity, I had almost said innocence, that is almost never seen in our hard-featured

Yankees. Mr. W—— talked very agreeably, but he
had some curious theological ideas which he brought
forward with the best possible good-nature and ease,
— about the fulfilment of Hebrew prophecies and the
Scarlet Lady, and the coming grand consummation
of all things, — queer ideas of one kind and another,
which I suppose he grew up with in one of those quiet
English homes sweet with the sanctities of extinct
beliefs as the tombs of dead Pharaohs with the
balsams of ancient forests. Well, we liked Mr.
A—— W——, who has been here two or three times
since he dined with us, and pleased us even more than
at first. . . . I had a very agreeable talk with an old
friend of yours at the Club the other day — Lord
Dufferin — whom I sat next to and found a good
person to have as a dinner-table neighbor. I am fond
of those brief prandial intimacies with the better sort
of people, used to society, *maniable*, malleable, plastic,
receptive, "simpatico" (choose your adjective — the
last is your own) on the one hand, and suggestive and
communicative on the other. I am afraid the M. P.
is, as a general thing, better company than the M. C.,
who calls one "Sir" when he addresses him, and
scorns any form of adjective below its superlative.
My English visitants, at any rate, and most, not all,
of those I have met at the Club, have been lighter in
hand than my own average beloved countrymen. I
always tell you about the Club, but I have nothing
special to say about it now, that I can think of. I
dined with our country's friend, Mr. Forster, at Mr.
Adams's a fortnight or thereabouts ago. I could not
do much with him, and I did not try to, for he — as
Mrs. Adams told me [he] was — seemed more like an
uncouth, strong-bodied, strong-minded American than

like my typical Englishman. I think it very likely
that Judge Hoar, who sat next him at table, got on
with him well enough — there is something of the
plain Saxon in both of them, which each would soon
find out. . . .

I have another little matter to mention, which relates to you personally. Last Tuesday evening the
present publishers of *The Atlantic*, Messrs. Houghton
& Co., gave a very handsome dinner at Parker's to
the contributors, etc., to the magazine. Emerson was
not there, nor Longfellow, whose oldest son is ill with
pneumonia, nor Lowell, whose wife's sister is very ill.
But it was a pleasant gathering, though the *Dii mino-
rum gentium* were the chief part of the company. I
was asked, among other things, to speak of the dead
and absent contributors. When I came to your name,
and alluded to the way in which you had been treated
by the government, the response was so universal and
energetic that it showed the very strong feeling for
you entertained by the assemblage, and would have
done your heart good to hear. . . . Wishing you all
a happy Christmas, I am with all kind remembrances,

Faithfully yours.

April 18, 1875.

MY DEAR MOTLEY, — I read your letter with feelings I could not restrain — how could I read such a
letter unmoved? I feel too strongly now, as when
writing to you before, that there is nothing I can put
down in words beyond a few imperfect expressions of
tender sympathy and the assurance that you are constantly in my remembrance. Every word you say
goes to my heart as to that of a friend who knows

better than most can know what She was who was the life of your life. I keep picturing you to myself alone — in one sense alone in spite of dear companionships — with your memories. Henceforth I know how largely, how intimately, you must live in these. If your own health is confirmed, as we all trust that it will be, I cannot help hoping that the poignancy of grief will, by the kindly and at last perhaps cheering influences that surround you, soften gradually into a sweet remembrance of the many happy years that have gone before. But I dare not attempt to console a grief like yours. It must have its own way, and hush itself to the repose of exhaustion — "lie down like a tired child," as Shelley says in those sad and beautiful lines written near Naples.

If you were here I might sit by you in silence, just to give you the feeling that some one was with you in the shadow for a moment. I should listen to you, and you would not fear to speak freely with me from the fulness of your heart, for you know how every word would fall upon my ear. I feel now as if all I could do would be to listen, but no doubt after a little time we could exchange many thoughts and feelings and recollections, which it might not be ungrateful to you to give an hour to from time to time.

I speak as if I were claiming more share in your sorrow than perhaps I ought to — for I remember that there are those who will come very near to you in their affectionate intercourse, and I hope that their presence will prove soothing and comforting to your wounded spirit. Something, too, I hope from change of climate and of scene, if you find yourself at all equal to the voyage, as I trust you may. If you should be at Nahant, during a part of the time at

least, I hope to be your neighbor and to see you frequently, if you should find it agreeable to have me
visit you. . . . You see why I do not trust myself to
write more largely — so much can be said that it is
hard to set down on paper. Take these few words
kindly, with love and best wishes for you and all
yours. My wife wishes me to add her little message
of kindest remembrance.

February 18, 1876.

MY DEAR MOTLEY, — If I have not written for a
long time, it is because my life has been so monotonous and mechanical that I had next to nothing to
tell. The pendulum in my old hall clock can hardly
move more regularly and rigidly back and forward
than I do to and from the college, where for seven
months I am a plodding lecturer. I do not complain
of this, — if I could get a salary of twenty or thirty
thousand dollars for it — or such a one as some of our
factory agents get for losing our money for us — I
could almost be content to lecture until I came to the
last of the seven ages, if I held out so long. But except that I am galvanized by a dinner-party, now and
then, or meet an old .friend and call up spirits from
the vasty deep, my life is almost void of incident
beyond its every-day routine. I have nobody to visit,
as I could visit you last summer, — nobody to talk
with, as I could with you, and am not like to have
until you come back, as I trust you will one of these
days. One friend I do indeed go to see weekly, —
Dr. Edward Clarke, who is confined mostly to his bed
by a disease of the intestines, with regard to which
very grave fears are entertained. It is very hard for
a man like him, unquestionably at the head of his

profession in Boston, in the full tide of business, to
be chained as it would be thought cruel to chain a
felon, and tortured, from time to time, with wearing
pains. I do not know whether it is the recollection
of the many hours I passed with you, so full of the
deepest and tenderest interest to me, and in which I
could not help feeling and knowing that my sympathy,
at least, made me a welcome visitor, — I do not know,
I say, whether it is that which has given me the feeling which has come over me, that " it is better to go
to the house of mourning than to the house of feast-
ing," and that " sorrow is better than laughter." We
never know each other until we have come together
in the hour of trial. I have said many things to you
that I could not write, and I hardly expect to have
such intimate confidences with any other friend under
any circumstances; but I have learned that I can at
least do something to lighten the weary hours of suffering, sometimes by a pleasant look, or a lively half-
hour's talk about the outside world, but far better
than that, at the proper moment leaving all these
lesser thoughts, and going down into those depths of
consciousness where all of us bury out of sight our
hopes, our fears, our memories, our dreams, — that
pale and shadowy world of ours, into which it is the
supreme privilege of friendship to be admitted. No,
— not pale or shadowy to men of strong natures and
quick sensibilities. The world of imagination and
recollection, which makes the past like the present,
never seemed so real to me as it [did] during the
period of my frequent companionship with you last
summer. I cannot tell you all that I feel I owe to
you for making life more real, more sincere, more profound in its significance, during those hours I spent

with you. To be told, as I have been, that they were comforting to you is a great happiness to me. . . .

The Centennial people are worrying my life out of me, almost. The number of letters I have had to answer, declining to do this and that, of late, seems to me enormous — is really considerable.

Any time when one of your daughters writes, will you ask her to add, in a postscript, that you got my letter of February 18th — this present letter. That is all — I wish to make sure you got it.

May 8, 1876.

MY DEAR MOTLEY, — I am most devoutly thankful that my seven months' lectures are at last over, and I am gradually beginning to come to myself, like one awakening from a trance or a fit of intoxication. You know thát the steady tramp of a regiment would rock the Menai bridge from its fastenings, and so all military bodies break their step in crossing it. This reiteration of lectures in even march, month after month, produces some such oscillations in one's mind, and he longs, after a certain time, to break up their uniformity. If they kept on long enough, Harvard would move over to Somerville.

Your letter of 26th March gave me great pleasure. It relieved me from the fear that you were condemned to the disease of your eyes, which had seemed to me, under the circumstances, a trial too hard to think of. I am rejoiced to find that you can read, even though you have to use glasses (as I have had to do these sixteen years). I was pleased, too, to find that you were even thinking of a little possible work for the summer. If it is in place of another visit to America

— Boston — Nahant — *home* — I should personally
regret it more than I can tell you, for I count the
hours I passed with you last summer among the
sweetest, the holiest, the dearest, and in one sense
the happiest, of all my social life. It seems strange
to speak of their happiness, when I saw you so often
with all the freshness of grief coming over you. But
those are the hours when friendship means the most, —
when we feel that we come nearer than at any other
time to our intimates, and the sense that we are perhaps lightening another's burden makes even the com-
monest intercourse a source of satisfaction. Besides
this you must not forget that you, whose presence,
from your natural gifts, was always so peculiarly
agreeable to me, have known the world in such a way
that your conversation cannot help being interesting
to one who has lived so purely provincial a life as I
have. So when your sorrow came over you, my heart
was for the time full of it, and when you, for a little
while, were beguiled into forgetfulness, and talked
with the life of earlier times, I was sure of being
pleased with hearing a hundred things nobody else
could tell me. I have told you, and I must tell you
again and again, that my life has run in a deeper
channel since the hours I spent in your society last
summer. They come back to me from time to time,
like visitations from another and higher sphere. No,
— I never felt the depths and the heights of sorrow so
before, and I count it as a rare privilege that I could
be with you so often at one of those periods when the
sharpest impressions are taken from the seal of
friendship.

You would miss one of your old friends, if you were
to revisit Nahant this summer. I was visiting my

poor friend Dr. Clarke, eight or ten days ago, when
he said to me, "Dr. ——'s father is dead." "Dr.
——'s father" was our old friend ——. Whether
he left any intimates outside of his family to mourn
for him I do not know. H—— I—— said he should
miss him much. I had a certain pleasure in contact
with his hard, recalcitrant intelligence. His mind
grew tough and knobby, like an oak that did not know
how to stretch up and spread out kindly, broadly,
straight-grained. I asked your dear Mary once why
T—— D—— was not more of a general favorite,
having so many things to recommend him, and I have
always thought her answer, that it was because he
had no *abandon*, was the truth of the matter. I hope
his better qualities — for he had sterling ones — will
germinate in the heavenly latitudes like those grains of
Egyptian wheat which were buried with the Pharaohs
and bear their fruit for the Khedive.

You may be sure that I copied every word you said
about Dana and sent it to him. He was greatly
pleased with your remembrance, and with what you
had said. Dick stands it well — in fact it made quite
a great man of him. He has gone off at the head of
our delegation, and makes a fine figure in his halo of
martyrdom.

I am glad you breathed a little life into my waning
patriotism. I have got so sickened with this tearing
down of political caterpillars' nests that if I did not
know that there are worse social contrivances, and that
this is a more or less wicked world wherever one goes,
I should be in danger of becoming half a traitor to
the theory of self-government. Corruption, incendi-
arism, and child-murder and torture have been the
staple of our newspapers since the Brooklyn scandal

has ceased to darken the horizon for a while. This morning we had a great dynamite explosion at Jersey City, close to New York. That is the Devil's last invention, and I have a shuddering fear, which I keep to myself, that it is to be — with the torch — the great ally of communism. But we grow timid as we grow older, and the young generation is not to be scared with our bugbears.

We have had three new Boston books, since I have written, I think. Ticknor's *Life and Letters*, eminently readable, much sought for; a new life of Hamilton by my wife's nephew, J. T. Morse, Jr.; and within a few days Tom Appleton's *Nile Journal*, which I find very pleasant and lively, much more like his talk than the other little book. I dined with Longfellow at Mr. Fields's the other evening. He seemed pretty well, but still complains somewhat. Lowell was at my house the other day — he has been complaining, but is now better.

Do not forget my kind remembrances to your children. My wife will not let me close this letter without her postscript of kind remembrance.

March 14, 1877.

MY DEAR MOTLEY, — I should have acknowledged and thanked you for your letter of the 30th of January but for many unusual distractions. I cannot and I need not tell you what singular enjoyment I had in reading that letter. It is too good a letter — too striking a one, for any *particulier* to receive and appropriate. The account of your daughter's wedding was like a passage from a stately drama. It was — *is*, I ought to say — enough to thrill any American to his marrow to read of those whom he has known so long and well among the common scenes of our not over-poetical existence enacting one of the great scenes of this mortal life in the midst of such shadows, treading over such dust, in an atmosphere of historic immortality. I lived the scene all over, and I do sincerely pity the New England Major or the Western Congressman who has not enough of imagination and reverence for the past to be kindled into something like poetical enthusiasm, as much as Johnson would pity the man whose patriotism did not grow strong at Marathon, or whose piety did not warm among the ruins of Iona. Oh, this shallow soil of memory, on which we live! We scratch it, and we find — what? the Indian's shell-heaps and stone arrow-heads, overlaid by a couple of centuries of half-starved civilization. Don't be disgusted and outraged, as a patriotic American. I am patriotic and provincial to my fingers' ends, — but I do sometimes feel that, æsthetically speaking, America is after all a penal colony. It would be worth a year of my life (if I had a good many to spare one from) to walk once more under the high, groined arches of Westminster Abbey. I never expect to see England or Europe again, but it is something to say I *have* lived and looked upon Alps, cathedrals, and the greatest works of the greatest artists. . . .

Sarah Wendell Holmes (Dr. Holmes's Mother)

Elizabeth Stuart Phelps Ward

A Morning Walk, November, 1893

John O. Sargent

IV. TO HARRIET BEECHER STOWE

November 17, 1867.

MY DEAR MRS. STOWE, — I cannot thank you too
heartily for your very kind and frank letter. Do you
know how much I value your opinion, and your good
opinion? I will answer my question and say that you
do not, and cannot, know; for it is not only in virtue
of natural gifts that it means so much to me, but
because you have had some of those experiences which
perhaps too often betray themselves in my writings,
that I always feel that you understand as very few
can.

Your kind womanly words affect me more gratefully perhaps on account of the stinging phrases
which have been made for me by a writer in *The
Nation*, whose aim from the first seems to have been
to wound if possible, to injure at any rate. I suppose
I know who he is, and only wonder how he came to
take me for his *souffre-douleur ;* but I suppose he must
have somebody to show his smartness on, and I may
have directly or indirectly offended him. I would
give five cents to know how, for his accidental position enables him to reach many of my friends. He
has done his best to anticipate my story, to cheapen
me, and make me of no account, — and if I cannot
endure it I deserve it all.

But, my dear lady, I listen to all you say with such
confidence in your tenderness, your truthfulness, your
judgment, that I have hardly any word to reply, ex-

cept to thank you with all my heart for the interest you show in me and what I write.

Yes, I must say one or two things. First, I have no doubt that I show the effects of a training often at variance with all my human instincts, — not so much from the lips of my dear parents, in both of whom nature never allowed "Grace" to lead them to any inhuman conclusions, — but from outside influences, against which my immature intelligence had to protest, with more or less injury to its balance, very probably, always after. I suppose all I write may show something of this, as the lame child limps at every step, as the crooked back shows through every garment. My nature is not embittered against my fellow-creatures — on the contrary, I find it hard to hate those who entreat me despitefully — for any length of time, certainly. But I am subject to strong fits of antagonism whenever I come across that spirit of unbelief in God and strong faith in the Devil which seems to me not extinct among us. I know this will keep repeating itself in my writings. Some say it is wicked, for [that] it is true that there is to be a great atheistic world over which the Devil is to rule forever, and where mankind (a few people who understood "the scheme" — see N. Adams's sermon on Choate — excepted) are to live. always hereafter. Some say it is foolish, for these notions are obsolete. But, wicked or foolish, that is my *limp*. The wound heals, the scar is left. But do you know (how much it means !) even scars tend to grow less and less with the lapse of time ? So I think the stain of my boyhood may wear off in some degree by intercourse with sweet and straight and wholesome natures, whose nurses never let them fall, as they are wont to say of the poor hunchbacks.

I bow meekly to all your criticisms except the Dante paragraph. I believe I did not go to one of the " Inferno " séances, one or two of " Purgatorio," the others all " Paradiso." How often I have said, talking with Lowell, almost the same things you say about the hideousness, the savagery, of that mediæval nightmare! Theodore of Abyssinia ought to sleep with it under his pillow, as Alexander slept with the Iliad. You cannot use too strong language. What could be expected of a Christianity that has filtered through such a mass of cruel and wicked human conceptions, but the barbarisms which hanged our grandmothers in 1692, and which to-day — ?

Just where I made that mark my son came in with a message from Mrs. Gibbons (Mr. Hopper's daughter, the Quaker, you know her), thanking me especially for my story, most particularly for Rev. J. B. S., and offering her testimony to the truthfulness of the character. Pardon me the freedom of this letter, — you have a master-key that opens so many hearts!

Don't think that I do not love dear old Dr. Watts with his tender songs that lulled me when I was a baby (how exquisite that " Peace, my darling, here 's no danger! "), and will mingle I doubt not with my last wandering thoughts. But how utterly good men and women have sometimes lost their human bearings on that cold and cruel sea, the floor of which is strewed with dead theologies!

May 29, 1869.

MY DEAR MRS. STOWE, —

.   .   .   .

They plunge a chronometer into a steam-boiler and an ice-chest, they turn it this way and that way, and in time they get its balance-wheel to run true in all temperatures and positions. I think one of your un-counted experiences I have shared with you. I have been in the doctrinal boiler at Andover, and the ra-tional ice-chest at Cambridge. I have been hung with my head downwards, from the hook of a theological dogma, and set on my feet again by the hand of unin-spired common-sense. — I have found myself like a nursery-tree, growing up with labels of this and that article of faith wired to my limbs. The labels have dropped off, but the wires are only buried in my flesh, which has grown over them. The curse of ages of incompetent, nay, inhuman thinking, filtered through the brains of holy men and the blood of tender-hearted women, but still acting like a poison to minds of a cer-tain quality and temper, fell upon me when only the most thoroughly human influences should have helped me to bud and flower. I do not say you have been through all this, — I do not want you to say you have, — you are my confessor, but I am not yours, except so far as with all the world I listen to your voluntary revelations and guess the history that lies beneath them.

Yet, I say we have had some experiences in com-mon, and however imperfectly I express myself by word or by letter, now or at any time, there are mental and emotional states which you can understand as none can do who have not been through the chronometer experience.

I am getting tired of *words*, — which makes me feel sure there must be a future in which states or conditions will be immediately, intuitively, communicable. Indeed, is there not something like it now? When I write to you, I know I shall not say what I want to; but I shall *signify* it, and I shall not take the trouble to look over what I said, just as it came, trusting to your interpretation.

What higher compliment can I pay to the story that has so profoundly interested Mrs. Holmes and myself, than by throwing open the folding-doors of my heart in this careless way to you, as I am doing! It is your own fault. You have yourself become an intimate through these fictitious realities you have made a part of our consciousness. It is no longer a question of exact agreement in this or that belief. I may not accept next year the article of faith which I hold to-day. My belief in health may be one thing, and in sickness another; in one mood I may be all belief and trust, in another, all doubt and despondency, — I say, *may be*, — not that I am much given to these alternations. But I know that you will remain always thoroughly and entirely womanly, charitable, hopeful; and what a preacher you have been and are of the real good tidings which have been so often misinterpreted!

I read your story not only for its narrative, its characters, and its thought, but with my critical eye open, and noticed a point or two which may possibly be worth looking at.

. . . .

Your books, being immortal, must be purged from every earthly stain. So you will pardon my minute criticisms.

With the warmest thanks from Mrs. Holmes and myself, to both of whom you have endeared yourself by your noble writings,

I am always your friend.

September 25, 1869.

MY DEAR MRS. STOWE, — I have been meaning to write to you for some time, but in the midst of all the wild and irrelevant talk about the article in *The Atlantic*, I felt as if there was little to say until the first fury of the storm had blown over. I think we all perceive now that the battle is not to be fought here, but in England. I have listened to a good deal of talk, always taking your side in a quiet way, backed very heartily on one occasion by Mr. Henry James, Senior, — reading all that came in my way, and watching the course of opinion. And first it was to be expected that the Guiccioli [family?], and the model-artists, and the cancan dancers would resent any attack on Lord Byron, and would highly relish the opportunity of abusing one who, like [you], had long been identified with all those moral enterprises which, by elevating the standard of humanity at large and of womanhood in particular, tend to render their callings unprofitable and their tastes unpopular. After this scum had worked itself off, must almost necessarily follow a controversy, more or less sharp and bitter, but not depending essentially on abuse. The first point the recusants got hold of was the error of the two years, which contrived to run the gauntlet of so many pairs of eyes. Some of them were made happy by mouthing and shaking this between their teeth, as a poodle tears round with a glove. This did not last long, — no sensible person could believe for a moment *you* were mistaken in the essential character of a statement, every word of which would fall on the ear of a listening friend like a drop of melted lead, and burn its scar deep into the memory. That Lady Byron believed, and told you, the story will not be questioned by any but fools and malignants. Whether her belief was well founded, there may be positive evidence in existence to show affirmatively. The fact that her statement is not peremptorily contradicted by those most likely to be acquainted with the facts of the case is the one result, so far, which is forcing itself into unwilling recognition. I have seen nothing in the various hypotheses brought forward which did not to me involve a greater improbability than the presumption of guilt. Take that, for instance, that Byron accused himself, through a spirit of perverse vanity, of crimes he had not committed. How preposterous [that] he would stain the name of a sister whom, on the supposition of his innocence, he loved with angelic ardor as well as purity, by associating it with such an infandous accusation!

Suppose there are some anomalies hard to explain in Lady Byron's conduct; could a young and guileless woman, in the hands of such a man, be expected to act in *any* given way, or would she not be like to waver, to doubt, to hope, to contradict herself in the anomalous position in which, without experience, she found herself? As to the intrinsic evidence contained in the poem, I think it confirms rather than contradicts the hypotheses of guilt. I do not think that Butler's argument, and all the other attempts at invalidation of the story, avail much in the face of the acknowledged fact that it was told to various competent and honest witnesses, and remains without a satisfactory answer from those most interested.

I know your firm self-reliance and your courage to proclaim the truth, when any good end is to be served by it. It is to be expected that public opinion will be more or less divided as to the expediency of this revelation. There is one argument which will come forward more and more as tempers cool down; namely, that the true character of a man, who has diabolized the literature of his century and hung his pure and injured wife in chains to dangle before all the unborn ribalds of coming generations, ought to be known in his true character to posterity.

Hoping that you have recovered from your indisposition,

Faithfully yours.

September 25, 1871.

MY DEAR MRS. STOWE, — I occupied a great part of my Sunday (yesterday) in reading your story, which I had just received with the author's compliments. Let me thank you first for the book, and secondly for the great pleasure I have had from it. Would you believe that to this day I do not read novels on Sunday, at least until "after sundown"? And this not as a matter of duty or religion, — for I hold the sabbatical view of the first day of the week as a pious fraud of the most transparent description, — but as a tribute to the holy superstitions of more innocent years, before I began to ask my dear good father those *enfant terrible* questions which were so much harder to answer than anything he found in St. Cyprian and Turretin and the other old books I knew the smell of so well, and can see now, standing in their old places.

Well, I cannot feel as if I were wicked to read one of your books, no matter what, on a Sunday. Besides, you promised this was not to be a novel, in your preface. To be honest, that was the last page of the book I read, but on general principles I should read anything of yours, a farce even, if you should write one, " between meetings," — (not that I go afternoons, but I *do* go mornings).

Who knows the New England man and woman as you do? Who writes to their needs and to their hearts as you have written and write? You have belief enough for the Christian world, and charity enough for that great and growing class who await the future with their hands folded on their breasts and their lips closed, caught as they are at the turning of the tide, when many old beliefs are impossible and the new faith is but half formed.

This new story of yours is very keen — some will say cruelly sharp, perhaps — but I am afraid it tells the truth. I think we had more than one " Lillie Ellis " even among those " who, born in Boston, need no second birth." I got to hate her so, I wished she would die, and thought she would, and that John would marry Rose; but you have a woman's heart and could not give up the poor sinner.

Do you know that when I see the tenderness of you sweet kind women, I can understand Theodore Parker's insisting on the *maternal* element in the Divine Being? I think the most encouraging hint with reference to the future of these helpless infants, whom we call men and women, is that He who made the heart of a mother would find it hard to quite give up a child. You see, now, I should have smitten Lillie and her offspring and have done with the bad lot. You women are all Universalists.

I will tell you here what I was told the other day of my own dearest mother — wife of the Reverend, etc., member of a good Orthodox church, who taught me the Assembly's Catechism: " Well, Mary [to an old friend and servant], I don't know but I am as good an Universalist as any of you." This is only for *you*, — I never told it before.

There is nothing in this note I have not said to you before about the hold you have on my feelings — most peculiar and exceptional, really perhaps shared to the same extent in the same way by no other person. I read all your books with tears in my eyes. " She, too, is the New England elm with the iron band welded round it when it was a sapling! But how *she* has grown in spite of it ! "

March 31, 1872.

MY DEAR MRS. STOWE, —

.   .   .   .

Well, I have myself comforted a good many people in my time. I have not been a great moral reformer, like yourself. My readers have been units where yours have been hundreds if not thousands. But I have stuck by humanity after my poor fashion, and have been told by a great many people in a great many places that they were better and happier for my having lived. That helps me to bear the hard words, which may be as necessary to help us digest our moral food as stones and gravel are to some birds with their other nourishment.

Lastly, I thank you for your frank criticism and advice, against which — for a wonder, now, is n't it? — I have not a single word of any kind to say, either of denial, or of justification, or of palliation.

I don't doubt you are quite right, and that I have fallen too much into the way of thinking and feeling which you so fairly called my attention to as partial and one-sided, and becoming false in virtue of new conditions. I shall not forget your criticisms. I have my doubts, as I look at what I have written, whether I should have offended you in the sequel of my story, if story you can call it, even if you had not written; but I am very thankful to you for your delicate and sufficiently distinct hint.

I wonder how you can write so much as you do. I don't know how it would be if I had not something more than a hundred lectures to give every year; but I often feel ashamed when I see what others can accomplish. Bigger brains, and more blood in them, I suspect. Anything but utter self-condemnation, organization, old age, stupidity. What a blessing if one could be told in the next world: "Mortal, you thought you had five talents; you had but one, my poor child!" But what an immense capacity for work there is in your family! I believe you could have run Noah's ark — which must have been a hard hotel to keep — among you. Pardon me for my vivacity — of a Sunday, too! — but I have been to "meeting."

February 19, 1875.

MY DEAR MRS. STOWE, — "Better late than never," say you. "Better half a loaf than no bread," said I, when I got the first instalment of your most welcome letter. By and by came the other half, — as I felt sure it would, and so possessed my soul in patience. In the mean time, it was not very hard to guess whence it came, for I had the handwriting to guide me, and I out with my little pocket-lens, and identified yourself and Dr. Stowe in less than no time. The photograph was pasted over the name of the place and the date, but I managed just now to get the corners up, and found that the letter was dated January 26th.

It gave me real pleasure. It is so hard to make it palpable to one's self that he is remembered by any who have lost sight of him for any time, and especially that any words one has written have still a value! I have been losing so many friends lately that I prize more and more every day the tokens of kind feelings from those who are left. Agassiz, with whom I have been so long intimate, Sumner, of whom I have seen a good deal in these last years, Wyman, whom I greatly delighted in, though I did not meet him very often, and recently my dear and early friend, Mrs. Lothrop Motley, — these losses have sadly impoverished my outer life. You are of a far more expansive nature than I am, I suspect, and can make new friends more easily than I do. Women glide into each other's confidence and assimilate to each other, I think, more easily than men, a great deal. Men are out-of-door and office animals; women are indoor creatures essentially, and so come together more naturally and entirely than their husbands and others of the male sort. I make a new *acquaintance* not rarely, but as for new friends in the full sense of the word, after a certain age it seems almost like these stories one reads of octogenarians cutting a third set of teeth, and I hardly think of such a thing.

After all, if a man will look into the circumstances that make him what he is, or help to, he will be able to account for himself much more nearly than he

might at first have thought possible. You think I
am wedded to the pavement. True, but I am also
passionately fond of the country, only I am so liable
to suffer from asthma when I get off the brick sidewalk that I am virtually imprisoned, except when I
can arrange my conditions in the most favorable way,
in a place that happens to agree with me; and of the
various places where I have been of late years in
summer — Newport, Nahant, Princeton, only one, Mr.
Brewer's house at Newport, *has* agreed with me. So
about visiting: I find that a cold draught of air, a
late supper, bad air, and perhaps I might add anything of any kind that fatigues — say rather bores me,
sets me all wrong, and wastes health and spirits for
nothing. Few people enjoy better health than I do
just so long as I am let alone and regulate my own
habits; but when others want me to wear their shoes,
how they do chafe and pinch! I think, if I am unso-
cial, it is quite as much by constitution as it is by
any want of the social instinct, and I have learned
to judge others very charitably in the study of my
own weakness.

One pleasure I have enjoyed largely, not nearly —
not a tenth part — as largely as you must have enjoyed
it — but still more than I ever expected to. It is the
words of commendation, of confidence, of affection
and gratitude even, that I receive from many whom I
have never seen and never expect to see. I did not
mean to speak of your letter in this connection, but
do let me say how it touched me to think of my poor
dead Elsie living her shadowy life over again in your
consciousness. I have received some very interesting
letters lately from young persons, men and women,
single and married, in this country and in England,

that spoke out so naturally and simply what was in their hearts, that I felt so pleased and so humble — for what humbles one like the praise which makes him think what he might perhaps have been and done? at any rate, what others have been and done — that I loved myself for my humility, until all at once I found I was getting vain beyond endurance on the strength of it. I think we could compare many experiences of correspondence with unknown friends. I feel as if you must have been the depositary of an infinite number of confidences, and even I myself have had so many that I have been amazed, and almost overwhelmed sometimes, at finding what a web of fine filaments I had spun from my thinking glands, that radiated all round me like the spokes of a spider's wheel.

Some of these correspondents have literary aspirations, and these very soon betray themselves, generally before they get to the fatal postscript informing you that they have a manuscript novel, or that they wish to send you some unpublished poem — lucky if they do not enclose a few specimens! Some have troubles, and want sympathy; some have perplexities, and want advice; some ask strange questions about their love-affairs (as, May I marry an own cousin? etc.). Some have religious doubts and questions. Some have the oddest requests. I answered one this week from Texas from a young lady who wanted to come North and defray her expenses by selling mocking-birds and other cage-birds. Many — poor things! — want to get money for translations or literary work of some kind for the magazines. But of late my letters have been mostly simple expressions of interest in various writings of mine, especially the Breakfast-

Table Series. I always answer all of them, which shows that, after all, their number must be limited; but it takes a good deal of time, as it is. Nobody's autographs will, I think, be cheaper than mine, if anybody should ever want such, by and by, for I am very good-natured about sending them even to the wretches that do not enclose a stamped envelope with the blank for my name.

You are pleased to ask me two or three questions, which I am more pleased to answer. The "experiments at Greylock," about which you inquire, were not related to me by a *Cambridge* Professor, but by Professor Alonzo Clark, of New York, who was at Williams College close by the mountain, as you know. He it was who told me of the woman bringing the "rattlers" to him in her apron, which story you find transferred to my true narrative. As for the experiments of Dr. Hering at Surinam, I only remember vaguely some notice of them in one of the journals, but I am wholly unable at the present moment to give an exact reference to them.

I have just written, to come out, probably, in the April *Atlantic*, a long article, which I want to call "Moral Automatism," and may call so, although taken strictly, the two words contradict each other. In this I notice at some [length] an extraordinary work published a few years ago, M. Prosper Despine's *Psychologie Naturelle*. You do not know what a favor you have just done me. For, taking down my story from the shelves to look out the points you refer to, I read the Doctor's letter in reply to Bernard Langdon's inquiries, and I confess I was astonished to see how far I had anticipated the general aim of M. Despine's book, and in fact much that I have said in another form on the subject fifteen years ago.

The more I study the facts of life, the more I am
convinced that the Oriental anthropology, which we
have so long accepted, as we once did the Oriental
cosmogony, does not correspond with the realities of
human nature. I am contented still with my old
image, which Dr. B——[1] mildly attacked me for, if
I remember right, of the drop of water in the crystal,
as representing will imprisoned in personal conditions
and outward circumstance; the farther removed I am
from the possibility of entertaining for a moment the
idea that Man is responsible for the disorders of the
world in which he finds himself, the more I pity him
for his suffering, the less I wonder at his "sin."
This I suppose is an organic heresy running in my
maternal blood, and driving my inherited Connecticut
theology out of me at every pore. But it is a heresy
which I believe will in due time supersede that confused system of half-beliefs, which calls itself Orthodoxy, — a bird of sable aspect, which is constantly
smoothing its oily plumage, but which has lost more
feathers than it can spare of late years. (You will
not mind this, will you? I think you have a very
large heart for all honest confessions of faith.) . . .

What sweet visions your Florida picture raises;
oh, had I the wings of a dove! Well, I enjoyed your
letter almost like a visit. With kindest remembrances to you all,

        I am always truly yours.

March 3, 1876.

MY DEAR MRS. STOWE, — How could you have
given me greater pleasure than by asking me to copy
the verses which I enclose? I shall set this request
by the side of a reminiscence very dear to me. A

[1] Apparently Bushnell.

cousin of my wife — Miss Sally Gardiner, — older than myself, unmarried, fastidious, a lover of Emerson's writings, a good and delicately organized woman, on whose gravestone I read " She loved much," once said to me or one of my friends that there was a poem of mine she often read the last thing at night, — as children say " Now I lay me." This was " The Chambered Nautilus." You have given me the one memory to store with that. How grateful we ought to be for our better moments, that lift infirmer natures, for the time at least, to the level of those whom they admire and reverence !

Your letters always touch me, but I hardly know how to answer them without following their own suggestions. And this last falls in remarkably with many of my own thoughts during the past year. Out of our Saturday Club we have lost Sumner and Howe. I paid my small tribute to both, — that to Howe will be in the April *Atlantic*. Last summer, as I may have told you, I was in daily relations for some weeks with Motley, who is still in the valley of the shadow of death, the death of one whose life was dearer to him than his own. He himself was in shattered and precarious health, and to be with him was to read very deep into the human soul in its sincerest realities. What yearning there is in tender natures, knitted in with the life of others, often nobler and purer than themselves, for that unquestioning child-like belief which is so largely a divine gift, and for which many pray without ever reaching it ! If God will make such good women as he does every day, he must not quarrel with his poor creatures for making too much of his earthly manifestations. The Catholics idealize and idolize a bambino, a virgin, a saint; and is not

a living fellow-creature, full of all that we conceive
makes an angelic, one might say divine, character,
more naturally and easily made an idol — *eidolon* —
image, to a common imagination, than a stuffed doll,
or a picture, or an abstraction? Father, mother, wife,
sister, daughter, — if these do not furnish me the elements out of which I put together my poor limited
working conception of the Divine, I know not where
to look for them. It is not by a parcel of adjectives
without nouns, multiplied by the sign of infinity, that
I can get at the conception, for which I am to keep
all my respect and affection.

I have only stammered out in my own way what
you have said in simpler phrase in your letter. All
that you say of the Infinite love and pity is the very
substance of such belief as I cherish in the midst of
the doubts and difficulties around us, all which imper-
atively demand new forms for that universal and
undying sentiment, without which life is the pitiful
melodrama which would make us ashamed of its author for making anything above a vegetable, — anything with possibilities of suffering. To you, I suppose, sin is the mystery, — to me suffering is. I trust
Love will prove the solution of both. At any rate
no atomic philosophy can prevent my hoping that it
will prove so.

I have another friend, whom I visit weekly, struck
down by chronic disease which threatens a fatal issue,
and confined for many months to his bed. What sermons his bedside preaches! Pity! I feel as if that
would be all that would be left of me, if I live but
a few years longer. Here is a man at the very head
of his profession, Dr. [Edward H.] Clarke, in full
business, trusted, looked up to, depended upon in an
extraordinary degree, and all at once a most painful,

mysterious, and threatening internal disease seizes upon him as the fox gnawed into the vitals of the Spartan boy. From the very height of active, useful, happy occupation, he is thrust into miserable inaction, imprisoned in his chamber, fettered to his bed, with nothing but paroxysms of bodily anguish to give variety to his existence. Oh, if there were but one walking our streets to-day, who could say to him, " Take up thy bed," and lift his infirmity from him with a look or a word ! Perhaps he might lose a lesson he may yet learn the meaning of, — certainly I should lose a lesson which is good for me in many ways to learn. But it does seem very hard to see such a man, who has healed so many by his skill and soothed so many by his presence, tortured in this way by a disease as cruel as a ravenous beast, and that gives so much cause for fear of its issue. I ought to say that he takes it all very calmly and sweetly, and that my regular visit to him is one that I look forward to with much interest. I sometimes think I might almost have a vocation to visit the sick and suffering, were I self-denying enough, which I fear I am not. But I do have the satisfaction of knowing that I have done something of late to lighten the burden of others in their sorrow, — not much — very little compared with what hundreds of women are doing all the time. I go and sit now and then with Dr. [Jacob] Bigelow, Senior, now close upon ninety years old, stone-blind, utterly helpless, and bedridden. Would you believe it ? He is one of the most cheerful, lively, and seemingly happy, or at least serenely tranquil, persons I ever met. If all suffering and privation were borne as he and Dr. Clarke bear theirs, it would be easier to contemplate human existence.

Educational suffering I can to a certain extent understand. But the great solid mass of daily anguish which the sun looks upon — and looks away from, as if he could not bear it, — antedating man, including everything that has a nerve in it, — that I can do nothing with. "Sin," or the failure of an imperfectly made and imperfectly guided being to keep a perfect law, seems to me to be given in the mere statement of the conditions of humanity, and could not be a surprise or a disappointment to a Creator with reasoning powers no greater than those of a human being of ordinary wisdom. But I must not weary, perhaps worry, you with my theological or anti-theological notions — say rather, convictions. Some time I may have the chance to talk about these with you.

I wish I could take the wings of the morning and fly to the shade of your orange-trees, for a few hours at least. But I am a fowl that keeps his roost, and my wings are more like those of a penguin than of an eagle.

Do you want me to send you any of my books? If you do, and will tell me what you should like, I will get Osgood to forward copies of them to you.

I am afraid of the great book you mentioned just now, for I am overrun with books I must read. Besides, I lecture steadily four times a week, and my correspondence, chiefly with people I do not know, has become very burdensome, — I suppose because I am too good-natured and give everybody advice, and thank everybody who says a pleasant word to me.

You will read this letter charitably, I know; it is carelessly worded, and only hints many things I could talk better. I rarely have the patience to write so much as this, and it takes a woman to write a real letter.

Remember me very kindly to Mr. Stowe.

May 8, 1876.

MY DEAR MRS. STOWE, — An "autograph letter," just received, inquires of your whereabouts, which I have given as Hartford, where I hope this scanty scroll may find you. It is the third time your name has been on my inner lips, — those silent but never resting ones, — this morning. First, having got through my seven months' lectures, and a week of deferred urgencies which followed, I was thinking that I would write and ask about you and your husband, and so perhaps get another of your *real* letters, which always make me think more deeply and feel more warmly. Secondly, I was writing this morning to an unknown English correspondent, a lady, who has twice written me very interesting letters, not the commonplace ones of mere expressions of liking and all that, but serious, though most kindly questionings, whether I had not been sometimes too sharp in speaking of unmarried women, — all which I took to heart, as I hope I do every well-intended criticism, especially if I think it may be just. I told her, what is true, that I like to face the accusing angel. The accusing and fault-finding devil is another matter; but what is there we cannot bear if the spirit of love is in it? Thirdly, this "autograph letter," with its questions, has given the slight tap which has set me going with this little scrap of a letter.

I feel like one awakening from a long trance, now that I have got through my lectures at the college. It seems as if it would take me some weeks to stretch my limbs and get them back to their natural supple-ness. I suppose I have lectured about long enough, — twenty-nine years here at our college, besides two years at Dartmouth. The young generation is on our shoulders looking beyond our horizon. Fortunately for me, there has been no change in human anatomy since Adam lost the rib from his side, and somehow or other I always find a full dozen on both sides in his male descendants. But when I say there has been no change, I am thinking of the grosser facts which the unaided eye can detect. I have seen grow up, under my own view, a universe of the lesser world as wonderful as that which the telescope has revealed in the infinite spaces. What a quaint comment one might make on that expression of the Apostle's, " seeing *through a glass darkly!* " So we did fifty years ago, but since that we have put *two* pieces of glass together, — a piece of flint-glass and a piece of crownglass, and now we see through our double glass *clearly* — how amazingly clearly!

How could I have written so far without recurring to your letter of March 8th? It touched me very deeply when I read it, and it has troubled my eyes a good deal in re-reading. As for Sir Robert Grant's hymn, I agree with you that it is altogether lovely, and I feel greatly obliged to you for taking the trouble to make me acquainted with it, especially in your own handwriting. Let me at this time, instead of trying to answer your letter as it deserves, with the best I could find in the depths of my heart, thank you for all its sweet and strengthening influences, of which I could not say more than I feel.

With kind remembrances to Mr. Stowe,

Always faithfully yours.

No date.

At the end of this letter — and of every human life — write in large capitals, as the merchants do at the foot of their accounts, — *E E*. [Note at the head of the letter, by the Doctor.]

MY DEAR MRS. STOWE, — Here lie *three* different letters begun in answer to your own, and left off as unsatisfactory, as leaving loopholes for new questions, as failing to express that which I feel to be the root of the matter in my own convictions. I begin to doubt whether I *can* convey my thoughts in a letter as I could in conversation, — no, not in one conversation, but in repeated talks, such as gradually shape out the conceptions and feelings of two friends, until they come to a perfect understanding at last of their bearings to each other in certain regions of thought. How well I know all the working and thinking formulæ of this good companion of mine, from whom I have learned so much more than she is conscious of having ever taught me! how well she knows all my mental movements, — how each of us can read life, as it looks to the other's eyes! I am afraid it is impossible fully to present the intricate conditions of an inward life, our sense of the relations we sustain to the Infinite, except through the inflections of speech and those sudden surprises of our own thought, which the immediate contact of another intelligence so often forces upon us.

I must try to say a few words, or I fear you would misinterpret my silence.

My creed, as I said in my book of ten years ago, is to be found in the first two words of. the Pater Noster. I know there is a great deal to shake it in the natural order of things, but my faith is strong enough to stand against all the untowardness of the blind elements amidst which we are placed here, and out of which our earthly tabernacles are shaped.

I see no corner of the Universe which the Father has wholly deserted. The forces of Nature bruise and wound our bodies, but an artery no sooner bleeds than the Divine hand is placed upon it to stay the flow. A wound is no sooner made than the healing process is set on foot. Pain reaches a certain point, and insensibility comes on, — for fainting is the natural anodyne of curable griefs, as death is the remedy of those which are intolerable.

Never, until the idea of a world without hope and without God — a world where wounds did not try to heal, where habit did not dull the sense of torture — was introduced among men by men, as you well know, was there any impossibility of recognizing the fatherly character of the Creator. If the Christian religion is in any degree responsible for this, you and I must change our natures before we can call it "good tidings." We cannot conceive of a Father's allowing so limited a being as his human child to utterly ruin himself. I see the perplexed condition (will you forgive me?) into which this dogma has thrown your brother Edward, who had to shape a past destiny for the race to make it tolerable, and another brother of yours whose inward conflicts I suspect to have been more severe than most of those who know him would believe. I do not believe you or I can ever get the iron of Calvinism out of our souls, — but see a woman bred as this companion of mine was, by a gentle-hearted father to whom all such ideas were simply shocking, inadmissible on any legendary evidence, unworthy alike of God and man, and you will find in such a woman that the great obstacle to the belief in God as a father has never existed. To this utter rejection of a godless universe, which is to run parallel forever with a *happy* world of dehumanized intelligences, I believe the leading souls of this century are pointing the belief of our whole race. I say *dehumanized* intelligences, for if there is anything human left about the spirits of *just* men made perfect and tender women turned to angels, they can never be quiet until they have got a drop of cold water to the tongue of Dives, and colonized those children who, according to our old friend Michael Wigglesworth, were assigned to " the easiest room in Hell." (How strange to think of! I knew here and in Paris a great-great-grandson of old Michael, yellow-haired, light-eyed, with the oddest of squints, whose face used to turn to a flame over the Burgundy, whose muscles were those of a prize-fighter, and whose worship of more than one of the heathen divinities in the days of his lusty youth was devout beyond all common measure. Peace to the dust of poor ——! He lies for many a year under the green sod at Mount Auburn. Long sickness sobered if it did not change him, and a saintly woman, herself struck with blindness, became his wife. But in what room of the Eternal Holy Inquisition Mansion would old Michael have placed his great-great-grandchild?) (Old Michael's descendants are generally excellent people.)

To me the Deity exists simply in his human relations. He is a mere extension of what I know in humanity. So he must be to every human being, it seems to me; at least all *communicable* ideas of him, — all but the ineffable contemplations, which visionaries, as we call them, and some others, claim — are obviously human. For no term is applied to him which has not shaped itself out of human experience. What does " good " mean but what " Uncle Cook " who takes care of the poor children, and certain women I know, show me in their lives ? What does " Father " mean but somebody who is bound to take care of you in the exact ratio of his power and knowledge to your weakness and ignorance, and who *will do it*, whether you know enough to understand all he does, or have sense enough to trust him implicitly, or not ? Every man makes his God, — the South-Sea islander makes him of wood, the Christian New Englander of ideas. — " No! the Bible makes him ! " But a thousand different Gods have been made out of the Bible ; you might as well say the quarry makes the temple. — Michael Wigglesworth made his frightful Deity out of the Bible. Cotton Mather made his, — and would have hanged my mother and yours to please him. The God of the Romanist and the God of the Quaker both are got out of the Bible. I have got just as far in my creed as I had ten years ago, — namely, as far as those first two words of the Pater Noster. There are difficulties, I know ; but it appears to me on the whole : —

1. That the Deity must be as good as the best conscious being he makes.

2. That it is more consonant with our ideas of what is best, to suppose that suffering, which is often obviously disciplinary and benevolent in its aim, is to be temporary rather than eternal.

3. That if the Deity expects the genuine love and respect of independent, thinking creatures, he must in the long run treat them as a good father would treat them.

4. That to suppose this world a mere trap, baited with temptations of sense, which only Divine ingenuity could have imagined, with the certainty that the larger part of the race would fall into it, and that to the tortures of a very helpless, ignorant, ill-educated being is to be added the cruellest sting of all, that he brought it on himself, does not seem a probable course of action on the part of "Our Father."

5. When I, as an erring mortal, am confronted with Infinite purity, it appears to me an absurdity to talk of judging me by that standard.

God made the sun too strong for my eyes — but he took care to give me eyelids.   He let the burning, all-devouring oxygen into my system, but he took care to dilute it with $\frac{4}{5}$ of nitrogen.

And a fellow-creature tells me that after this world, where all these provisions are made, where all accidents are repaired, or attempted, at least, to be repaired, there is to be another, where there are eyes without lids, flame to breathe instead of air, wounds that never heal, and an army of experts in torture in the place of that ever-present God whom I used to call "My Father!"

I only say it does not seem probable to me.   Nehemiah Adams seems to feel sure of it, — but, thank God, I can read history, and when I remember that to doubt the horrid legendary doctrines of witchcraft a century and a half ago was to be a Sadducee, I must think that in a century and a half from now, I hope a good deal sooner, his writings, if read at all, will be read with the same feelings we entertain to the witchcraft ravings of Cotton Mather.

6. Either my moral nature will remain human in another life, or it will be changed to something not human.

Edwards and others have supposed it would be changed to something not human, for they have thought one of the delights of the blessed would be to witness the just vengeance of the Almighty on their late friends and neighbors, — to say nothing of relatives. Why not a pleasure to accompany the Arch-tormentor himself on his clinical visits to the tormented? Why not love lies instead of truth — hatred instead of love — devils instead of angels — if our human qualities are to belong to us no more after the great change? I cannot accept this supposition. I am obliged to think that I shall love the same qualities in another state that I love in this. *Can* I love a father who lets me ruin myself?

What if I happen to love another as well as myself? *Can* I love a being who lets that other ruin himself — (I mean go to everlasting torment)?

What if I happen to be so human that I love and pity all my race, and cannot be happy if they are to be writhing in agony forever, and nobody suffered to go near them to help or pity? *Can* I love the being who has arranged the universe so that they shall come to this?

But I *must* love my Creator, for he is as kind as my father was, and as tender as my mother was. Otherwise he has made a creature better than himself, according to our human definition of better, — which is contrary to all reason, as it seems to me. How absurd to declaim against the lawless passions of Jupiter, or the jealous rages of Juno, as sufficiently disproving their Divinity, and then call on mankind to believe in a being who has established an almost infinite laboratory, where the vivisections and *viviustions* of sensitive organisms are to set forth his glory forever to creatures that were once men and women — men with tears in their eyes — women with milk in their breasts!

I grant all that can fairly be said about the suffering we see here on earth. I should not have expected to find so much. But I see compensation in some form trying to restore the balance; I see apparent misery solacing itself in unforeseen ways; I see habit rendering tolerable what seemed too much to be borne; I see sleep with its sweet oblivion, and death with its certain release from the unfit tenement and its at least possible solution of every doubt and cure for every ill. In all this I see nothing like Hell. I see ignorance and ill-training make men act like demons; to me they are as the insane and the idiots are. Mary Lamb was in *deed* a murderess, — but she might, after stabbing her mother, have plunged her bloody knife into her own heart, and yet have been carried straight by pitying angels to the company of the blessed.

Was there ever such a prayer as that one: —

"Father, forgive them, *for they know not what they do!*"

Your little Iroquois knows not what he does. *No* sinner truly knows what he does.

We do not "come into the world with a bias to vice," except relatively to society. Any bias we bring into the world comes, mediately it is true but just as really, from the Creator. A clear intelligence, a just balance of bodily, mental, and moral instincts, a wise training, are a complete human outfit. Withhold any one or more of these conditions, and it shows itself in a man's life, in error, in excess, in sin, in vice. Who withheld it?

I believe much, I dare not say how much, of what we call "sin" has no moral character whatever in the sight of the great Judge. I believe much of what we call "vice" is not only an object of the profoundest compassion to good men and women, but that the tenderest of God's mercies are in store for many whom the so-called justice of the world condemns.

More and more I feel that God is all in all, that the pride of man has shown itself more fearfully in his over-estimate of his own capacity for sin than in any other way. Do not mistake me for what is popularly meant by an "antinomian." "For every idle word" — yes, I am ready to adopt that too. God lets me move my limbs — these he would trust me with. But he shut my heart and my breathing organs and all the wondrous mechanism by which I live, in a casket beyond my rash meddling, of which he keeps the key. So I know that he has entrusted me with many precious interests which I can use well or ill; but I will not believe that he has ever trusted the immortal destiny of my soul out of his own hands.

If the doctrine of a world of endless torture had come in with the Christian religion, it might have been very differently received. But men's minds were familiar with it through the fables of a cruel mythology. Prometheus and Tantalus and Sisyphus, the lower world with its river of fire, came out of the same imaginations that contrived the heathenisms we are in the habit of denouncing as baseless superstitions.

I am satisfied that we shall never properly understand Christianity until we take the exact inventory of what was in the world when it came. I hope you have read the famous article on the Talmud in the last *Lon don Quarterly.* We must remember that our sacred writings are simply legends, — that is, written from memory after the events occurred, sometimes long afterwards. If — and I am afraid it is so — Christ *is said to have* taught, as the heathen taught before him, that there is a universe of torture to match the universe of bliss, with a sovereign and an aristocracy of "his angels;" if he is said to have taught that the greater part of our race were to become the subjects of this potentate and exposed forever to the brutalities of himself and his crew, — then how thankful we should be to Strauss, to Renan, to anybody, who will add to our doubts as to the exactness, the authenticity, the authority of the legends on which this belief reposes! That is the reason why such a quiet statement as that of M. Sainte-Beuve, quoted in one of the last *Literary Gazettes*, brings with it a feeling, not of simple horror that the world is doubting its old beliefs, but of inward question whether the total overthrow of the Godless Universe, as a counterpart of Heaven in the belief of mankind, would not be as great a blessing to the race as the rooting out of the scriptural doctrine of witchcraft was to the trembling old women of Essex County a hundred and fifty years ago.

I do not think Nehemiah Adams's Universe is anything to be grateful for. I do not think his gospel is "good tidings." I believe his belief to be a lurid reflection of old heathenisms. Romanism is to me infinitely more human than Calvinism — which when I once spoke of as "heart-rending" to a high-souled and long-suffering Christian woman, she said "*heart-withering!*"

Faith! faith! faith! In what? In the character

of my Maker. I cannot see the great church of Christendom as so many holy people do, — I cannot worship the Virgin Mary; I cannot see "the scheme" as Nehemiah Adams does, — seeming to think Mr. Choate was safe, if he only comprehended that. But I do believe that good people, kind fathers, kind mothers, are the type of the Creator, and not cruel, jealous, vindictive ones. You remember what Father Taylor said to one of the sterner sort, — "Oh, I see! your *God* is my *Devil!*"

I will send this note or letter — it is not what I want to send, but it may give a hint here and there.

Do I not ask for light? God knows I do.

May 17, 1880.

MY DEAR MRS. STOWE, — A thousand thanks for all the trouble you have taken to copy the poem. It is a beautiful poem and a precious autograph. In an article published many years ago in the *Foreign Quarterly Review,* I think, — its title was "Hymnnology," — "Rock of Ages" was set down as the best hymn in the English language. I recognize its wonderful power and solemnity. If you asked me what is the secret of it, I should say that of all the Protestant hymns I remember it is richest in material imagery. We think in getting free of Romanism we have lost our love of image-worship, but I do not think so myself. Thirty years ago I remember seeing a great gilt cross put on top of the steeple of a *Baptist* meeting-house in Pittsfield, and since that time you know how symbolism has come into the Episcopal Church and overflowed it into the Congregational and other denominations.

The imagination wants help, and if it cannot get it in pictures, statues, crucifixes, etc., it will find it in words. That, I believe, is the reason why "Rock of Ages" impresses us more than any other hymn, — for I think it does. It is the Protestant "Dies Iræ"!

> "Quid sum miser tunc dicturus" —
> "Could my tears forever flow" —

the utter helplessness of the soul and its passionate appeal are common to both. Our hymn has more of hope and less of terror, but it is perfectly *solid* with material imagery, and that is what most of us must have to kindle our spiritual exaltation to its highest point.

V. TO ELIZABETH STUART PHELPS WARD

BEVERLY FARMS, *July* 6, 1879.

MY DEAR MISS PHELPS, — I was very glad to hear that you reached your little resting-place comfortably, and I hope rest of body and mind will restore you soon. I trust you will not busy yourself just now with the problem of human existence. Be a vegetable, — a flower, I mean, of course, — taking nourishment from the earth *via* its most nourishing products, and looking into the sleepy and contented eyes of the cattle and all creatures that live without worded thought, — not into those of the worrying stars which have no eyelids, and stare you into asking questions they will not answer.

I am getting to believe that your first title is quite as good as any that has been since suggested. I don't quite like the " Mustered In." In the first place my impression is that Captains of *war-ships* carry out " sealed orders," while *land-troops* are said to be " mustered in." In the second place I have no great liking for fancy titles unless they are specially appropriate, as was most certainly the title " Gates Ajar." So, as at present advised, I should say

Sealed Orders and Stray Stories,

or

Sealed Orders and Other Stories,

which last is at least inoffensive.

I suppose you must have found the change of weather very trying. I never experienced anything

like it in my protracted existence — so far as my feelings were concerned. I may have known more
change in the thermometer, possibly, but here on the
4th the heat was almost intolerable, and yesterday, the
5th, we were thankful to have a good winter fire.

I never feel well for some little time after coming
to the country, and I am staying at home from
"meet'n," — where I like to go and hear worthy Mr.
Redding, the " Babtist " (Novanglice) preacher, — it
does me some kind of good, I think. There is a little
plant called *Reverence* in the corner of my Soul's
garden, which I love to have watered about once a
week.

Hoping that I shall have the pleasure of seeing
you some time during the season, I am, dear Miss
Phelps,

Faithfully yours.

BEVERLY FARMS, *August* 31, 1879.

MY DEAR MISS PHELPS, — It is my turn now to
send you my kindest regards and remembrances on
your reaching what you call " the half-way house,"
but which I think of as one of those " arbors " where
Christiana rested — at least Christian did, as I remember ; and I am sure the trees would stretch their
branches over your head if you sat down near them,
as they did over Buddha. And this reminds me that
I have been reading and writing a long review of one
of the divinest poems I ever read, *The Light of Asia*,
by Mr. Edwin Arnold. It embodies the legends of
that wonderful personage whose religion is the most
prevalent of any on the face of the earth — so we
are told. You may look for my review in the next

number of the *International*, and I hope it will make you wish to read the poem.

I had a great many visitors on my birthday and many letters; I wrote twenty-two letters in reply yesterday. My house was turned into a bower of roses, and everybody looked as pleased as possible to recognize the fact that I had at least reached the natural limit of human existence. Threescore and ten is a different matter, however, since the invention of spectacles and various other contrivances, which in many cases take away the meaning of the words "I have no pleasure in them."

I thank you most cordially for your kind remembrance. I hope life will grow easier and sweeter to you as you go on your way, softening, sweetening, illuminating it for others.

Believe me, dear Miss Phelps,

Faithfully yours.

BEVERLY FARMS, *September* 27, 1879.

MY DEAR MISS PHELPS, — I must say a word before pulling up my tent-pegs and pitching my tent once more on the shore of the Charles. I should have liked to pass an hour or two with you before going, but I have done almost no visiting out of our immediate neighborhood. Yesterday, as a final excursion, we went to Gloucester, — I did not think of it when we started, — drove round the town, looked at the fire, or tried to, — turned round and came home.

My vacation is over, and I only regret that it has not been as idle as it ought to have been. I have done a good deal of reading, some studying, and struggled with a correspondence which is growing almost too much for me. Among other things I have sat in judgment on an *epic* written by a celebrated professional man and sent me by his nephew. It came pretty near going over the ground that the old school-master, Mr. J. Milton, treated in a poem you may have heard of. I had to say to his relative, who wished to know whether this posthumous work should be published or not, that he had better keep the reputation he had honestly got in another line of labor, and not enter into competition with J. M. Another experience was with a Western "poet," who sent me a duodecimo of some hundred pages of verse, and requested my opinion. I gave it — not very flattering, but civil and honest, as I supposed he wanted it to be. In due time I received the most impertinent, in fact, insolent letter I ever got, — with one exception, many years ago, — a similar return for an honest criticism from another Western bard. And Horace was a heathen sinner — was he? — for saying —

> "Odi ignobile vulgus."

But my summer has been placid, on the whole, and if my duties did not call me back, I might perhaps stay until the leaves had fallen.

I am really sorry you should be turned out of your sea-shell. There was so much good sense and good taste in your little arrangements for summer rest, that it seems a pity you should be disturbed. You have seen our little place. It serves our turn well enough, and we are going to keep it at present, perhaps for years.

If I could make you well, I believe I would turn doctor again. I hope that dear, good old physician

who cures more patients than all the M. D.'s — I
mean *Time* — will make you strong and hearty again,
or at least will lighten that burden which makes
life hard to bear for you. At least you can look
back and think of all you have done for others. I
believe if He who made His home with the good
women of Bethany were walking our highways, yours
would be one of the doors where He would knock for
entrance. Would not that be enough?

BOSTON, *October* 29, 1879.

MY DEAR MISS PHELPS, — Many thanks for the
story-book, the title of which you did me the honor of
discussing with me. I have read eleven of the seventeen stories, and shall read the others very soon; but
I cannot wait any longer before acknowledging your
kindness. Besides, this is an off day — no lecture
— and I have a little leisure for my distant friends.

The stories I have read, I have read carefully.
They all come out of your true woman's heart, and
some of them have brought the tears out of my eyes
— not the tears of weakness, for the wheel is not yet
broken at the cistern, or the pitcher broken at the
fountain.

Do you ask me which I like best of those I have
read? Perhaps I should say "Doherty," — a very
simple story, shame, misery, ruin, — as it seems, —
but at the last a ray of Divine love, and a feeling in
the reader [such] as he remembers in " Margaret "
(Faust's): " She is saved ! "

The stories of emotional complications between
lovers, and between married people, like " Running
the Risk," will passionately interest many women. I

do not think men ever come to understand all the hair-springs, the oscillating machinery, the compensation balances of a woman's nature in a state of unstable equilibrium.   There is a kind of music — sometimes it is a strange discord — which can be re- solved to a woman's ear, but not to a man.   Indeed, there are single tones a woman hears too acute for the masculine organ of hearing.   (You know many persons cannot hear the bat's squeak.)

I know life shows itself to you in some of its most saddening aspects, but though I am commonly busy and cheerful, I like to sit down in silence with you at times, and lose myself in tender sympathies.   I wish that, with twice your length of days, I had done half as much to lighten the world's burdens!

Boston, *December* 10, 1879.

MY DEAR MISS PHELPS, — Your few words are more than eloquent — they are precious.   If the In- finite Love needs to be pleaded with in behalf of its own children, it will be the voice of a woman — a true woman — a tender-hearted woman — that reaches it and is listened to.   Need I say more than that I thank you and bless you for your kind and sweet remembrance?

Boston, *May* 4, 1888.

MY DEAR MISS PHELPS, — I have just received your kind letter, and I must write you a few words about myself, knowing that you will be pleased to hear from me under my new conditions.

All was gradual and gentle in the passing away of my dear wife.   The last sad stage, which I feared, was spared her and us. There was no paralysis, no help-lessness, no *painful* mental disturbance; that is, she remained quiet, amiable, docile, tractable, comely in aspect, gracious in manner, cheerful, easily pleased, until within a few days of the end, when she grew weaker very rapidly, and presently left us with that sweet smile on her face which the parting soul some-times leaves on the features. To the few who looked upon it, it was like a celestial vision.

Forty-five years we lived most happily together. Then came the cloud, — not a sullen storm-cloud, but a silvery one. Her illusions were pleasant ones, — she enjoyed living, was interested in all around her, and oftentimes seemed to be with the dead whom she had loved just as if they were living, in the most nat-ural and simple way.

We were fortunate in finding a companion for her, — a widow lady of intelligence and amiable disposi-tion, to whom she soon became attached. If you had happened to call at almost any time before the last week, I should have carried you into the parlor and said, "Amelia, here is our friend Miss Phelps," and you would have left her after a few moments, hardly realizing that she was the subject of any mental in-firmity, she looked and spoke and smiled so like her-self as you must remember her.

I have every cause to be grateful that, after so many happy years, when the inevitable came, it was so mercifully ordered.

My daughter, Mrs. Turner Sargent, has come to live with me, and we are necessarily hard at work arranging our new household. It was her own pro-posal to come, and she lets her own beautiful house (59 Beacon Street), to which she was greatly attached. But she is a very cheerful woman, and accommodates herself admirably to our new conditions. We keep the place at Beverly Farms which we had last year, and where I hope I shall see you. I am glad my little book pleased you.

This letter is all about my own experiences. I hope when you write you will fill your letter with yours. I have never got over your story of "Jack." It is a *great* story.

Boston, April 13, 1889.

My dear Mrs. Ward, — I thank you for your very kind and sympathetic letter. The loss of my daughter is a heavy blow and a great *disappointment*. We had made out a very pleasant programme for our joint lives, had learned to know, to love, and to justly value each other in the relation of father and daughter, and were full of hope, when her summons came. It came as did that of her mother, very gently. Some weeks of suffering there were, made almost happy to her by the kindness of more friends than she could have believed would have so tenderly remembered her. Then came a change, which looked like an approach to recovery. Bodily ease, restored appetite, improvement in pulse, easy respiration, the delight of returning life, rekindled hope; she and all of us could not help hoping and almost believing that she was to be with us again, active, joyous, giving and receiving pleasure among her numerous friends.

Dis aliter visum. In the midst of this apparent improvement she had a sudden convulsion, followed by insensibility and coma, in the deep slumber of which she breathed her life peacefully away.

I am not left alone. My daughter-in-law, a very

helpful, hopeful, powerful as well as brilliant woman, is with me, and my household goes on smoothly, and not without a cheerful aspect. Her husband the Judge will soon be established in the house, and I trust we shall live as happily as we ought to, if my large allowance of years should be a little farther extended.

Pray come and see me, and bring Mr. Ward with you, the next time you are in town. We shall, both Mrs. Holmes and myself, — for the Judge is a good deal away from home, — be most happy to see you.

With kindest regards to Mr. Ward, I am, dear Mrs. Ward,

Affectionately yours.

Sunday Afternoon, *May* 31, 1891.

My DEAR MRS. WARD, — One who is very dear to me said to me yesterday: "I want you to read Mrs. Ward's story, 'The Bell of St. Basil.'" And so I have just been reading it. Not for the first time, though. I remember well that I read it in a previous volume, and that it produced a deep impression on me. But *how* deep it would be on this second reading I did not suspect. I may as well confess that the pathos of your story quite overcame me. I did not know I had so many tears in my emotional fountains. Either I have come to the " streams of dotage," or that is one of the most touching stories that even your tear-compelling imagination ever gave birth to. — No matter! Marlborough was ten years younger than I am when he died; and Swift died four years younger than I now am, after having been " a driveller and a show" for I don't remember how many years. So I think it is not my imbecility, but your command of the springs of sensibility, which is to blame for my exhibition of weakness. Of course the "exhibition" was all to myself, thank heaven, for I would not show myself in such a moment of weakness if every tear were to be turned into a pearl.

It did me good to have a good, long cry. I was happy to find myself, as old books have it, "dissolved in floods of tears." When we ought to cry, we don't. When we want to cry, we can't. In the mean time the internal cisterns are filling up ready to burst. What a relief when — from an apparently totally insufficient cause — a woman's fanciful relation of something that never happened; a picture of some people that never lived, in a place not to be found in the Gazetteer — all at once something gives way, and down comes the freshet, with such a sense of sweet, delicious, stingless sorrow and sympathy, and withal of our own loveableness for being so tender-hearted, that it seems as if

"Angels alone that soar above"

were fit company for such amiable creatures as we feel ourselves.

I could not help writing on the spot, while the impression of your story was still tingling all through me. The ink on the first page of this note and the tears on my cheeks dried at the same moment.

I thank you, then, for all these most welcome and most wholesome tears, and for all the sweet and ennobling influences which I, with so many others, have felt from your admirable writings.

With kindest regards to Mr. Ward and yourself, I am

Always faithfully yours.

BEVERLY FARMS, *July* 5, 1893.

MY DEAR MRS. WARD, — I am glad that any season can induce you to let me have a letter from you,
— a luxury I have not had for a good while. As for
me, you see I have come to a card and a ready-stamped
envelope. My secretary is among the mountains.
My eyes are getting dimmer, and my fingers have
taken to cramps, so I am making everything as simple
as possible.

Nothing would delight me more than to talk over
time and eternity with you and your husband, but as
to saying anything on these subjects to be *reported*, I
would as soon send a piece of my spinal marrow to
one of those omnivorous editors. I may very possibly
dictate to my secretary some of my notions on such
matters, but I am disposed to keep out of the market-
place and bide my time for talking. Perhaps I may
not think it worth while to express myself with absolute freedom on the deepest question. It is obvious
to me that the order of things is adjusted on a basis
which is to last for a good while, and afford a staging
for good men and women, and even for some whom
we might call great men and women, to be useful in
their day and generation. You may find my philosophy in this regard in a poem of mine called "The
Organ - Blower." Wherever you are, you see the
handle of the organ-bellows; take hold and blow —
the Lord will play the tune as He pleases.

So you see I am quite obstinate, not to be lured, or
*Ma*clured. But I want to see you and talk with you,
and, above all, listen to you and know how *you* feel
with reference to certain great problems. I would be
at home almost any afternoon that you and your
husband would honor me with a call.

BOSTON, *September* 29, 1893.

MY DEAR MRS. WARD, — My visit to Gloucester was the most delightful incident of my summer. The weather was perfect, and I enjoyed the long drive very much. When I got to your new place and looked around me, I was enchanted. It is a most remarkable and a most lovely prospect you have before you and all round you. Your home is an ideal, so truly realized that I had to rub my eyes to know whether I was dreaming or awake, — looking at a true landscape or reading a story-book. The hour I was with you passed so quickly that I was taken by surprise when I was told that my driver was at the door. There are many things I should like to have said, many questions I should like to have asked; but they will keep, and you will drop in on me some day, and we will finish — or rather continue — our talk.

I am glad to be back, for I find myself much better in town than in the harsh Beverly winds. I come back, however, to all sorts of lesser cares and bothers, — letters, letters, letters, callers who do not know when to go, books asking to be read and criticised, and the accumulation of literary stuff of all sorts that has piled itself up during my absence from town. However, I can see tolerably, and I have a new gas illuminating contrivance which gives me a wonderful bright and steady light to read and write by. The "writer's cramp," which troubles me from time to time, does not affect me at all to-day, as my hand-writing shows you.

I am interested in many things, — most of all in the Congress of all Religions. I want to get the full record of that — not that I think it will amount to much directly; but in its indirect influence upon the

Christian Church, which has attempted to confiscate every advance of humanity to be its own private property, it may be useful. I am sure such an influence is needed. The hideous inhumanity which practically takes away all hope for the great majority of the human race may find itself put to shame by the gentle faiths of more enlightened, less brutally *theologized-ecclesiastized* peoples. I really look on that Congress as the longest stride towards the Millennium that I have seen, or am like to see if I last till the —— [illegible].

You and your husband look very happy, and no doubt are so, now that the *yacht* is laid up. But what a romance it is! You looking out for the returning sail — he driving in before the blast — two hearts, one leaping landward, one seaward! Long may peace and happiness be with you both.

Always affectionately yours,
OLIVER WENDELL HOLMES.

VI. MISCELLANEOUS LETTERS

TO JAMES FREEMAN CLARKE.

May 11, 1836.

DEAR JAMES, — Since I have been home, I have repeatedly inquired after you, and heard of you at other times without asking. Everything which I heard was exceedingly gratifying to me, — not merely because you were my classmate and friend, but because in your success I saw my own prophecies fulfilled, and because the favorable opinion which you always seemed to entertain of myself carried with it a value in proportion somewhat to the rate at which I found your own abilities were estimated by others. But although I have never forgotten the praises and encouragements you sometimes used to give me, and which, with their very words and circumstances, I believe I have recalled more often and more faithfully than any others I have received, I should have been by no means certain that all these little recollections had not passed from your mind, as the opera airs which we hear for a week or two give place to some other novelty. I was surprised and delighted to find that, after an absence and silence of nearly three years, you could still recognize and be pleased with a little sketch which I claim as mine with far greater pleasure than I ever expected to, when I gave the poor " Grisette " to the pages of the *American Monthly*. Like everything tolerable I ever wrote, it

was conceived in exultation and brought forth with
pain and labor.   The time at which any new thought
strikes me is my Sibylline moment, but the act of
composition, so exciting and so easy to some people,
is a wearing business, attended with a dull, disagreeable sensation about the forehead, — only from time
to time it is interrupted by the simultaneous descent
of some group of words or some unexpected image,
which produces a burst of the most insane enthusiasm
and self-gratulation, during which I commit puerile
excesses of language and action.   As I am determined
to make you understand this, I will give you an instance or two, — marking the lines which came in this
sudden way and occasioned a paroxysm, — in a little
piece called " The Last Reader," one of four which I
have published since my return : —

> They lie upon my pathway bleak,
>   Those flowers that once ran wild,
> *As on a father's careworn cheek*
>   *The ringlets of his child.*

And in another part of the same : —

> What care I though the dust is spread
>   Around these yellow leaves,
> *Or o'er them his sarcastic thread*
>   *Oblivion's insect weaves.*

The little piece from which I take these lines did
not seem to be as popular as the " Grisette," though
more elaborate and, as I supposed at the time, better.
My pet expression in the two last quoted lines was
changed by the New York editor on his own responsibility into : —

> Or o'er them his *corroding* thread —

which occasioned immense indignation on my part,
and a refusal to write until he would promise to keep

hands off. The four things which I said I had written were all published in the *American Monthly*, and were as follows : some " Lines written at Sea " (a Smith-like title for one's verses), beginning, —

> If sometimes in the dark blue eye
> Or in the deep red wine.

After this a patriotic affair, called " Our Yankee Girls ; " then " The Last Reader," and last of all the one which pleased you, " La Grisette." I had not written a stanza while abroad, and I felt on first sitting down as if the power of writing had passed away as completely as poor Zerah Colburn's talent for calculation, and left me high and dry upon the sand, my sails and pennons all flapping in the wind — my keel wedged into the solid shore of fact — and with no hope of ever bounding again over the billows of poetry. So it was, however, that, after writing one or two of these pieces, particularly " Our Yankee Girls " and " The Last Reader," I thought them remarkably good — at least for me, and was in hopes other people would think so. But several of my friends seemed to think I had fallen off, — and one in particular, who always professed a great liking for my verses, stopped me one day to tell me that the " Grisette " was poor stuff, — namby-pamby, " such as young Buckingham used to write." This troubled me somewhat — I supposed I was running to seed — and when I found one of my offspring altered and mutilated in the magazine, where it was published, it settled the matter, and I determined not to write any more at present. Some time since I was appointed Φ B K poet for the coming anniversary, and, as I accepted, this occupation will be enough to keep me quiet. You

would suppose from what I have said that I have
been thinking a great deal about poetry; it is not
true, — perhaps there is no one among the young men
who has been more ardently engaged in medicine than
I have for the last three years.   And on this account
I determined to publish whatever I did anonymously,
that nobody might suppose I was ambitious of being
considered a regular scribbler.   If you ask me then
what I am thinking about, I will answer you — Medicine — which finds me regular occupation — which
can support me and give me a hold on the community
in which I live, and which my love of observation and
the habits which I have formed for the last few years
have rendered to me the most delightful of employ-
ments.   Thus I have answered one or two of your
questions, and prattled something too wildly about
myself.   But your very kind letter so soothed and
pleased my perturbed spirit that I could not help falling into this ecstasy of egotism.   Write again, and
give me an account of yourself and your situation,
and the next time I send a letter to Louisville it shall
be filled with something else besides my own insignificant history.

TO JAMES FREEMAN CLARKE.[1]

March 17, 1838.

MY DEAR JAMES, — The fates have sent a triple-
headed Cerberus, or hydra, this week in the shape of
three special requests for verses.   I have seriously

[1] Mr. Clarke had requested Dr. Holmes to give him something
to print in *The Western Messenger*, a monthly magazine of which
he was editor.   This poem (The Parting Word) was printed in
the May number, 1838.

reflected on each and all, and come to the conclusion
to repel two of my petitioners, — one by a churlish
silence and the other by an unctuous or rather sapo-
naceous refusal, and to dispose of the third — that is
yourself — by sending such a specimen of fancy work
as shall prevent you from too rashly repeating the request. If it were necessary now to sit down and card
and spin and weave a brand-new lyric, I should plead
utter incapacity. In my humble notion poetry is to
one's mind what inflorescence is to plants — a sudden
and occasional manifestation of bright colors — the
exhalation of an unwonted sweetness — which require
certain influences and naturally appear only at certain intervals. I am sure that three or four days
ago, when the air suddenly put on its summer soft-
ness and clearness, I felt that my buds began to ex-
pand, and I believe I should have leaved out charmingly, had not the nipping frost of two or three
habitual bores fallen upon the embryo petals and
corollas. *Dis aliter visum.* The week which is just
extricating its caudal extremity from the narrow
crack which we call the present — (here intervened a
visit to Salem to see a nephew, very ill — and I resume) — has been full of troubles and trials. Three
several times I have been remorselessly and relentlessly
victimized to the extent of *six consecutive hours*, at
the maximum, either by individuals who were over-
fascinated by my social attractions and particularly
convenient sofa, or by express combinations got together for amusement, into which my weakness suffered me to be wheedled. Such martyrdoms have a
most mildewing effect upon my faculties. The self-
exhausting process which takes place in the mind
and body of a man stretched hour after hour upon

the rack of conversational torture by he or she in-
quisitors leaves him — at least it does me — as lifeless
and spiritless as a clod. Adrift, for instance, in the
middle of a long evening, with a single heavy-witted
companion, of known and tried tenacity, whose ideas
I have many years since inventoried, whose faculties
I have weighed with unnecessary minuteness, whose
ultimate capabilities I perfectly realize, whose most
elaborate conclusions I assume as axioms, in short
with an individual all whose mental laws I have ana-
lyzed, and therefore with the right materials could
make just such another man or machine, — what has
life more unendurable! At ten o'clock to feel, like
the shipwrecked sailor on a raft, that as far as you
have floated from eight, so far must you toss and
hitch and worry without sail or oar, until you strike
upon the dark and distant shore of twelve! My week
receives a temper from a succession of such trials, and
though habitually very cheerful and I believe even
good-natured, my philosophy has shaken a little beneath an accidental series of such afflictions. Consequently it was the worst moment for your little
request, and indeed, from almost any other source
I should have rejected it with indignation as part of
a systematic plan of imposition, which the world had
got up to annoy me.

If I would fulfil my promise on this page, I must
condense both my meaning and my forms. First as
to myself, the cause of this vexation which I have
referred to is a want of synchronism in some of my
old friends and myself. Many of them have remained
idle while I have grown industrious; have held on
to prejudices I have outgrown; have given out all
the gas my agency is capable of extracting. I have

passed through the condition of college idler, and an apprentice in general society, and now for the first time in my life I find the true desire of knowledge growing up in my mind, and my instincts turning from the pleasures of conversation to those of books. Ten years have probably carried me once round my own intellectual orbit; I must drink in light from other sources. No graduate of Harvard — or at least very few — had ever read less at my age than myself. My ignorance one year since would have asphyxiated a legion of cherubim. In consequence of this feeling I have been secretly throwing in knowledge; and, having confidence enough in my own powers of apprehension and diligence, shall probably be a pretty well-informed man some time or other. When I have ploughed and sowed my little intellectual territory, if there spring up any Arethusa from the ancient fountains, well and good; if not, — the most important transactions of life, fortunately, are carried on in prose.

Now as to yourself, — you must judge by the manner in which I have always spoken to you about myself that I cannot rank you among those common companions or friends who judge of one by looking to see how the hour and minute hands of fortune and favor stand, but neither care to look into the inward machinery nor are worthy of such confidence. I have always placed the highest value on your good opinion. Many years since, when you among the very first praised one of my earliest efforts, it gave me more sincere pleasure than all the other little flatteries I received; for, although scarcely known beyond one or two small coteries, I have been directly and indirectly flattered by men, and especially by women. But I

felt certain you knew and meant what you said. I am
going to make one or two criticisms on the pretty
verses you sent me, supposing that you kept a copy,
and that the stanzas are numbered in the same order.
The first two are neat and epigrammatical, and would
indeed make a clever epigram, taken alone. Is the
train of sad feeling expressed in the next four verses
true? Or is it in an imaginary character, and under
the influence of the sentimental feeling rhyme is apt
to bring on, that it was written? The illusions of
poetical feeling so often lead us away that I cannot but
hope you have exaggerated the desolation of your own
condition. In the seventh verse I don't like the idea
of a soul's "glittering," — the image of a soul looking
down upon us suggests a resemblance to the pure,
pale, and steady light of a planet, if you please, but no
such notion as glittering or twinkling, or indeed any
of the more ostentatious forms of effulgence. Nor
do I like the word "wiselier" in the last verse, if
there be indeed such an English word. I cut up a
poem, which a young gentleman is going to deliver on
a public occasion, at his special request and in his
presence last evening, so that I am critical to canni-
balism this morning.

The verses, which you have asked and I have promised, must come, I see, upon another piece of paper,
and, I fear, make you pay too dear for the whistle.
Single postage, like the common atmospheric pressure,
keeps up the just balance between the centrifugal
force of friendship and the centripetal one of interest,
— remove it, and our affections would ooze out like
the traveller's blood at the summit of Mont Blanc, —
but *double* it, and the warmest current of sympathy
stiffens, curdles, and is arrested in its channels. I

have by me one or two, especially one crack piece of poetry. You shall not have it; I will not give it away or sell it at present, because I can make it better if I keep it. I shall snub you with an insignificant little affair, to be called "The Parting Word," or some such name, and which, if you are ashamed of, you need not print. It is no great things, but for all that I am not run out nor used up, nor in a state of senility or caducity. I can write twice as well as I ever did before, but I will not write at present, — and, without looking your gift horse in the mouth, make the most of him, for I shall not have either colt or pony to spare for a year to come.

P. S. If you print — *print correctly.*

TO GEORGE TICKNOR.

December 19th.

MY DEAR SIR, — I thank you very heartily in my turn for the beautiful and interesting volume of *Calderon* you have kindly sent me. I am much interested in the study of "assonants," being well aware that the form of verse has much to do with the effect of the sentiment. I was never so much struck with this until I read Tennyson's "In Memoriam." It is truly extraordinary what freshness is given to a most commonplace rhythm by a return to that exceptional arrangement of the rhymes occasionally employed by earlier writers. If I mistake not, "Hiawatha" has borrowed something of its movement from *Calderon*, or some original of similar construction. I am impressed with this fact about all the exceptional measures : that though they please for once in our own dialect, they do not bear repetition. If you will pardon me for referring to the volume I sent you, I should like to have you notice the rhythm of one poem in it, "The Chambered Nautilus." I am as willing to submit this to criticism as any I have written, in form as well as in substance, and I have not seen any English verse of just the same pattern.

Lieutenant Holmes, of the 20th M. V., will feel honored to present himself at the headquarters of scholarship and hospitality in Park Street.

Very truly and respectfully yours.

TO JAMES T. FIELDS.[1]

PITTSFIELD, *June* 13, 1852.

MY DEAR MR. FIELDS, — I have just received your very interesting note, and the proof which accompanied it. I don't know when I ever read anything about myself that struck me so piquantly as that story about the old gentleman. It is almost too good to be true, but you are not in the habit of quizzing. The trait is so nature-like and Dickens-like, no American — no living soul but a peppery, crotchety, good-hearted, mellow old John Bull — could have done such a thing. God bless him! Perhaps the verses are not much, and perhaps he is no great judge whether they are or not; but what a pleasant thing it is to win the hearty liking of any honest creature, who is neither your relation nor compatriot, and who must fancy what pleases him for itself and nothing else!

I will not say what pleasure I have received from Miss Mitford's kind words. I am going to sit down, and write her a letter with a good deal of myself in it, which I am quite sure she will read with indulgence,

[1] Reprinted from *The Century Magazine*, February, 1895.

if not with gratification. If you see her, or write
to her, be sure to let her know that she must make
up her mind to such a letter as she will have to sit
down to.

I am afraid I have not much of interest for you.
It is a fine thing to see one's trees and things growing,
but not so much to tell of. I have been a week in the
country now, and am writing at this moment amidst
such a scintillation of fireflies and chorus of frogs as
a cockney would cross the Atlantic to enjoy. During
the past winter I have done nothing but lecture, having delivered between seventy and eighty all round
the country from Maine to western New York, and
even confronted the critical terrors of the great city
that holds half a million and P—— H——. All this
spring I have been working on microscopes, so that it
is only within a few days I have really got hold of anything to read — to say nothing of writing, except for
my lyceum audiences. I had a literary *rencontre* just
before I came away, however, in the shape of a dinner at the Revere House, with Griswold and Epes
Sargent. What a curious creature Griswold is! He
seems to me a kind of naturalist whose subjects are
authors, whose memory is a perfect fauna of all flying,
running, and creeping things that feed on ink. Epes
has done mighty well with his red-edged school-book,[1]
which is a very creditable-looking volume, to say the
least.

It would be hard to tell how much you are missed
among us. I really do not know who would make a
greater blank, if he were abstracted. As for myself, I
have been all lost since you have been away, in all
that relates to literary matters, to say nothing of the

[1] *Sargent's Standard Speaker.*

almost daily aid, comfort, and refreshment I imbibed from your luminous presence. Do come among us as soon as you can; and having come, stay among your devoted friends, of whom count

O. W. HOLMES.

PITTSFIELD, June 11, 1854.

MY DEAR MOTHER, — I received Ann's letter a few days ago, and would answer it direct to her but for two reasons — first, that writing to you is the same thing; second, that Amelia is actually writing at this moment to Ann herself. Two letters, from husband and wife, would be too much for a person confined to her bed. — And first, I hope you will stay at Salem as long as Ann can keep you; that is, until you feel ready to come to Pittsfield, if, as is likely, you make up your mind to give us that delight. At any rate, I hope you will make a good long stay in Salem; it must be one of the curative means that can be most relied upon to keep the mind cheerful and bright. I would give more for your being with Ann than for all the salves and 'intments that were ever stirred up. — Please read this sentence over twice, and believe it. Healing is a living process, greatly under the influence of mental conditions. It has often been found that the same wound received in battle will do well in the soldiers that have beaten, that would prove fatal in those that have just been defeated.

We are going on as pleasantly as ever. I did not tell you that I had been at work with electricity as a part of my summer plan of instructive amusements. The old machine is mounted on its ancient footing, or rather, with new splendor, and gives sparks an inch long. I have been making various kinds of apparatus, and really reminded myself of my young days more than by anything I have done for a long time. I find that many of my old tastes return upon me whenever they get a chance; chemistry will have its turn by and by, perhaps mineralogy, and the rest of them. I learn something new, and often learn things I can make useful in instruction. But perhaps the pleasantest thing about it is that I can do so easily what I used to find so difficult, — realize my ideas with my hands with so much comfort and satisfaction.

But in the mean time the garden has been growing into beauty in the most magical way under the hands principally of great A and little a. I am fairly astonished at the way in which they work. Would you believe it, — I was stopping to rest with a tolerably heavy wheelbarrow of gravel yesterday, when Amelia took hold of it and trundled it along as if she had been a Paddy.

Went to meet'n to-day — or rather to church — heard Mr. P——. Saw Mr. and Mrs. Newton, Judge Curtis, and others whom we have not met. Very glad to see the Newtons always — gentleman and ladies — scarce articles in republican America. We always keep dark and lie low for the first week or two, before beginning to visit and be visited. When we begin that series of operations you shall hear of the result. Infinitely pleased and delighted with Ann's letter — don't let her tire herself — John must write. I enclose a kiss to be fairly divided.

Your aff. son & bro.

TO JAMES T. FIELDS.[1]

8 MONTGOMERY PLACE, *July* 24, 1857.

MY DEAR MR. FIELDS, — I return the three poems you sent me, having read them with much gratification. Each of them has its peculiar merits and defects, as it seems to me, but all show poetical feeling and artistic skill.

"Sleep On!" is the freshest and most individual in its character. You will see my pencil comment at the end of it. "Inkerman" is comparatively slipshod and careless, though not without lyric fire and vivid force of description. "Raphael Sanzio" would deserve higher praise if it were not so closely imitative.

In truth, all these poems have a genuine sound; they are full of poetical thought, and breathed out in softly modulated words. The music of "Sleep On!" is very sweet, and I have never seen heroic verse in which the rhyme was less obtrusive, or the rhythm more diffluent. Still it would not be fair to speak in these terms of praise without pointing out the transparent imitativeness which is common to all these poems.

"Inkerman" is a poetical Macaulay stewed. The whole flow of its verse and resonant passion of its narrative are borrowed from the *Lays of Ancient Rome*. There are many crashing lines in it, and the story is rather dashingly told; but it is very inferior in polish, and even correctness, to both the other poems. I have marked some of its errata.

"Raphael," good as it is, is nothing more than Browning browned over. Every turn of expression, and the whole animus, so to speak, is taken from

[1] Reprinted from *The Century Magazine*, February, 1895.

those poetical monologues of his. *Call it* an imitation, and it is excellent.

The best of the three poems, then, is "Sleep On!" I see Keats in it, and one or both of the Brownings; but though the form is borrowed, the passion is genuine, — the fire has passed along there, and the verse has followed before the ashes were quite cool.

Talent, certainly; taste very fine for the melodies of language; deep, quiet sentiment. Genius? If beardless, yea; if in sable silvered, — and I think this cannot be a very young hand, — why, then . . . we will suspend our opinion.

TO CHARLES ELIOT NORTON.

BOSTON, *August* 12, 1859.

MY DEAR CHARLES, — I must write a line at least to thank you for my kind welcome and most delightful visit. Nothing but my own capricious infirmity [1] prevented it from being a week of unmingled pleasure. I begin to think I must have fed on (atmospheric) poisons, like Mithridates, so that the blessed air of Newport is to my perverted organs as chlorine to reasonable ones. All my troubles wear off in a few days after my return. This morning I am very nearly right. Did you ever think what a striking illustration such cases — which I think are not uncommon — afford of the relation of the sinful soul to the holy state of here and hereafter? "Carry me back! Oh, carry me back!" the sinner would cry by the waves of the River of Life or in the streets of the New Jerusalem; "I shall suffocate in this celestial air, — I am poisoned by these limpid waters!"

[1] The asthma.

But though my body suffered somewhat for its sinful second nature, my mind and heart were more refreshed than I can tell you. I had been stationary too long, — I wanted a brief change of some kind, and those few days in your bright home were like the drops of water dashed on the forehead of one whose eyes are just beginning to see twilight and his lips whitening.

Let me be just too to my own home-loving disposition — this brief absence made all around me fresher and happier than when I left it. I came back as the sick man to his chamber, to find that the windows have been opened and the bed has been shaken up, and he is a new creation in a new world. Such a week irons a year's creases out of one's forehead.

Remember me in all honor and love to your mother and sisters, and tell Miss Grace that I don't know whether to call her a diamond set in pearls or a pearl set in diamonds.

Your grateful and affectionate cousin.

TO JAMES T. FIELDS.[1]

$100.00.

MY DEAR SIR, — The above is an argument of great weight to all those who, like the late John Rogers, are surrounded by a numerous family.

I will incubate this golden egg two days, and present you with the resulting chicken upon the third.

Yours very truly.

P. S. You will perceive that the last sentence is figurative, and implies that I shall watch and fast over your proposition for forty-eight hours. But I

[1] Reprinted from *The Century Magazine,* February, 1895.

could n't on any account be so sneaky as to get up and recite poor old " Hanover " over again. Oh, no! If anything, it must be of the *paullo majora*.

" Silvæ sint consule dignæ." Let us have a brand-new poem or none.

Yours as on the preceding page.

TO JAMES T. FIELDS.[1]

21 CHARLES STREET, *July* 6, 8.33 A. M.
Barometer at 30$\frac{1}{16}$.

MY DEAR FRIEND AND NEIGHBOR: Your most unexpected gift, which is not a mere token of remembrance, but a permanently valuable present, is making me happier every moment I look at it. It is so pleasant to be thought of by our friends when they have so much to draw their thoughts away from us; it is so pleasant, too, to find that they have cared enough about us to study our special tastes, — that you can see why your beautiful gift has a growing charm for me. Only Mrs. Holmes thinks it ought to be in the parlor among the things for show, and I think it ought to be in the study, where I can look at it at least once an hour every day of my life.

I have observed some extraordinary movements of the index of the barometer during the discussions that ensued, which you may be interested to see my notes of: —

Barometer.

Mrs. H.

My dear, we shall of course keep this beautiful barometer in the parlor. *Fair.*

Dr. H.

Why, no, my dear; the study is the place. *Dry.*

[1] Reprinted from *The Century Magazine*, February, 1895.

Mrs. H.

I'm sure it ought to go in the parlor. It's too
handsome for your old den.   *Change.*

Dr. H.

I shall keep it in the study.   *Very dry.*

Mrs. H.

I don't think that's fair.   *Rain.*

Dr. H.

I'm sorry. Can't help it.   *Very dry.*

Mrs. H.

It's — too — too — ba-a-ad.   *Much rain.*

Dr. H.

(Music omitted.)

'Mid pleas-ures and paaal-a-a-c-es.   *Set Fair.*

Mrs. H.

I *will* have it ! You horrid —   *Stormy.*

You see what a wonderful instrument this is that
you have given me.   But, my dear Mr. Fields, while
I watch its changes it will be a constant memorial
of unchanging friendship; and while the dark hand
of fate is traversing the whole range of mortal vicis-
situdes, the golden index of the kind affections shall
stand always at SET FAIR.

TO JAMES T. FIELDS.[1]

296 BEACON STREET, *February* 11, 1862.

MY DEAR MR. FIELDS, — On Friday evening last
I white-cravated myself, took a carriage, and found
myself at your door at eight of the clock P. M.

A cautious female responded to my ring, and opened
the chained portal about as far as a clam opens his
shell to see what is going on in Cambridge Street,
where he is waiting for a customer.

Her first glance impressed her with the convic-

1 Reprinted from *The Century Magazine*, February, 1895.

tion that I was a burglar. The mild address with which I accosted her removed that impression, and I rose in the moral scale to the comparatively elevated position of what the unfeeling world calls a "sneak-thief."

By dint, however, of soft words, and that look of ingenuous simplicity by which I am so well known to you and all my friends, I coaxed her into the belief that I was nothing worse than a rejected contributor, an autograph collector, an author with a volume of poems to dispose of, or other disagreeable but not dangerous character.

She unfastened the chain, and I stood before her.

> I calmed her fears, and she was calm
> And told

me how you and Mrs. F. had gone to New York, and how she knew nothing of any literary debauch that was to come off under your roof, but would go and call another unprotected female who knew the past, present, and future, and could tell me why this was thus, that I had been lured from my fireside by the *ignis fatuus* of a deceptive invitation.

It was my turn to be afraid, alone in the house with two of the stronger sex; and I retired.

On reaching home, I read my note and found it was Friday the 16th, not the 9th, I was invited for. . . .

Dear Mr. Fields, I shall be very happy to come to your home on Friday evening, the 16th February, at eight o'clock, to meet yourself and Mrs. Fields, and hear Mr. James read his paper on Emerson.

TO JAMES FREEMAN CLARKE.[1]

June 28, 1864.

Ex dono auctoris. Thank you, my dear friend, for the volume you have kindly sent me, recalling many profitable hours — I think I am safe in saying *many* — which I have spent in listening to some among the discourses it contains.

I have been feeling your texts (which as you know are the pulses of sermons), and from these I have stolen my way along until I got my hand on the hearts of a good number of them. I think you and I are not ardent admirers of sermons in general. They are last year's bird's-nests, for the most part, — dried apples in loaded orchards, — the empty phials that sick men have drained, and died notwithstanding, — the skins of the wise serpents, out of which they have crept, carrying their brains with them. Nothing but a pile of old prescriptions is worse reading. If I did not feel very sure you agree with me, I should apologize for my prelude.

Now the beauty of your sermons is, that they have eggs in them, fragrant juices in them, strengthening cordials in them, sound brains in them, — and therefore you and I are logically bound to approve, to admire, and to applaud them. I have always done my part in the way of approbation, admiration, and applause; but as authors are apt sometimes to undervalue themselves, I want you to take my word for it that your discourses, read or heard, are the *aurum potabile* of spiritual medicine. Less fancifully, they are first perfectly *human* (which theology has not commonly

[1] In response to the gift of a volume of sermons, *The Hour which Cometh.*

been at all — still less divine) ; full of faith, full of
courage, full of kindness and large charity ; tender,
yet searching the realities of things with true manly
thought; poetical, yet with a great deal of plain common sense, — sermons that will always be good reading,
because they reach down even below Christianity to
that plutonic core of nature over which all revelations
must stratify their doctrines.

Thank you for being good, for being brave, true,
tender, brotherly to all mankind, sinners included, for
thinking such good thoughts, for preaching them, for
printing them, and once more for sending them to
your loving friend and classmate.

TO JAMES T. FIELDS.[1]

21 CHARLES STREET, *July* 17, 1864.

MY DEAR MR. FIELDS, — *Can* you tell me anything that will get this horrible old woman of the
C—— California off from my shoulders? Do you
know anything about this pestilent manuscript she
raves about? This continent is not big enough for
me and her together, and if she does n't jump into the
Pacific I shall have to leap into the Atlantic, — I mean
the original damp spot so called.

P. S. To avoid the necessity of the latter, I have
written to her, cordially recommending suicide as
adapted to her case.

[1] Reprinted from *The Century Magazine*, February, 1895.

TO JAMES FREEMAN CLARKE.[1]

January 25 (1865 ?).

MY DEAR FRIEND AND CLASSMATE, — I have not read the "Address" which you have kindly sent me, though I have taken a clairvoyant look through [it] and seen how greatly I shall delight to read it.

I know your fine critical sense, the many facets of your nature, which press, each in turn, so squarely against every side of human nature itself, living or reproduced in literature.

Therefore your talk about that rose diamond, who reflected everything, is of very great interest to me. The criticism of different minds is like the astronomer's parallax, — nay, it is the photographer's portraits. Did we not think our friend had one face, and has not the photographer taught us he has a hundred, a million — that he is all the time shedding faces, of which these artists catch a dozen or two, but which are in number as the sands of the seashore? So there are innumerous Shakespeares, and among them all there is none I want to know more than yours.

Thank you again for the great pleasure you promise me.

TO WILLIAM AMORY.

21 CHARLES STREET, *April* 22, 1865.

DEAR MR. AMORY, — I am promised my *Rebellion Record* next week, Monday, I think, and I will look it over for poems.

All I will mention now are these : —

[1] Acknowledging receipt of a printed copy of an address by Dr. Clarke before the Historic Genealogical Society of Boston, in 1864, on the tercentenary of Shakespeare's birth.

" The River Fight,"
" The Bay Fight,"
both by Henry Howard Brownell, of East Hartford,
Conn., who was with Farragut in his battles.

" The Old Sergeant,"
by Forceythe Willson, a wonderful poem for direct-
ness and literalness of narrative, combined with an
imaginative grandeur which makes it one of the most
impressive poems in our literature, — I should be
inclined to say in any literature.

"Sheridan's Ride," by T. B. Read, I suppose you
know. It is very spirited, but imperfect in execution.

Of the Rebel songs, the best I know are "Mary-
land " and " That 's Stonewall Jackson's way."

There are some verses beginning

"Whoop ! the Doodles are broken loose,"

which are very lively and stinging.

I take it for granted that you know the poems of
Longfellow, Lowell, Mrs. Howe, and the rest of your
neighbors, who have written more or less about the
war.

The Song of the war is, after all, the John Brown
song. To be sure some of the verses are nonsense or
worse, but the first stanza and one at least of the
others, with the tune, closing with Hallelujah, come
nearest to the " Marseillaise," in effect and as an expression of the feeling of the time, of all that the war
has produced. Mrs. Howe has written some good
words to the tune, beginning, —

"Mine eyes have seen the glory of the coming of the Lord."

Mr. Brownell has also written some good verses to
the same tune.

If you get his volume, be sure that it is the *second*

edition, 1864. The first has not "The Bay Fight" or "The River Fight."

. . . .

I have just copied off the Agassiz poem for you, — I am afraid you will be frightened when you see how long it is.

Very truly yours.

TO JAMES T. FIELDS.[1]

MONTREAL, *October* 23, 1867.

DEAR MR. FIELDS, — ... I am as comfortable here as I can be, but I have earned my money, for I have had a full share of my old trouble.[1] Last night was better, and to-day I am going about the town. Miss Frothingham sent me a basket of black Hamburg grapes to-day, which were very grateful after the hotel tea and coffee and other 'pothecary's stuff.

Don't talk to me about taverns! There is just one genuine, clean, decent, palatable thing occasionally to be had in them — namely, a boiled egg. The soups *taste* pretty good sometimes, but their sources are involved in a darker mystery than that of the Nile. Omelettes taste as if they had been carried in the waiter's hat, or fried in an old boot. I ordered scrambled eggs one day. It must be that they had been scrambled for by *somebody*, but who — who in the possession of a sound reason *could* have scrambled for what I had set before me under that name? Butter! I am thinking just now of those exquisite little pellets I have so often seen at your table, and wondering why the taverns *always* keep it until it is old. Fool that

[1] Reprinted from *The Century Magazine*, February, 1895.
[2] Asthma.

I am! As if the taverns did not know that if it was good it would be eaten, which is not what they want. Then the waiters with their napkins — what don't they do with those napkins! Mention any one thing of which you think you can say with truth, "*That* they do not do." . . .

I have a really fine parlor, but every time I enter it I perceive that

Still, sad "odor" of humanity

which clings to it from my predecessor. Mr. Hogan got home yesterday, I believe. I saw him for the first time to-day. He was civil — they all are civil. I have no fault to find except with taverns here and pretty much everywhere.

Every six months a tavern should burn to the ground, with all its traps, its "properties," its beds and pots and kettles, and start afresh from its ashes like John Phœnix-Squibob!

No; give me home, or a home like mine, where all is clean and sweet, where coffee has preëxisted in the berry, and tea has still faint recollections of the pigtails that dangled about the plant from which it was picked, where butter has not the prevailing character which Pope assigned to Denham, where soup could look you in the face if it had "eyes" (which it has not), and where the comely Anne or the gracious Margaret takes the place of these napkin-bearing animals.

Enough! But I have been forlorn and ailing and fastidious — but I am feeling a little better, and can talk about it. I had some ugly nights, I tell you; but I am writing in good spirits, as you see. I have written once before to Low, as I think I told you, and on the 25th mean to go to a notary with Mr. Dawson, as he tells me it is the right thing to do.

P. S. Made a pretty good dinner, after all; but better a hash at home than a roast with strangers.

BOSTON, *July* 10, 1869.

MY DEAR FIELDS, — I got your charming letter yesterday, with all its pleasant things, — who ever knew like you to find something to cheer and encourage everybody that he thinks will feel better for a kind word! And the daisy from Alloway Kirkyard too, — I think I see the very hillock it grew on in my stereograph. We are getting flowers from you at home meantime very often, for one comes with bouquets gathered from your Charles Street garden and leaves them for Mrs. H. every few days. Yet we miss you, be very sure; indeed, we could hardly pass your house for the first weeks of your absence without a turn of that form of homesickness one feels when others, whom he depends upon to make home what it is, are away. Very few friends can be so ill spared; believe me when I say it to you, for I have said it a hundred times to others.

You know what we have been doing about here, no doubt. How we have had a great Jubilee, the funny effect of which was the acute paroxysm of jealousy it excited in some of our neighbors. I don't know that anything better was said about it than that of the *Daily*, — viz., that New York had the Big Elephant (there is a monster one there just now) and the Green-Eyed Monster, — the latter the biggest in the *World* (which was specially malicious).

The "Peace Jubilee" was a mighty success, — a sensation of a lifetime. It subdued everybody to it self except the Great Pedlington malignants. They are beginning to talk about getting up one themselves, after having abused ours until the country laughed at them. The two worst papers were the *Tribune* and the *World;* some of the others — the *Herald* and *Frank Leslie's* among the rest — were all right.

I have been in correspondence with Mrs. Stowe about her Byron article coming out in the September *Atlantic*. She asked me to look over her proofs, which I did very diligently, and made various lesser suggestions, which she received very kindly and adopted. It will be more widely read, of course, than any paper which has been written for a long time.

．　．　．　．　．　．　．　．　．　．　．

You ask me about my new "venture." I wrote a good deal this spring, but of late I have not written, waiting until various matters were off my mind, and perhaps until the heats of summer are over. I cannot promise anything positively as yet, but as you know my habits and dispositions you can guess that there is a fair chance, and that I shall probably let you know in season.

I enclose you two copies of verses, as my friend of *The Nation* calls my versified misfortunes. The first consists of only four stanzas, read as a sequel to a longer poem written for our last class meeting, in which the "Boatswain of '29" gives advice to younger craft how to keep their crews and avoid shipwreck. The other verses will explain themselves. They were "written by request" of the committee.

With our best love, my own and my wife's, to both of you, and longing wishes for your safe and speedy return, I am

Always yours.

December 8, 1869.

MY DEAR DR. HEDGE, — You told me that I *need* not read the book which you have sent me, and for which I cordially thank you; but you did not tell me I *must* not read it. Now I have read it, every word of it, and I wish to say to you that I have had too much pleasure in reading it to be denied the privilege of telling you how I have enjoyed it. I am struck with the union of free thought and reverential feeling, — with the ingenuity of many of your comments and explanations, which yet commend themselves as having at least a reasonable degree of probability. Cain and Abel, for instance, became so naturally representatives of the nomadic herdsman and the tiller of the ground, with his fences and actions of trespass, that I have quite forgotten my primitive picture of the two men with rugs round their middles, one of whom is trying the then new experiment of hitting the other on the head, to see what effect it would have on their fraternal and celestial relations. It is strange how we read these stories, like children, until some wiser teacher shows us the full-grown meaning they hide under their beautiful simple forms. I will not say positively that I should agree with all your glosses; but they are incomparable in contrast with any others I have read. The truth is staring the Christian world in the face, that the stories of the old Hebrew books cannot be taken as literal statements of fact. But the property of the church is so large and so mixed up with its vested beliefs, that it is hopeless to expect anything like honest avowal of the convictions which there can be little doubt intelligent churchmen of many denominations, if not of all, entertain. It is best, I suppose, it should be so, for take idolatry and bibliolatry out of the world all at once, as the magnetic mountain drew the nails and bolts of Sindbad's ship, and the vessel that floats much of the best of our humanity would resolve itself in a floating ruin of planks and timbers.

I am struck, too, with the poetical style of many of your discourses. In truth, you have written more *verses* than you may perhaps be aware of. Here are some of them : —

"Our characters alone are truly ours," p. 20. "Not years but centuries chronicle its ebb," p. 64. "Marble and brass have crumbled into dust," p. 123. "As slow as that which shaped the solid earth by long accretion from the fiery deep," p. 144.

"Both are births of one creative word,
  Both agencies of one Almighty Power," p. 142.

"Are inconsistent with the crowded life
  Which such longevity must needs engender," p. 148.

. . . "A veritable piece of history,"
"Embracing centuries in its term and scope," } p. 220.
"That wondrous tower of Babel is a fact," }

"Still serves a landmark to the nomad tribes" (!).

Pray tell me if you knew you were writing verse, or were you in the case of M. Jourdain ? In the mean time, thanking you for your charming and noble commentaries on the grand old book,

I am always gratefully yours.

April 14, 1872.

MY DEAR FRIEND AND CLASSMATE, — A large part of my Sunday has been passed with you, — for I have been reading in the *Ten Great Religions* most of the afternoon (instead of going to church, sinner that I am (or not)), and I have just finished the Address at the Dedication, which I had not read until this evening.

I am not going to pay you cheap compliments about a work which embodies the studies and thoughts of so many years, but I am going to thank you for writing it. You could not have chosen any task which I should have been so grateful for, and you have performed it in a way which, if I can judge by my own impressions, must be in the highest degree acceptable to that very large class of readers who wish to have some clear idea of the comparative anatomy (to steal one of my own terms) of religion.

The book is full of interest, and ought to be read by all the millions of rural and metropolitan and cosmopolitan provincials, who think the Almighty never cared a shekel for any of his children except a pack of rebellious Jews and some fifty or sixty generations of squabbling and fighting Christians.

The Address is in the best taste, and made the water stand in my eyes, as Christiana had it stand in hers, you will remember. But I said I would not trouble you with praise, — only this I must say: I don't know anybody whose brain and heart have grown quite so steadily together as yours, — and if I could look back on such a record as you can, I should feel that I ought to be very thankful for having always been guided to the right side, and having always done good service to the noblest causes — truth, freedom, charity, human brotherhood.

I am very glad my lecture amused you.

TO MRS. CAROLINE L. KELLOGG.

BOSTON, *October* 27, 1872.

MY DEAR MRS. KELLOGG, — I was greatly obliged to you for the picture of the old Puritan Colonel, who got into the pulpit mistaking it for the saddle. He ought to have led a charge of dragoons shouting forth, "The sword of the Lord and of Gideon," and had that knotty old frontispiece of his ornamented with half-a-dozen good sabre-cuts. There are a good many soldiers who had better have preached, but it is only now and then that one sees a preacher who was clearly meant for a trooper. However, I don't doubt that he has charged on the hosts of Satan as lustily as he would have pitched into the ranks of the Southern fire-eaters.

I was not a little pleased too that you and Mrs. Stowe agreed in a charitable opinion about such a heretic as I am. The real truth is, these Beechers are so chock-full of good, sound, square-stepping, strong-hearted humanity that they cannot shut the doors of their sympathies against Jew or Gentile. I find everywhere, except among the older sort of people — (you and I must be old too, in time, but even I am not old yet) — and the smaller kind of human potatoes, there is much more real "catholicism," much more feeling that we are all in the same boat and the boat in a fog, than there was when I was studying Calvin's essence of Christianity in the Assembly's

Catechism. So I can understand how a couple of good-hearted and large-souled women manage to tolerate the existence of such a person as I am. But to be spoken of so very kindly as you say Mrs. Stowe spoke of me made me color up so that I thought at first you had written on pink paper, — it was the reflection of my blushes.

You had a good time at your celebration, as I knew you would, without getting me up there to tag rhymes together after the eloquent and elegant George had exhausted all your sensibilities. Spunky town, Pittsfield! Jubilees and celebrations are sure to go off well there. How I sometimes long for a sight of Saddle Mountain! But then I should have to go down to our old place, and I could not make up my mind to do it. I should (want to) cry so as to make Sackett's Brook run over its banks, and there would be danger of a freshet in the Housatonic. A thousand thanks again, and remember me to your husband and children, and to Mrs. Newton when you see her.

TO BISHOP LEE.

December 6, 1879.

MY DEAR BISHOP-SCHOOLMATE-FRIEND, — I was more pleased — I *am* more pleased, I should say, for I have just read your letter — at receiving your kind message of remembrance than I can tell in the few words to which my tired right hand restricts me. I cannot forget the interest you showed in my early papers in *The Atlantic*, or the friendly admonition, not unwelcome, sweet and gracious as it was, that I should be careful in dealing with the great subjects on which I had sometimes ventured. I think you will agree with me that since that time a remarkable change has taken place in the attitude of men towards each other in all that relates to spiritual matters, especially in this respect: that Protestantism is more respectful in its treatment of Romanism, Orthodoxy in its treatment of Heterodoxy, supernaturalism in its treatment of naturalism, Christianity in its handling of humanity. The limitations of men are better realized, the impossibility of their thinking alike more fully recognized, the virtue of humility found to include many things which have often been considered outside of its province, — among others the conviction of the infallibility of our own special convictions in matters of belief, which appeal differently to different minds. I have tried to do my share in enlarging the spiritual charity of mankind, and though it is delicate, perhaps dangerous work, as our well-being in this and all other worlds rests in faith and obedience, I hope, if I have done anything, it has been useful, not harmful. It was well, I think, that you and others should have given me affectionate cautions, and I love you all the better for having done it.

Believe me, my dear old friend, sincerely and affectionately yours.

TO JOHN O. SARGENT.

June 8, 1877.

MY DEAR JOHN, — It sounded so good — or looked so good — to be addressed as Wendell! Few, few are there who call me by that name. Herman Inches, James Russell Lowell, — who else besides these and yourself? I got your letter two or three days ago,

and read it at once.   Now I have just read it again,
aloud to my wife, and the whole poem too, which I
find mighty pleasant, really Horatian in its whole tone
and spirit.   You write better than you did in the days
of *The Collegian,* — you wrote remarkably well then,
but there is an ease about this version which only
a somewhat mellow stage of life can give to prose or
verse.   Those graceful adaptations of Roman life to
New York scenes and persons are very taking.   I
shall go to bed and dream that

> " On terrapin and Clos Vougeot
> I 'm lunching with Delmonico."

I return Barnes's letter to you, — it is full of good
feeling, — its only fault is that it is hard to read.   I
did n't know that *men* ever criss-crossed their letters,
— don't I know that women do!   I have had fifty
bushels (more or less) of letters from women, since I
have been somewhat known as an author.   If I had
been as good-looking as you, I suppose I should have
been made a fool of, but I am 'umble about personal
advantages.   Besides, I remember Alexandre Dumas
or some other Frenchman says that the women who
write to authors are for the most part " laides pour
faire fuir l'armée Russe."   But as I said before, they
do criss-cross their letters in such a way that I feel in
looking at them that the age of miracles is not past
after all.

Do you know why I write in this flippant way?   I
will tell you: this is the eleventh letter I am writing
without stopping to take breath between them, and
my hand has got going like *planchette.*   I am sure, but
for that, I should have written in a different vein, for
I have had enough to sadden me within the past few
months.   The death of ——, to whom I was really

attached, and whose most pleasant companionship I
miss very much, was soon followed by that of my
sister, Mrs. Upham.   Edmund Quincy was not so
much an intimate with me, though an agreeable acquaintance.   But Motley I have been in the closest
relation with, and especially of late since his wife's
death.   Two years ago he spent the summer, or a large
part of it, at Nahant, and I passed generally two
hours or thereabouts with him every day for weeks.
I have also been in constant correspondence with him
for many years.   It is a large gap he leaves in my
friendships, for one makes few new friends in the
later decades of life, and the tap-root of early intimacy reaches deeper down than the looser fibres of
later growth.   Constant occupation leaves none too
much of leisure for mourning over our losses when
they do not invade the circle of daily life.   Perhaps
it is best it should be so, but I sometimes feel as if
I had not waked up to all that I have lost.

I enclose the account of our Unitarian festival, or
rather of my own part in it, — also a copy of " The
First Fan," which you were good enough to speak
well of.

TO JOHN G. WHITTIER.[1]

June 19, 1878.

MY DEAR WHITTIER, — It was very kind in you
to tell me that my Andover poem pleased you.   I
wrote the poem rather as a duty than as a pleasure,
and yet here and there I found myself taken off my
feet by that sudden influx of a tide that comes from
we know not whence, but which makes being, and

[1] This letter has been already printed in Pickard's *Life and
Letters of John Greenleaf Whittier.*

especially internal vision, so intense and real. You, as a poet, know so well what that means! But I will give a trivial illustration, which to my mind is much better than a grander one. In the intensified state of retrospection which came over me, a fact reproduced itself, which I do not believe had come up before for *fifty years.* It was "the upward-slanting floor" of the school-room at the Academy. Not a poetical fact, — and all the better for that, — not an important one, but still a fact which had its place in the old fresco that seemed to have utterly faded from the wall of memory. What an exalted state of vitality that is which thus reproduces obsolete trivialities as a part of its vivid picture, — flashes, — just as in the experience a hundred times recorded of drowning persons who have been rescued! We may become intensely conscious of existence through pleasure or through pain, but we never know ourselves until we have tried both experiences; and I think that some of the most real moments of life are those in which we are seized upon by that higher power, which takes the rudder out of the hands of *will,* as the pilot takes the place of the captain in entering some strange harbor; and I am sure I never know where I am going to be landed from the moment I find myself in the strange hands of the unknown power that has taken control of me. Not that there is much, if any, of what is called "inspiration" in the particular poem that pleases you, — but there are passages, for all that, which I could not write except in the clairvoyant condition. To cover my egotisms, let me say to you unhesitatingly that *you* have written the most beautiful school-boy poem in the English language. I just this moment read it, because I was writing to you,

and before I had got through "In School-Days" the
tears were rolling out of my eyes. Yes, I need not
have said all this to you, as if you did not know it all,
— perhaps I said it because you know it so well.

I am very glad you are interested in Dr. Clarke's
book. I watched him during its preparation, and
discussed many points with him. To me the book is
in every way full of interest, — and it will always be
memorable as having been written in the valley of the
shadow of death. I have left no room for all the feelings I wish to express to you; perhaps they are better
imagined.

TO JOHN G. WHITTIER.[1]

BOSTON, *October* 10, 1878.

MY DEAR WHITTIER, — I know how to thank you
for the poems, but I do not know how to thank you
for the more than kind words which make the little
volume precious. I never was so busy, it seems to
me, what with daily lectures and literary tasks on
hand, and all the interruptions which you know about
so well. But I would not thank you for your sweet
and most cheering remembrance before reading every
poem over, whether I remembered it well or not.
And this has been a great pleasure to me, for you
write from your heart and reach all hearts. My wife
wanted me to read one, — a special favorite of my
own, "The Witch of Wenham," but I told her "No,"
— I knew I should break down before I got through
with it, for it made me tearful again, as it did the first
time I read it.

I was going to say: I thank you; but I would say,

[1] This letter has been already printed in Pickard's *Life and
Letters of John Greenleaf Whittier.*

rather, _ thank God that He has given you the thoughts
and feelings which sing themselves as naturally as the
wood-thrush rings his silver bell, — to steal your own
exquisitely descriptive line. Who has preached the
gospel of love to such a mighty congregation as you
have preached it? Who has done so much to sweeten
the soul of Calvinistic New England? You have your
reward here in the affection with which all our people,
who are capable of loving anybody, regard you. I
trust you will find a still higher in that world the
harmonies of which find an echo in so many of your
songs.

TO GEORGE ABBOT JAMES.

296 BEACON STREET, December 26, 1879.

MY DEAR GEORGE, — We — for we do not know
each other apart very well — are greatly obliged by
your kind remembrance, and mightily pleased with the
Royal token of it. Louis Philippe, " le Roi Citoyen,"
was my monarch for nearly three years. I remember
visiting his palace at Fontainebleau, but he did not ask
me to stay, — not being there, probably, at the time.
I cannot help recalling a French lesson I got *apropos*
of that visit.

With two other students — Sam Wigglesworth was
one of them — I was seated in front of the Diligence on the imperial, if I remember the name correctly. The great vehicle entered a courtyard at
Fontainebleau, making a sudden turn, and if we had
not bobbed our heads very quickly and very humbly,
there would have been three letters with black seals
sent to America by the next sailing-vessel. As soon
as we were inside the courtyard I exclaimed in loud
tones to the driver : " Vous avez manqué de tuer trois

gentilshommes." I got consumedly laughed at for using the word I have underscored, — *noblemen*, they said it meant — when speaking of *trois étudiants*.

See, now, how your beautiful gift wakes up old recollections — the stately palace, the noble park-forest; rather, the great trees, — I remember one in particular, *le bouquet du Roi*, — the weeping rock (*la roche qui pleure*), and the pale woman with her sick child, catching the drops to give him; *Ça donne de la force*, she said. All these, and many another recollection, are summoned as I read the word "Fontainebleau" on the exquisite Sèvres porcelain.

But better than all this is the feeling that the cup, which held — or may have held — the coffee for a king's breakfast, comes holding what kings cannot always command, the kind wishes of one whose friendship we are sure of.

With our love to yourself and Lily, from both of us, for both of us.

TO JOHN GREENLEAF WHITTIER.[1]

March 6, 1881.

I have sweetened this Sunday afternoon by reading the poems in the precious little volume you sent me a few days ago. Some were new to me; others, as you ought to know, are well known. I have not forgotten your kind words for my evening breakfast. If you happen to have seen an article in the March — or was it February? — *North American*, you will have noticed, it may be, my reference to "The Minister's Daughter," and to yourself as preaching the Gospel

[1] Reproduced from Pickard's *Life of John Greenleaf Whittier*, ii. 667.

of Love to a larger congregation than any minister addresses. I never rise from any of your poems without feeling the refreshment of their free and sweet atmosphere. I may find more perfume in one than in another, — as one does in passing from one flowery field into the next. I may find more careful planting in this or in that, as in different garden-beds, but there is always the morning air of a soul that breathes freely, and always the fragrance of a loving spirit. Again that sweetest "Minister's Daughter" brought the tears into my eyes — and out of them. Again I read with emotion that generous tribute ["The Lost Occasion"] to the man whom, living, we so longed to admire without a reservation; of whom, dead, you write with such a noble humanity. I must not speak too warmly of the lines whose kindness I feel so deeply, only wishing I had deserved such a tribute better. But of the poem which comes next, "Garrison," I can speak; and I will say that it has the strenuous tone, the grave music, of your highest mood, — which, I believe, is the truest and best expression of the New England inner life which it has ever found, at least in versified utterance. I have forgotten to thank you for remembering me, and especially for the way in which you remember me, for I did not miss the words which made my blood warm, as I read them on the fly-leaf. Let me say — for it means more than you can know — that no written or printed words come into our household on which my wife, a very true-hearted woman, looks with so much interest as on yours.

TO JAMES FREEMAN CLARKE.[1]

April 6, 1881.

My DEAR JAMES, — Many thanks for your book, in which I have read a good deal, selecting the parts which most interested me, and have found them full of interest, carefully studied and vividly presented. I should think this book must have a wider circulation than anything you have written, and though many readers will say they accept more of the Christian story as fact, and others less, than you do, yet all will agree that the narrative is admirable, the sweet reasonableness that runs through it all enough to disarm all angry criticisms. There is only one grave objection to so wise and good a teacher as you are, — it is, that he renders the supernatural less probable by showing us what excellence a man may reach without being born out of the natural order or endowed with more than the human divine attributes.

TO BISHOP LEE.

January 25, 1883.

My DEAR BISHOP, — I am sorry that you should have been put to the trouble to answer a letter about me. I know nothing of the writer except that he applied to me for my experiences of life. I offered him the same outline of its chief epochs as I do to others who are curious about my personality, and told him that another gentleman, a man of some literary standing, was beforehand with him, and that I had promised him the incidents to help out his narrative.

[1] Acknowledging the receipt of *The Legend of Thomas Didymus.*

This pursuit of the biographers is like the poor young prince's "baptism of fire," — a kind of necessity to authors who reach a certain amount of publicity. To shield myself from the fusillade I had some copies of the main facts of my life made, and I dodge behind these when they open fire.

There is one pleasant thing about it, — it brought me a letter from an honored and beloved old school-mate of my tender years. I am very glad to hear that you are well and happy, as you ought to be, with a long, diligent, useful, and dignified career to look back upon.

I did not give up my professorship from any kind of infirmity, mental or bodily, but because my services in literature were called for on such terms that I could not resist the advantages they offered. Like all the rest of us, I feel the effects of age; but I enjoy life and work, and may possibly do a good deal of writing before I am done with. I have become quite attached to this particular planet, with which I have been so long acquainted. I wish I could believe that we may be able to take a peep at it now and then from the height of a future existence. I can hardly conceive of its losing its interest for those who have been cradled on it. I do not know whether this is quite Orthodox, but it is mighty human.

I hope I may some time have the pleasure of meeting you at one of our Harvard Commencements, but I suppose you find, as I do, that every year makes it harder and harder to get away from the fireside. Wishing you, in return for your kind expressions, all the blessings that the evening of life can bring, I am

Your once little schoolmate, now your old friend.

May 15, 1887.

MY DEAR JOHN, — Isn't it a comfort to be called by your Chris'n name by one to whom it "comes natural" to do so? Yes, you are John and I am Wendell till the stars are opposite our names in the Quinquennial.

I delight in finding that [you] are as much alive as ever. If there are two of you, so much the better ; — we can't have too many John O.'s. I did not see your double at the Governor's, and I never saw Wade Hampton ; so whether he has the honor of looking like you I cannot say.

> "Cope could not cope, nor Wade wade through the snow,
> Nor Hawley haul his cannon to the foe."

Wade would have liked to wade through the blood of our soldiers, I suppose, as far as Bunker Hill, — but he didn't. No, my dear John, look like yourself, — you were never an unhandsome-looking fellow.

I am so glad to see that you stick to your Horace. I read your translations with great delight as soon as they came, and have them lying by me to read again. I found them admirable. The fact is, you have lived in Horace so intimately and so long that you have got his flavor into your very marrow, and feel and talk just as that grand Roman gentleman did. You would have been good company for Mæcenas. I wish I had become as familiar with some classic author as you are with Horace. There is nothing like one of those perennial old fellows for good old gentlemanly reading ; and for wit and wisdom, what is there to compare with the writings of Horace? You make me envious, — I vow I shall have to get up Juvenal or Catullus, naughty but nice, or somebody that nobody else knows about — Silius Italicus — or mediæval Vida " on whose classic brow," etc., etc., or George Buchanan. I get so tired of the damp sheets of all sorts of *literati* just out of the press, — of screeching rhymesters (worse than the " screeching women of Marblehead "), and clamorous essayists, that I want something always by me, calm, settled beyond cavilling criticism, — a cool, clear draught of Falernian that has been somewhere near two thousand years in the cellar.

I hope you will go on and translate all the Odes and as much else of Horace's as you have the courage to attack.

TO JOHN O. SARGENT.

November 16, 1888.

DEAR JOHN, — Next to a good poem is a good criticism on it. I have been reading the Ode " Justum et tenacem " carefully, and your translation and commentary. I feel as if I had never taken the noble poem in before. How brave a scholiast was in Sargent — no, not *lost* by ever so much, for you will live to print that volume of "Translations " with notes critical and explanatory, and I hope I shall live to receive a presentation copy.

I find the translation and the elucidation of the poem admirable. I shall catch your Horatio-mania, I am afraid, for I have so many irons in the fire that I dread a new temptation.

" Si fractus illabatur orbis
Impavidum ferient ruinæ."

I remember contrasting that magnificent utterance of old Pagan manhood with the abject terrors of the

Dies irœ. Which is the nobler attitude for one of God's human creatures ?

It seems to me that we are both pretty bright for old friends that can begin their old stories with the second title of Waverley, " 'T is sixty years since."

September 2, 1889.

Here I am at your side among the octogenarians.

. . . .

You know all about it. You know why I have not thanked you before this for your beautiful and precious tribute, which would make any birthday memorable. I remember how you were overwhelmed with tributes on the occasion of your own eightieth birthday, and you can understand the impossibility I find before me of responding in any fitting shape to all the tokens of friendship which I receive. . . . I hope, dear Whittier, that you find much to enjoy in the midst of all the lesser trials which old age must bring with it. You have kind friends all around you, and the love and homage of your fellow-countrymen as few have enjoyed them, with the deep satisfaction of knowing that you have earned them, not merely by the gifts of your genius, but by a noble life which has ripened without a flaw into a grand and serene old age. I never see my name coupled with yours, as it often is nowadays, without feeling honored by finding myself in such company, and wishing that I were more worthy of it. . . . I am living here with my daughter-in-law, and just as I turned this leaf I heard

[1] Reproduced from Pickard's *Life of John Greenleaf Whittier*, ii. 741.

wheels at the door, and she got out, leading in in triumph her husband, His Honor, Judge Holmes of the Supreme Court of Massachusetts, just arrived from Europe by the Scythia. I look up to him as my magistrate, and he knows me as his father, but my arms are around his neck and his moustache is sweeping my cheek, — I feel young again at four-score.

TO JOHN C. TRAUTWINE, JR.

BOSTON, *April* 29, 1891.

MY DEAR SIR, — Your letter was — is, I should say — in many respects very gratifying to me. I try to remember Bacon's precept always, and I apply it specially to this letter of yours ; — it is well worn, but you will let me repeat it : —

"Read not to contradict and refute; not to believe and take for granted; not to find talk and discourse; but to weigh and consider."

I notice that you are J. C. T. *Junior*. Do you suppose I want you, a young man, to take the severe views of the future that I, a confirmed octogenarian, do? No, I am very willing to see you and other young persons more sanguine than myself in their views of a possible condition of humanity which I cannot believe in as they do, but *towards* which, as an unattainable ideal, many practical measures may be instituted which will prove serviceable. The best examples I can find of a truly realized communistic society are to be looked for among the Shakers, who have no wives nor children, and the ants, who have no brains. But I would get a lesson from both, — adopt some things from the Shaker communities and some from the excellently ordered and thoroughly socialistic ant-villages.

I do not pretend to answer all the letters I receive with my own hand, as it would take all my time to do it, but I was unwilling to hand your letter over to my secretary, and I thank you personally for your friendly way of [showing me] what you think is my error, — an error, if it be one, of no great consequence in a writer who has survived his generation, and can hardly be expected to see the future with the eyes of his children and grandchildren.

TO JOHN G. WHITTIER.[1]

[1891.]

I congratulate you upon having climbed another glacier and crossed another crevasse in your ascent of the white summit which already begins to see the morning twilight of the coming century. A life so well filled as yours has been cannot be too long for your fellow-men. In their affections you are secure, whether you are with them here, or near them in some higher life than theirs. I hope your years have not become a burden, so that you are tired of living. At our age we must live chiefly in the past: happy is he who has a past like yours to look back upon. It is one of the felicitous incidents — I will not say accidents — of my life, that the lapse of time has brought us very near together, so that I frequently find myself honored by seeing my name mentioned in near connection with your own. We are lonely, very lonely, in these last years. The image which I have used before this in writing to you recurs once more to my thought. We were on deck together as we began the

---

[1] Reproduced from Pickard's *Life of John Greenleaf Whittier*, ii. 755.

voyage of life two generations ago. A whole generation passed, and the succeeding one found us in the
cabin with a goodly number of coevals. Then the
craft which held us began going to pieces, until a few
of us were left on the raft pieced together of its fragments. And now the raft has at last parted, and you
and I are left clinging to the solitary spar, which is
all that still remains afloat of the sunken vessel.

I have just been looking over the headstones in Mr.
Griswold's cemetery, entitled *The Poets and Poetry
of America*. In that venerable receptacle, just com-
pleting its half century of existence — for the date of
the edition before me is 1842 — I find the names of
John Greenleaf Whittier and Oliver Wendell Holmes
next each other, in their due order, as they should be.
All around are the names of the dead — too often of
forgotten dead. Three which I see there are still
living: Mr. John Osborne Sargent, who makes Horace
his own by faithful study, and ours by scholarly translation; Isaac McLellan, who was writing in 1830,
and whose last work is dated 1886; and Christopher
P. Cranch, whose poetical gift has too rarely found
expression. Of these many dead, you are the most
venerated, revered, and beloved survivor; of these
few living, the most honored representative. Long
may it be before you leave a world where your influence has been so beneficent, where your example has
been such inspiration, where you are so truly loved,
and where your presence is a perpetual benediction.

TO CHARLES ELIOT NORTON.

296 BEACON STREET, *October* 17, 1891.

MY DEAR *Friend*, — You must feel the meaning
of that word more and more, as I do certainly, as, one

after another, those whose friendship means most for me are taken away. I think I know what this last supreme loss [1] must be to you, and I assure you I have thought a great deal of your bereavement, and felt a sympathy for you which I have rarely known for any one out of my own family circle. I am sure that his intimacy must have made a large part of your interest in life. During the delivery of his noble poem, read under the Washington elm, I could not keep my eyes from following the expression of your countenance. No Dante in the presence of Beatrice could have shown more truthfully in his features the delight with which he looked at her and listened to her. It impressed me more than all else on that occasion, and I never think of you without seeing your portrait in that exalted state of feeling — I will not say

"breathless with adoration,"

for the phrase might not please you, — but entirely absorbed in the delight which you were experiencing.

I could claim no such intimacy as yours with James, and yet I feel his loss very deeply. He always showed a very kindly feeling towards me, and I owe to him more than to almost any other friend. He early tried to interest me in some of those larger movements in which he was himself active. I recognized the generous aim of his effort, and received his communication not ungraciously. But the little fruit on my poorly built espalier was very slow in ripening, and after that first attempt of his he left me for a long interval to ripen as I might. It was not until 1857 that he appealed to me again, not so much trying to change my ways of thinking and acting as to stimulate me to

[1] The death of James Russell Lowell.

use certain gifts, which he believed I had from nature, for the use of the public.   Though almost a decade younger than myself, I recognized his literary experience and wisdom, and began to believe in myself because he thought so well of me.   From the impulse he gave me I date my best efforts and my nearest approach to success in literary pursuits.   His praise I always felt to be one of my best rewards.

I am rejoiced to know that you are to write the Memoir, for which the world of letters will be impatiently waiting.   No one else could have been thought of, and I hope most sincerely that I may live to see it finished.   But I am lagging beyond my time.   I looked forward to having a few kind words said for me, when I should be gone, by him for whom I have lived to write a requiem such as it was given me to put in words, inadequate, but not falsely colored.

Perhaps I should not have written at this particular moment had I not found on my table your Translation of the first Part of the *Divine Comedy*.   You must finish your work without his eye to review its closing portions.   But his presence will be with you still, as in some degree it is with us all who knew and loved him, luminous, benign, helpful, and rich in thought and learning beyond all others in our circle of knowledge.   I sent you my In Memoriam lines, directed to Ashfield, where I hope they reached you.

TO MRS. JAMES T. FIELDS.[1]

Where this will find you, in a geographical point of view, I do not know; but I know your heart will be in its right place, and accept kindly the few barren words this sheet holds for you. Yes; barren of incident, of news of all sorts, but yet having a certain flavor of Boston, of Cape Ann, and, above all, of dear old remembrances, the suggestion of any one of which is as good as a page of any common letter. So, whatever I write will carry the fragrance of home with it, and pay you for the three minutes it costs you to read it. . . . I find great delight in talking over cathedrals and pictures and English scenery, and all the sights my travelling friends have been looking at, with Mrs. Bell. It seems to me that she knew them all beforehand, so that she was journeying all the time among reminiscences which were hardly distinguishable from realities.

My recollections are to those of other people around me who call themselves old — the sexagenarians, for instance — something like what a cellar is to the ground-floor of a house. The young people in the upper stories (American spelling, *story*) go down to the basement in their inquiries, and think they have got to the bottom; but I go down another flight of steps, and find myself below the surface of the earth, as are the bodies of most of my contemporaries. As to health, I am doing tolerably well. I have just come in from a moderate walk in which I acquitted myself creditably. I take two-hour drives in the after-

[1] Mrs. Fields prints this in her article in *The Century Magazine*, February, 1895, explaining that it was written to her by the Doctor when he was eighty-three years old.

noon, in the open or close carriage, according to the weather; but I do not pretend to do much visiting, and I avoid all excursions when people go to have what they call a " good time."

I am reading right and left — whatever turns up, but especially re-reading old books. Two new volumes of Dr. Johnson's letters have furnished me part of my reading. As for writing, when my secretary comes back, I shall resume my dictation. No literary work ever seemed to me easier or more agreeable than living over my past life, and putting it on record as well as I could. If anybody should ever care to write a sketch or memoir of my life, these notes would help him mightily. My friends, too, might enjoy them, — if I do not have the misfortune to outlive them all. With affectionate regards and all sweet messages to Miss Jewett.

Always your friend,

O. W. Holmes.

INDEX

works, 240; connection with the Saturday Club and love for it, 241–245 (see Saturday Club); his table-talk, 245–252; a few of his sayings, 249, 250; writes *The Professor at the Breakfast-Table*, 252; *The Poet at the Breakfast-Table*, 253–255; comments on sundry symptoms of the times, 255; publishes *Elsie Venner*, 256; objects to dramatization of it, 257; corresponds with Dr. Weir Mitchell about snakes and their venom, 259–262; receives from him a present of a rattlesnake's skin, 260; letter to Mrs. Stowe about the *motif* of *Elsie Venner*, 263; publishes *The Guardian Angel*, 265; *A Mortal Antipathy*, 266; letter to Mr. Ireland about the latter, 267; his relations with religion and the religious world, 267; interest in theology, 268; his humanity, 269; "Americanizing religion," 273; the making of gods, 273; duties of the Creator, 274; kindly to the "crippled souls," 277; sets Science against Free-will, 278; never formulated his own faith, 278, 279; repudiates the "Deity of ecclesiastical commerce," 279; a church-goer, 280; apropos of this, his letter to Bishop Phillips Brooks, 280; would like to have written enduring hymns, 281; remarks about ghosts and psychology, 281; about the orthodox hell, 282; his letters to persons in affliction: to P. Barnes, 283; to W. R. Sturtevant, 284; to Mrs. Dorr, 286; striking letter on immortality to John Lindley, 288; more on same topic, 289–291; his influence in bringing about toleration of varying opinions, 292; letter to J. R. Lowell, defending his abstention from "causes," reforms, etc., 295, and see 326; attitude towards slavery, 296, 300, 303, 304; effect

of the war on his opinions, 305; but he continues to refuse to join associations, apropos of which his letter to Dr. J. F. Clarke, 305; his Fourth of July oration, 1863, 307; efforts with President Cleveland on behalf of James Russell Lowell, 308; feelings towards the South after the war, 309–313; apropos of which are his letters to Alex. P. Morse, 310; and to Paul H. Hayne, 312, 313; demands upon his time by correspondents and others, 313 *et seq.*; conscientious accuracy in giving advice and praise, 316–319; anecdote about his advice to Bret Harte, 318; and to T. B. Aldrich, 318; his liking for simple language, 319; an indifferent writer of letters, 319–321; but a prolific writer of short notes, 321; specimens of short letters and notes, of replies to requests, etc., 322–357; announces birth of son, 322; recipe for the contributor of a rejected article for the *Atlantic*, 325; refuses to appear at a public meeting, 326; describes composition of a lyric as "having a fit," 327; to Dr. E. E. Hale, about the "great unwritten article," 328; recommendations to editors, 329; to Mrs. Kellogg, who asked him to take part on a public occasion, 330; to Miss Sherwood, ditto, 331; about the "Old South," 332; does not wish reëlection as President of Alumni Association, 333; notes concerning writings sent to him for criticism, 334, 339–344; notes about the dinners of the Dental Faculty, or Association, 336–338; declines to write a Gettysburg poem, 338; opinion about editorial right to alter contributor's language, 340; efforts to get the use of his name, 346; his position as to the expulsion of homœopathists from Massa-

own remarks about his personal appearance, 100–103; *Vanity Fair's* caricature of him, 303; his letter to James Freeman Clarke about the *Envoi*, 104; group of letters to James Russell Lowell, 107–138; about *A Fable for Critics*, 107; about *The Vision*, 109; about *The Biglow Papers*, 112; declining invitation to cattle-show, 114; he is chosen president of the Phi Beta Kappa, 119, 123; his life at Beverly Farms, 131; teeth, 135; group of letters to James William Kimball, on sundry tenets of religion, 139–152; group of letters to John Lothrop Motley, 153–222 (remarks on the war and public affairs, *passim*, through these letters); about his son's wound, and Ball's Bluff, 157–159; about relations of United States with England, 159; remarks on death of his mother, 164; remarks on Grant, Stanton, Farragut, and others, 174–177; about Mrs. Stowe's article charging Lord Byron with incest, 179, 183, 209, 228, 295; about the "Coliseum," 179; about President Eliot and his innovations in Harvard University, 187, 188, 190; political predictions in 1872, 194, 195; description of the "Great Fire" in Boston, November, 1872, 196–198; at Nahant, 200–202; about the Beecher-Tilton scandal, 209, 210; about the manners of Englishmen, 212–214; group of letters to Harriet Beecher Stowe, 223–255; remarks about correspondents, 236, 259; article on "Moral Automatism," 237; group of letters to Elizabeth Stuart Phelps Ward, 256–268; early letter to James Freeman Clarke about some lyrics, and about his methods of work, 269; to same, replying to request for some verses, 272; to

same, about bores, 273; to same, thanking for *The Hour which Cometh*, 288; to same, 290; to same, about *Ten Great Religions*, 298; to same, 309; to George Ticknor, 277; to James T. Fields, 278; to his mother (about Pittsfield), 280; to Mr. Fields, about some poetical effusions, 282; to Charles Eliot Norton, about visit to Newport, 283; to same, about death of James Russell Lowell, 316; to Mr. Fields, 284, 289, 294; to same, thanking for a barometer, 285; to same, about mistaken date for dinner-party, 286; to same, about tavern at Montreal, 292; to William Amory, about war-poems, 290; to Rev. Frederic H. Hedge, D. D., 296; to Mrs. Kellogg, 299; to Bishop Lee, 300, 309; to John O. Sargent, 301, 311, 312; remarks on his friendship with Motley, 303; to G. A. James, thanking for Sèvres cup, 306; to J. G. Whittier, 303, 305, 313, 315; to J. C. Trautwine, Jr., 314; to Mrs. James T. Fields, 319.

Holmes, Mrs., the Doctor's wife (Amelia Lee Jackson); descended from Dorothy Quincy ("Dorothy Q."), i. 14; marriage, 170, 171; mentioned by him, 194, 198; remarks about his letter-writing, 319; her death, ii. 71; the Doctor's letter about her death, 261.

Holmes, Oliver Wendell, the younger; i. 5; class poet, class of 1861, Harvard University, 63; wounded, 170, 311, ii. 24, 157; his career, i. 171; his birth announced by his father, 322; a judge of Supreme Court, Massachusetts, 322; comes to live with his father, ii. 71, 263; ill, in the army, 172; visit to Europe, introductions, 177.

Holmes, Mrs. Oliver Wendell; the younger, ii. 71, 86, 263.

Holmes, Sir Robert; i. 4, 5.

Holmes, Temperance; i. 9–11.

Holmes, Thomas; i. 4.

Homœopathists; expelled from Massachusetts Medical Society, 348; and Dr. Holmes's letter thereon, 349.

Homœopathy; Dr. Holmes's relation to, i. 162–164.

Homœopathy and its Kindred Delusions; i. 162–164, 350.

Hooper, Robert W.; i. 83, 87, 104, 110, 117, 130, 142; death, ii. 79.

Horace; ii. 311; compared with Dr. Holmes, i. 230; one of his odes compared with *Dies Iræ*, ii. 312.

Houghton, Mifflin & Co.; ii. 214; relations with Dr. Holmes, i. 221–224.

Houghton, H. O.; the publisher; remarks about Dr. Holmes's "copy," ii. 22.

Howe, Mrs. Julia Ward; her war-lyrics, ii. 291.

Howe, Dr. Samuel G.; i. 144.

Howe, M. A. De W., junior; letter to, declining request, i. 335.

Howells, William D.; ii. 182; of Dr. Holmes and *The Atlantic Monthly*, i. 205; his introduction to Dr. Holmes, 358; at the Atlantic Breakfast, ii. 43; praised by Dr. Holmes in 1865, 177.

Hughes, Thomas; i. 244.

Humboldt Celebration; ii. 184, 185.

Hundred Days in Europe; quoted, i. 90, ii. 103; written, 66.

Hunt, Dr. William; letter to, ii. 24.

Hunt, William M.; ii. 211.

Hutchinson, Ellen M.; ii. 135.

Inches, Herman; ii. 81.

In Memoriam; its metre, ii. 277.

Innocents Abroad, The; anecdote about dedication, ii. 22.

"Institute of 1770;" i. 306.

Intermittent Fever, Essay on; takes prize, i. 162, 168.

International Review, The; Dr.

Holmes's contributions to, i. 219; review of *Light of Asia*, ii. 257, 258.

Ireland, Alexander; letter to, about *A Mortal Antipathy*, i. 267; letters to, about life of Emerson, ii. 58, 62.

Irving, Rev. Edward; described by Dr. Holmes, i. 134.

Jackson, Amelia Lee, wife of Dr. Holmes. See Holmes, Mrs.

Jackson, Andrew; i. 96.

Jackson, Judge Charles; Dr. Holmes's father-in-law, i. 171.

Jackson, Edward; i. 14.

Jackson, Dr. James, senior; i. 82, 168; Dr. Holmes's esteem for 143.

Jackson, James, junior; i. 98, 104, 107, 110, 120, 123, 142, 143, 151; illness and death, 122, 143.

Jackson, Dr. John B. S.; i. 324.

Jackson, Jonathan; i. 14.

Jackson, Mary; i. 14, 16.

James, George Abbot; note to, thanking for Roman wine-glass, i. 351; note to, about book-binding and C. Sumner, ii. 2; note to, thanking for Sèvres cup, 306.

James, Henry, senior; approves Mrs. Stowe's Byron article, ii. 228.

Johnson, Samuel; chronological parallel, i. 20.

Kane, Dr. E. K.; i. 189.

Kellogg, Caroline L.; letters to, i. 18, 195, 197, 201, 320, 322, 330, ii. 68, 86, 90.

Kemble, Charles; i. 83.

Kemble, Fanny; i. 83.

Kemper, G. W.; note to, i. 326.

Kimball, James William; i. 279; letter to, quoted, 281; series of letters to, on religious topics, ii. 139–152.

King, Rev. Thomas Starr; ii. 170.

King's Chapel; i. 280, 281; Dr. Holmes's funeral, ii. 92.

Kirkland, John Thornton; i. 39.

JOHN T. MORSE, JR. (1840-1937), was a native of Boston. After graduating from Harvard in 1860, he practiced as a lawyer in Boston for nearly twenty years. He found himself devoting more and more time to writing and editing, and in 1880 he conceived the American Statesmen series, contributing five of the volumes himself. He wrote his biography of Oliver Wendell Holmes for the American Men of Letters series in 1896 and was also the author of several legal works.

EARL N. HARBERT is Professor of English and Chairman of the Department at Northeastern University. He is the author of *The Force So Much Closer Home: Henry Adams and the Adams Family.*